# Name, Rank, and Serial Number

# Name, Rank, and Serial Number

*Exploiting Korean War POWs at Home and Abroad*

CHARLES S. YOUNG

# OXFORD
UNIVERSITY PRESS

Oxford University Press is a department of the University of Oxford.
It furthers the University's objective of excellence in research, scholarship,
and education by publishing worldwide.

Oxford    New York

Auckland    Cape Town    Dar es Salaam    Hong Kong    Karachi
Kuala Lumpur    Madrid    Melbourne    Mexico City    Nairobi
New Delhi    Shanghai    Taipei    Toronto

With offices in

Argentina    Austria    Brazil    Chile    Czech Republic    France    Greece
Guatemala    Hungary    Italy    Japan    Poland    Portugal    Singapore
South Korea    Switzerland    Thailand    Turkey    Ukraine    Vietnam

Oxford is a registered trademark of Oxford University Press
in the UK and certain other countries.

Published in the United States of America by
Oxford University Press
198 Madison Avenue, New York, NY 10016

Library of Congress Cataloging-in-Publication Data

Young, Charles S. (Charles Steuart), 1959-
Name, rank, and serial number : exploiting Korean War POWs at home and abroad / Charles S. Young.
pages cm
Includes bibliographical references and index.
ISBN 978–0–19–518348–1 (hardback)
1. Korean War, 1950–1953—Prisoners and prisons.    2. Prisoners of war—United States.
3. Prisoners of war—Korea (North)    4. Korean War, 1950–1953—Public opinion—United States.
5. Public opinion—United States.    I. Title.    II. Title:
Exploiting Korean War POWs at home and abroad.
DS921.Y68 2014
951.904′27—dc23
2013040056

1  3  5  7  9  8  6  4  2
Printed in the United States of America
on acid-free paper

*For Lisa Van Donsel*
♫ *It was Christmas Eve, Babe.*

# CONTENTS

# ACKNOWLEDGMENTS

My committee members, Lloyd Gardner, John Chambers, Marilyn Young, and the late Dee Garrison, were encouraging, helpful, and got the manuscript to the top of the pile at Oxford. My editor Susan Ferber took a wrench to the manuscript and tightened all the loose places. My gang, Dan Katz, Kathy Stratton, Tami Friedman, Bill Haywood, and Lisa Van Donsel, were coaches of writing and the soul, and Lisa also transcribed interviews. Bruce Franklin and Elliot Gruner broke trail in POW territory and made incisive comments. Elliot's warm encouragement helped give a nonmilitary author confidence in his subject, and he also lent an *Outer Limits* tape. Several anonymous manuscript reviewers made acute suggestions. Collection and reproduction of photographs was made possible by the Southern Arkansas University Research Committee. Barbara Constable at the Eisenhower Library was a dream archivist, while Donna McCloy at SAU managed a never-ending stream of interlibrary loan books. James Matray and William Stueck used their vast knowledge to catch a number of errors. David Buck answered questions about things Chinese while Daehwan Cho was my Korean consultant. The estate of my eldest brother, William Roland Young, provided a research grant and my father, Charles W. Young, found useful articles. I would never have gone the academic route without my high school debate coach Jim Holt, who provided Ivy League instruction in a cow town in Wisconsin (my research methods are little changed). The sweetest assistance came from my son Lukas, who intently helped print 4x6 evidence cards, which still bear smears from his moist, two-year-old hands. The card printing was over by the time Abbie and Quinn Young came along, but they helped restore my energy for editing. This book has been a long process, so I am pleased to fulfill the wish of my mother, Linda Rehm Young, 92, to "hurry up and finish before I die."

# Name, Rank, and Serial Number

# Introduction

## *The Cold Welcome*

> History has a stutter. It says wa-wa-wa-watch out.
> —The Mekons

This book began as a question: Why were returning prisoners of war treated so differently after the Korean War than Vietnam? I was aware that prisoners of Vietnam were perhaps that war's most successfully heroicized group. President Nixon lavished attention on them late in the war and then welcomed them home with a banquet at the White House, all in headlines. With POW/MIA flags still popular 40 years later, it was surprising to learn that in 1953, prisoners returning from Korea got the opposite treatment. They were deplored as a group, even despised. Instead of their own flag, they got FBI files. Korea POWs reportedly helped the enemy; revealed more than name, rank, and serial number; preyed upon each other; and gave in to the new dread, brainwashing. Where did all that come from? Even if there was a partial truth within, scandal-mongering was an odd departure from patriotic tradition. Much of the explanation can be found in the political uses K-POWs were put to, first in communist Chinese propaganda during the war, then again at home. Research reveals an official hand behind the ignominy. Government criticism of ex-POWs' character was then amplified by a general recoil from apparent softness, a special preoccupation of 1950s Cold War culture. Korea introduced the difficulty of maintaining ardor for fighting limited, drawn-out wars. Limited war created novel trials for K-POWs, and also bound them to the other prisoners. Captured North Korean and Chinese soldiers were used intensively in a psychological warfare operation that was surprisingly consequential for American GIs.

The story emerged out of civilizational clashes, but it begins and ends with the prisoners themselves. When the Korean War ended in late summer 1953, Staff Sgt. Jack Flanary had spent nearly three years in a Chinese prisoner of war camp.[1] Flanary was bursting to get home to Harlan County, Kentucky, but first he had to endure two weeks on a military transport ship. The just-freed prisoners were handed leaflets explaining that they would be taking the sea route home, so they could "receive good food and plenty of rest."[2] There was also another concern, one that had prompted generals in Washington to issue careful instructions on the handling of repatriates. Believing that some POWs were tainted by communism, the army decided to bring them home by sea instead of air so they could be observed. The enemy was expected to have recruited spies or agitators who might make embarrassing criticisms of the war. Investigators wanted to know about the POWs who had written antiwar letters home, broadcast polemics on shortwave radio, and published articles in the communist press. Psychiatrists, sociologists, counterintelligence officers, and criminal investigators clustered around the repatriates, poking and probing with multipage questionnaires in one of the largest mobilizations of academics in a single military operation. Who had helped the enemy, and why?

Sgt. Flanary endured the swarm of sleuths and social scientists until docking stateside. The journey quickened, and on September 12, 1953 he caught a flight to Knoxville, Tennessee, not far from his Kentucky home. His local reception was warmer. The Tennessee State Patrol provided an honorary escort to the border, where a Kentucky state police caravan took him the rest of the way to the town of Benham, near the border with Virginia. Flanary's return thrilled the coal town. People poured out of the Appalachian hills and an estimated 10,000 lined the main road in a town of 3,500. They honored Flanary in a parade with three marching bands, 200 cars, Boy Scouts, Girl Scouts, the Lions Club, and people who just joined in.[3] The governor of Kentucky greeted an estimated 5,000 people in the Benham stadium, where a speakers' platform with a military color guard was set up. Presents and honors awaited the young sergeant: a $50 savings bond from the American Legion and a nomination from the Veterans of Foreign Wars to become a Kentucky Colonel.

As the event was getting started, something unexpected happened. A rumor rippled through the crowd, and when it reached the speakers' platform the organizers stepped down and went into a huddle. The tale was so troubling that they decided to halt presentations on the spot. The word was that while in prison camp, the sergeant had buddied up to the Chinese communists. He was a collaborator. The town leaders decided they could not risk honoring someone who might have given aid and comfort to the enemy. The governor's staff may have prompted the decision—a town leader explained to the *New York Times* that "we just couldn't take a chance on embarrassing the governor." No one seemed to know where the rumor started, but the honor guard was sent home, the savings bond rescinded, and Flanary's membership in the VFW put on hold. Town elders said they would decide what to do with the awards after an investigation.[4]

The snap judgment about Flanary was repeated in various forms for years to come. Returned prisoners were suspect as a group and shadowed by the FBI, fumed over in Congressional hearings, whispered about by neighbors, and dissected by pundits and researchers. A government board used secret evidence to deny cash bonuses to some returnees.[5] This was the cold welcome. Repatriated POWs were exhibits in a systematic scolding of the nation for not being tough enough. Nearly half died in captivity, but this was blamed less on disease and starvation than on the presumed weakness and bad character of the younger generation. The dead succumbed because of "too much mama," according to the *Saturday Evening Post.*[6] One canard still being repeated is that they lacked the gumption to try and escape. The most agitated critics claimed that one in three POWs was a collaborator. They were seduced by the enemy with "fantastic ease," claimed Irving Kristol, a prominent conservative commentator.[7] For the first and last time, American prisoners as a group were said to have been weak and cowardly.

Prisoners in Korea responded as human beings to a unique situation. There had been no collapse of manhood in the few years since World War II. Some were heroic, others craven, or a combination thereof. Even those who did gravitate toward Chinese views almost always snapped back to their previous selves once removed from the environment. The disproportionate reaction to Korean collaboration can also be seen in the case of the 21 prisoners who went to live with their captors in China after the war. As the armistice approached, the Chinese and North Koreans faced a public relations calamity with thousands of their own prisoners reportedly refusing to return home to communism. To parry this embarrassment, the Chinese invited a number of United Nations prisoners to stay with them, including a handful of Americans. The 21 were about .025 percent of the total—too tiny a sample to prove anything, much less a generational unraveling of moral fiber. Nonetheless, the 21 prompted years of hand-wringing and truckloads of copy.

The instances of collaboration in Korea are better attributed to the environment rather than a sudden national malaise. As a rule, determined captors get what they want out of captives. The difference in Korea was that prisoners were pressured to do different things than in previous wars—public, political things, such as delivering propaganda broadcasts over shortwave radio, or writing articles blaming capitalism for Jim Crow segregation in the United States. The POWs' off-key denunciations of Wall Street warmongering were regularly taken at face value and considered signs of conversion to communism, not signs of being prisoners of war. There were 14 courts-martial of prisoners returned from Korea, but none from Vietnam, even though there was enough collaboration in Vietnam to fuel a scandal if that had been the intent of American authorities.

Instead, they made a conscious decision—embraced by the public—to heroicize all the prisoners freed in 1973 and indict none.

The curious thing about Korea was not collaboration, but the stir about it after the war. The initial dismay was amplified by officials who scripted news events, rewrote Hollywood movies, cultivated reporters, and planted stories. Much of the POW's "march to calumny" was in fact generated by the Pentagon, although there were plenty of armchair heroes and pundits happy to help.[8] But calling a generation of soldiers milksops was risky, and it provoked a new set of complications for opinion makers. Plenty of families resented the cold welcome and felt that their sons were being punished a second time. Sniping at the manhood of troops eventually generated a public backlash powerful enough to stop courts-martial in their tracks. The roots of this blowback can be seen by returning to the homecoming of Sgt. Flanary in Harlan County, Kentucky.

Despite what turned out to be an unwelcome-home party, many locals still considered Flanary a hero. An aunt angrily denied any red hue and predicted that "some people are going to be sorry that rumor got started." In place of the revoked $50 savings bond, sympathizers passed the hat and gave Flanery ten times that much in cash. More agreeable civic clubs provided a watch, luggage, and clothing. Then the celebrating began. "I didn't get to sleep until 4 Sunday morning," Flanary told a reporter, "so I didn't get to church." Within a day of the stadium incident, the patriot groups tempered their rhetoric. The VFW backtracked, and the American Legion commander announced that they backed Flanary 100 percent, "until his loyalty has definitely been disproved."[9]

The Flanary case is useful not so much for what he did or did not do, but because it represents a debate that was repeated throughout the 1950s. Convinced that soldiers had gone soft, blue-ribbon committees began chiding the communities that raised them. This culminated in a new Code of Conduct that demanded more forcefully than ever that prisoners reveal only name, rank, and service number. Standing against this indictment were families and supporters who rejected a code so Spartan it shamed a young man in front of the whole county, based on speculation. Flanary was never charged with a crime, although he did admit to willingly reading and discussing literature provided by the Chinese, but denied that they influenced him, including on the subject of segregation: "I was against racial discrimination when I went in the Army and I am now."[10] Any Chinese indoctrination Flanary might have accepted seemed to have been shed on the boat home. Kin were just glad to have him home and were little interested in what might have happened in the parallel universe of captivity. Whatever had gone on was over now, and it was time for ex-POWs to resume normal lives. In this way, patriotic communities found themselves strangely at odds with the Cold War state, despite being unsympathetic to communism. A contest had begun between government and families over ownership of the freed sons. Were returned prisoners in a sense still in uniform, to be martialed as evidence in Cold War debates? Or could they return to private life?

Offending the POWs' home communities revealed the difficulty of managing public opinion in an era of limited wars. At its root was not the weakness of prisoners, but the fact that combat could occur anywhere on the planet, without immediate threat to America. The Cold War was over which social system would appeal to the world the most. Moscow and Washington led the blocs, but the outcome would be decided by which side other nations chose. This competition involved the entire body politic on cultural and ideological levels, as well as military. The most important prize was not territory, but perception—which system was the most dynamic and humane, which should other countries choose?

The cold welcome was one way in which prisoners were used as objects. A related issue was what exactly their lengthy imprisonment accomplished. It is commonly thought that the sacrifice of soldiers and POWs saved the South Korean government. That it did. But although North Korea's invasion was shattered by fall 1950, the war continued for 30 months. After the United States and United Nations allies beat back the initial attack, they made the fateful decision to conquer North Korea. This was such a different mission that it could be called a second Korean War. Most of soldiers' time in captivity and half of all casualties occurred during the second war. Since securing the South had already been accomplished, the continuing sacrifice served new purposes. It is this later phase that needs closer examination. As is well known, the US/UN invasion of the North was defeated by China. Each side's attempt to reunite the peninsula had failed, and by summer 1951 they resigned themselves to a stalemate and entered truce negotiations. Since winning outright was off the table, American decision-makers intended to negotiate as tough an armistice as possible. Both sides turned to political warfare over the peace talks and used prisoners in a propaganda rivalry that replaced an elusive military victory. When talks reached the details of how prisoners of war would be exchanged, American delegates dug in their heels over a novel issue. A number of prisoners held on a South Korean island had emerged as anticommunists. They were encouraged to press their views inside the camps, which would have been dangerous if they were returned home after the war. US representatives insisted they would not force home prisoners who rejected repatriation, and demanded armistice protocols that would insure what they dubbed "voluntary" or "nonforcible" repatriation. The Chinese and North Korean negotiators considered this a transparent trick to kidnap soldiers and embarrass their governments with mass desertions.

The anticommunist prisoners did in fact join a large program generating defections, which included terror in the prison compounds. How much is part of the historical debate. Voluntary repatriation was a broomstick stuck in bicycle spokes that brought talks to a tumbling halt, and American POWs quickly felt the impact. Not only was their captivity lengthened by the impasse, the Chinese used them more urgently in propaganda. The blizzard of accusations that the United States used bacteriological weapons was based on coerced prisoner confessions, and began directly after voluntary repatriation was formally proposed. Since the communist countries rejected an embarrassing armistice, the other part of the American strategy was to wear them down with massive bombing. Washington wanted peace, but on its terms—and prolonging the war had other benefits, such as quadrupling the military budget and solidifying defense pacts like the North Atlantic Treaty Organization (NATO). This was not a preconceived scheme, rather, the rewards of fighting on were always more promising than enemy truce offers.

The logjam over a POW exchange doubled the length of the war. Soldiers fought longer and POWs stayed longer so that anticommunist Chinese and Koreans were not sent home at bayonet point. How much did the added sacrifice accomplish? An answer depends in part on the authenticity of the defections. It is known that there was some degree of coercion. Intelligence operatives from South Korea, Taiwan, and the US Army worked inside the barbed wire to build the community of defectors. The camps broke out in civil war between loyal communists and opponents of repatriation. Were nonrepatriated warriors mainly defending themselves, or forcing other prisoners to join them? Unsurprisingly, considering that there was a peak of 170,000 held in chaotic conditions, both occurred. The analytical task is to find the mix. Was the large number of nonrepatriates best explained by coercion, or opposition to their governments? This book will answer whether American POWs' extra time in captivity served to protect their counterparts, or keep them from their families.

POWs bear on another issue. Korea is called "the forgotten war" so often that I once heard historian Marilyn Young remark that it is "remembered as the forgotten war." Its unpopularity and lack of clear victory certainly made it less memorable, but the prisoner repatriation issue suggests an additional explanation. Voluntary repatriation produced stunning numbers: Nearly 50,000 North Korean and Chinese POWs were not handed over after the armistice. This was a remarkable triumph for the program's patrons. Eighteen additional months of war had succeeded in a grand rebuke of the enemy by salt-of-the-earth foot soldiers. Curiously, this received scant notice from Americans at the time, and has since vanished from common wisdom. CIA director Allen Dulles called it "one of the greatest psychological victories" ever, but it failed to displace any of the negativity that made the war so forgettable.[11] Chapter 13 will explain why.

While a number of books have addressed the shoddy treatment of ex-POWs returning to America, this study explains the circumstances.[12] The obsession of the early Cold War was weakness within, and freed prisoners were an example. Resistance to captivity was a parable for the national will. Like prisoners being interrogated, the country could either capitulate to the Kremlin or fight back. Being tough reduced the elaborate conduct of foreign relations to a question of individual manliness and simplified home morale. Voluntary repatriation was a mainspring driving these developments. It made prisoners into reluctant propaganda stars abroad, and, by delaying peace, kept the squeeze on them to cooperate. Time, pressure, and exposure turned collaboration from a footnote into a scandal that dominated K-POWs' reception after the war. The fact that Korea became a war over prisoners is not well known. This book seeks to make them a central consideration of the history. In no other American conflict have the terms of a prisoner exchange been so pivotal in conducting and ending the war, or assessing its results. Despite their significance, many POW issues were so secret or obscured by government misdirection that the real war was unrecognizable to most citizens.

The chapters of the book demonstrate how American POWs were used by their government in two ways: First, their captivity was prolonged and possibly cheapened by the partial repatriation of enemy prisoners after the war. Second, returning GIs were shamed by propaganda at home in a psychological warfare program that targeted the public. Policymakers avoided daylight when they calculated POW policies and prolonging the war, demonstrating how even basic national priorities can be set in the dark. Chapter 1 explains how the global Cold War shaped the Korean conflict and limited its scope. Psychological warfare and international public relations overshadowed military victory in Korea and pulled prisoners into their maneuvers. The experience of American POWs is detailed in Chapter 2. A terrible mortality rate established the brutality of Korean captivity in current events, and also raised some prisoners' susceptibility to enemy blandishments. Several subsequent chapters go back and forth between prisoners in northern and southern camps, showing how their fates became entangled. In Chapter 3, a psychological warfare operation began recruiting defectors among North Korean and Chinese prisoners and recast the conflict. It prolonged the war and put prisoners of both sides in jeopardy. Chapter 4 explores Chinese indoctrination of United Nations prisoners and their use in publicity. Chapter 5 details how stalemate in battle intensified dueling propaganda campaigns. China used POW confessions to accuse the United States of bacteriological war crimes, while the United States claimed that prisoners were renouncing communism. Meanwhile, the deadlock in peace talks burned down the landscape. Chapter 6 challenges the perception of widespread collaboration by American POWs. They were bored by indoctrination, not brainwashed. Next, Chapter 7 weighs the results of the voluntary repatriation campaign over which the war continued. It answers whether a few or a lot of POWs were prevented from returning home. In Chapter 8, freed American prisoners came back to a country that considered them collaborators, but was undecided whether to blame enemy mistreatment or the GI weakness. In Chapter 9, a postwar propaganda campaign about communist murder and brainwashing raised sympathy for K-POWs and created the "brainwashing dilemma." As a result, detailed in Chapter 10, public outcry halted prosecutions of collaborators because brainwashing seemed to have erased their culpability. In Chapter 11, the public's "misplaced sympathy" for weak POWs was pounced on by military pundits, principally by accusing repatriates and their communities of effeminacy and even mother–son incest. In Chapter 12, I explain how Hollywood tried to school resistant audiences about duty in captivity, but created action films that were unrealistic and courtroom parables that were too dry. However, the attempt revealed movie producers and Pentagon consultants combining in sophisticated efforts to manage public opinion. Chapter 13, "The Hidden Reason for Forgetting Korea," explains why the seemingly successful voluntary repatriation program could not be used to redeem the conflict. The concluding chapter tracks how different Washington's Korean War was from the one described to the public. Military objectives shifted dramatically, with little explanation. The nature of limited war made it harder to maintain public support, and the basic goals of the war went unannounced.

The title of this book comes from the directive that POWs identify themselves to the captor with name, rank, and service number. While "service number" is the more correct phrase, I have used "serial number" because of its frequent appearance in popular culture.

# PART ONE

# OVER THERE

# 1

# Limited War Sets the Stage for the POW Odyssey

We have been engaged in full-scale psychological warfare with the Soviets since 1946.

—The Joint Chiefs of Staff, August 1950

In late 1950, a column of American prisoners trudged north through snow and ice. Swept up with them was a civilian missionary from Texas named Larry Zellers. The POWs were being evacuated ahead of American troops who were rolling up the peninsula after the victory at Inchon. The North Korean troops marched the prisoners at night to avoid air attack. There was no reliable source of food beyond what guards scrounged from villagers. To sleep, POWs were packed so tightly into flimsy buildings that stale air snuffed candles out, forcing them to open windows. But that let in winter winds well below zero, requiring them to rotate turns in the warm spots. Prisoners tried to sleep through the pain of wounds, thirst, hunger, frostbite, and dysentery. According to Zellers, "a normal person has to resort to rather vigorous and unpleasant means to take his life, but in the winter of 1950 all that one of our group had to do was to miss three or four meals." Guards were expected to move the columns swiftly and not lose any strays. Anyone who collapsed could not be left behind, so they were shot. Zellers described how men unable to continue would drop down at the side of the road and silently wait for a guard to bring deliverance. He saw two GI buddies helping each other along, one with boots, one without. The man who still had shoes collapsed. A guard approached with his rifle, but paused to allow the friend to remove the boots of his resigned companion.[1] As he walked away, the crunching of his new footwear in the snow was interrupted by a shot.

The emergency evacuations were deadly for many prisoners, but they also meant the war should be over soon. North Korea was falling rapidly and captives could expect liberation directly. Then China entered the war from the north and victory was replaced by full retreat. The new conflict was larger and deadlier, but it moved quickly, and by the end of spring 1951 leaders of both sides saw nothing ahead but stalemate. The beginning of truce talks offered Larry Zellers and the rest of the POWs another chance for relatively quick freedom. Unexpectedly, armistice negotiations went so poorly that a one-year war stretched into three. From July until December 1951 representatives settled point after point of the armistice agenda, until they got to the mechanics of exchanging prisoners. That was not resolved until July 1953, an additional year-and-a-half of captivity for Larry Zellers. A detail that usually falls quickly into place after the portentous parts of a truce had become the most difficult.

How could a dispute over exchanging prisoners of war double the length of the Korean conflict? As good a place to start as any is in the physics of uranium, because splitting the atom also divided Korea. During World War II, before the Manhattan Project succeeded, the United States wanted the Soviets to join the war against Japan as soon as possible. American officials dreaded the human cost of invading the home islands and wanted Soviet manpower to deal with the Japanese army in Manchuria and the Korean peninsula below. But this would enhance Soviet influence in East Asia after the war and make the USSR the sole hegemon of the Korean peninsula. Once the United States had a working atomic bomb, it lost enthusiasm for Soviet help. Washington canceled the planned joint occupation of Japan and insisted on a shared presence in Korea. The permanent division at the 38th Parallel of the peninsula began as a way to manage the surrender of Japanese troops stationed there. Americans received the surrender and maintained order below the 38th, while the Soviets did the same above. Temporary surrender sectors soon became separate occupation zones, which subsequently diverged into different social entities. In the south, the Americans helped a stubborn conservative named Syngman Rhee take power. Rhee allied himself with Korean traditional elites and collaborators of the Japanese and attacked the left-leaning peasant associations that were popping up. To the north, the Soviets nurtured a communist guerrilla fighter named Kim Il Sung, who won the loyalty of a segment of society by expropriating land and nationalizing industry. Both autocrats suppressed rivals and declared separate governments in 1948, though each also longed to rule over all. Regimes in both North and South considered themselves the only legitimate authority and pledged to unite the land. Civil strife and armed clashes began, especially in the south. After the Rhee government defeated a two-year guerrilla insurgency, Kim Il Sung took stock. It was clear that the United States was rebuilding Tokyo as a regional power, and Korea would likely again become an adjunct of the Japanese economy. Kim calculated that he had to move fast before South Korea was permanently entwined with Japan. That meant invading.

It is easy to see that the North–South division created a local antagonism between Korean parties, but why would the great powers risk triggering a nuclear war by getting deeply involved? And how did that eventually lead all the way to the cold welcome for American POWs at home?

Prison camps in North Korea were in desolate, icy places, but their origins were international. After World War II, Washington took on the ambitious task of intervening wherever Russian accents were overheard. The need to confront the Soviets was put succinctly in the government blueprint for containment, National Security Council Document 68. NSC-68 argued that the mere existence of American freedom threatened the Kremlin because it might incite the captive nations of the Soviet empire. The United States was the strongest obstacle to communism and therefore the target of a "peculiarly virulent blend of hatred and fear."[2] Communism represented a total threat, not just a military danger, for it could spread laterally through space or vertically through culture and class. The Kremlin would be confronted on whatever terrain it advanced, whether cultural subversion from within or military expansion from without. The essence of the containment policy was preventing expansion. NSC-68 defined communism as a monolithic conspiracy centralized in the Kremlin; there was little appreciation of regional variations and rivalries.

Underlying Washington's postwar outlook was tremendous new strength and ambition. Much of European industry was in ruins, while American production emerged not just intact, but larger. The Second World War destroyed Old World empires and created a power vacuum in their former colonies, which the United States, USSR, and some combination of local forces would try to fill. World War II catapulted the United States from a largely continental power to one with alliances and military bases ringing the world. Washington sought to lead the world toward a prosperous order of liberal capitalism. The Soviet Union also sought expanded military and political alliances. Leninist millennialism convinced Soviet leaders that socialism would displace capitalism, which they could hurry along by building influence in the Third World. Most of all, the Soviets sought security against a feared capitalist encirclement.

Containment was meant to be flexible, with a continuum of methods from trade networks and cultural ties, to arming Soviet enemies and fighting its allies to—at the extreme—nuclear war. In order to respond prudently to any development, Washington sought to maintain a "preponderance" of power.[3] This meant military superiority in both nuclear and conventional weapons. By having unmistakable strategic superiority, Washington could risk intervening in regional situations. The Soviets would know that they were trumped by American nuclear force, which remained far superior into the 1960s. The American strategy was thus carefully constructed to include what came to be known as "limited wars." From a position of strength, it could pursue political objectives such as encouraging Chinese and North Korean prisoners to renounce their allegiances to home. The Americans and Soviets both wanted to be the shepherd of nations, but their rivalry had one overriding constraint: the danger of Armageddon. Even a conventional third world war would be more devastating than anyone wanted to contemplate. Their competition would have to be limited to small steps over an indefinite period of time. This made the duration of the Cold War especially unpredictable and would require that resources not be overspent on local clashes. The Cold War was conceptually expansive, but militarily constrained.

The term "limited war" is used to distinguish a type of military action from two other conditions: peace and general war. "Limited war" characterizes the conflicts fought by the United States during the era of Soviet contention, though it could also apply to post-Cold War engagements. Limited wars were those in which it entered local combat while avoiding direct confrontation with the USSR. Put another way, limited war was when Pentagon officials had the luxury of doing cost-benefit analysis in an office, not a bunker. The phrase "limited" is not a measure of the violence of a conflict. Korea and Vietnam were the classic limited wars, but they both surpassed World War II in the volume of explosives used, one lasted twice as long, and early casualties in Korea topped those at the start of the war in the Pacific. These struggles were certainly not limited from the point of view of East Asians, who lost more people than the United States in all its wars combined. Limited war is defined not by the intensity of fighting, but by the narrow intentions of the great powers.

Although American planners sought military strength, they saw the Cold War as an ideological struggle first. Officials understood the Cold War in much the same way as their adversaries—an epic battle of civilizations for the soul of humankind. American leaders were keenly worried that the wretched of the earth might turn toward socialist collectivization in order to escape endemic poverty and oppression. Even in Western Europe, the most immediate danger was the political challenge of indigenous Marxists, not Soviet tanks. None concerned wanted world war to be the method of triumph—the competition was very much about image and perception. American cold warriors thus played to both governments and peoples. They reassured local leaders that the United States was a vigilant, capable ally, and tried to persuade the people that their aspirations were best met under free enterprise. If capitalism showed itself to be more vibrant than communism—militarily, economically, and culturally—that would prove where the future lay. The great powers felt their every move being followed by an international audience. In the global competition, image was reality; the stronger social system would be the one able to publicize the best record of achievement.

For both superpowers, Europeans were the most important allies. Populous and advanced, Europe could easily tip the balance in the global competition.

Both sides put their biggest armies in Europe, but never fought; competition was political and economic. Prosperity was the heart of the American grand strategy. If peoples' lives improved, they would not turn to collectivization in Europe or anywhere else. Thus, the United States invested huge sums rebuilding European economies. For both blocs, European priorities restricted developments in Korea.

The American plan for a flourishing Western Europe included one highly controversial measure: reviving Germany. Getting allies to accept it would require great creativity, but Germany was the greatest industrial power of the continent, the biggest market for neighbors, and had critical resources, especially coal. Washington believed West Germany would have to be rebuilt in order for Western Europe to thrive, and probably rearmed. This, however, was potentially destabilizing because a rehabilitated West Germany would threaten the Soviets twice—once with its military potential, and again with its economic might. Militarily, Russia had been devastated twice in one century by Germans, and Bonn's prosperity might make East Bloc populations disgruntled. Like Russia, France had also repeatedly been overrun by the Germans, and getting French acceptance for rebuilding Germany was one of Washington's touchiest postwar challenges. France and the other Western European nations would accept a strong West Germany only if they were certain that the United States would maintain an army in Europe to keep both the USSR and Germany in line. America would have to prove its credibility to prospective allies in the rest of the world, as well. But credibility is a perception, not a new weapon or a fortress on high ground. Containment, therefore, was not so much about holding territory or building missiles, but about giving psychological reassurance to allies that the United States was in it for the duration. This meant that a country with little strategic significance in strict military terms might become important for building credibility. This and another form of credibility—deterrence—explain most of Washington's decision. Since Korea was a fight for credibility, the terms of the conflict were constrained. Korea was a means to an end, not the end itself. While the superpowers were willing to fight a world war over Europe, neither would risk all over a sideshow. If fighting in Korea enhanced the appearance of power, they would do so. If credibility could be established in some other fashion, such as a propaganda coup using prisoners of war, then that was another way.

A competition for prestige and credibility was the ideal arena for new concepts of psychological warfare. Theories of human communication had recently been formalized into a school of thought dubbed "psychological operations" or "psyops." Great hopes were invested in this political/ideological form of conflict, as psy-warriors attempted to turn propaganda into a potent, modern technology of mind compulsion. Psychological warfare went beyond battlefield tactics; it could be anything that affected the thoughts of the intended target, from surrender leaflets dropped in battle to the overall perception of American strength. A report advocating bigger and better psyops defined it as "the sum total of our current efforts—political, psychological, economic and military."[4] The phrase "political warfare" was largely interchangeable with psyops. The rise of fascism decades earlier seemed to prove the potency of propaganda and what became psychological warfare. The fascists seemed to have exploited mentally weak masses using the new media of radio, talking pictures, and outdoor amplification.[5] Television debuted at the 1936 Berlin Olympics, and electronics were thought to spread potent psychological symbols that stimulated near-clinical hysteria in thousands of people at once. World War II sold defense officials on psychological warfare, and the Cold War was the time to perfect it.

Since the Cold War was more ideological struggle than bullets, targeting minds was a natural. As a universalist creed, communism jumped boundaries of nation, ethnicity, and religion. America was "engaged in full-scale psychological warfare," declared the Joint Chiefs of Staff (JCS).[6] Everything could impact the psychological condition of the enemy or the allies, making the purview of psyops very broad. The rest of the world would choose sides according to the whole package offered by a political-economic system, as transmitted by mass communications. Psyops rose on the same wave as the Voice of America (VOA) and the US Information Agency. Political warfare was elevated to a strategic place alongside nuclear deterrence and securing natural resources. At its most ambitious, psychological warfare would bring down the USSR. The Soviets' Achilles heel was thought to be their unpopularity, especially in the occupied nations of Eastern Europe.[7] Captive peoples could be encouraged to reject the Soviets using propaganda, political posturing, and display of consumer riches in the west. The Marshall Plan was considered a model of psychological operations. Rebuilding Western Europe brought prosperity and undercut communist-led unions, as well as demonstrating American leadership. With the success of the Marshall Plan behind them, psy-warriors had astonishingly high hopes. If conducted well, "psychological operations could prevent total war," according to a Pentagon policy brief.[8] Persuading an enemy populace not to participate in aggression would be the ultimate achievement.

Academic communications theories augmented psychological warfare. University research centers, often funded by the Pentagon, concentrated on the methods of persuasion, not content. Like their blood relatives in the advertising industry, they assumed that people would accept almost anything if the package was attractive. This "instrumentalist" approach was ideal for propaganda; it avoided constraining fixations on truth and concentrated instead on results. One cunning document discouraged direct criticism of Marxism in broadcasts to Eastern Europe because the ideology remained popular. It suggested arguing that Stalinist occupiers had forsaken true Marxist principles. This was not exactly the official view, but the point was to use what worked.[9] Psy-warriors lost little sleep over the accuracy or morality of their messages since the shadiest propaganda was preferable to the brutality of war. Their results-oriented approach to mass communications was applied domestically as well, where persuasion was calibrated with the new polling techniques.

Psychological warfare was nurtured by the National Security Council, which in early 1949 recommended expanding "foreign information programs and overt psychological operations." Thus was born "Project Troy," whose very name reflected the ambitions of psywar—a weapon that might collapse an enemy from within. Troy research led to the suggestion of creating a "single authority for political warfare," since any government department from Agriculture to the CIA might impact psychological postures. Significantly, the report included the public in psychological warfare and sought ways to gain "acceptance of foreign policy decisions." Troy helped prompt the formation of the Psychological Strategy Board (PSB) in April 1951, and the PSB became the NSC's largest department and a nerve center for POW matters.[10]

By 1948, American cold warriors had successfully confronted communism in Berlin, Greece, and Iran, but still worried the winning streak might be over. In Europe, the French and Italian communist parties used their consistent records of antifascism to keep a stubborn hold on voters. The Soviets built an atomic bomb in 1949, long before Americans expected them to, and were making strides in heavy industry. That same year, the Chinese Communist Party took power in the world's most populous nation, despite American assistance to the nationalist army of Chiang Kai-shek. China was a fearful premonition: Third World millions might willingly choose the other side. Then in early 1950, it appeared that spies had infested the government. The arrest of Klaus Fuchs and the Rosenbergs revealed that atomic research was penetrated by the Soviets. Alger Hiss's conviction suggested that even the upper reaches of government were infiltrated by spies. There was an urgency for action.

Given that Europe was the focus of the Cold War, it is ironic that war came not there but on the periphery. As part of the draw down from the Second World War, both the United States and the Soviet Union pulled combat troops out of Korea: the Soviets by the end of 1948, the United States six months later. Both, however, left behind advisers, diplomats, and the apparatus of influence. Washington left equipment and ammunition for its ally Syngman Rhee, but curbed his adventurism by withholding heavy offensive weapons like tanks. Conflict between the two halves of Korea intensified, especially along the 38th Parallel, where both sides probed and fought some significant battles. With the southern regime becoming more entrenched, Kim Il Sung resolved to invade and began a lengthy courtship of Stalin to get arms. Stalin worried about the response of the Americans, but Kim assured him that the south was so weak he could overwhelm it before the United States could respond. With the victory of the Chinese Communist Party, Stalin could contemplate greater risks. Eventually, with the concurrence of the Chinese, he agreed to bankroll an invasion, but warned Kim that no Soviet troops would save him if the plan backfired.[11] The Soviets provided tanks, artillery, aircraft, and veteran generals to make the intricate plans. Another boost came from thousands of battle-hardened Korean troops who had helped win the Chinese civil war. Soviet assistance accelerated a comparatively low-intensity civil war. On June 25, 1950, a modern, well-trained, and equipped army swept across the 38th Parallel. While much of the Korean Peoples Army (KPA) was on foot, a regiment drove the Soviet's highly regarded T-34 tank. The attackers rapidly overwhelmed South Korean troops and seized the capital, Seoul, in three days. They then rushed down valley roads toward the key southern port at Pusan, which had to be taken quickly before the United States decided to intervene. While on the move, the KPA incorporated more than 80,000 South Koreans into combat and labor units. Some were captured soldiers, and many were civilians press-ganged (drafted) into service.

When the White House learned of the invasion, the first thought was about the big picture. The administration's immediate assumption was that the Kremlin had ordered the invasion, as opposed to enabling a North Korean initiative. They wondered if Korea might be designed to divert attention from Europe, or if it was a feint before attacks on Iran or Taiwan. An NSC analysis concluded that the USSR was probing American resolve and seeking control of the immediate peninsula, not trying to provoke general war or direct confrontation with the United States. Confident in the preponderance of American power, the White House began preparing a response under the assumption that the conflict could be kept small. Truman's first public statements were vague about who was to blame and did not directly criticize the Soviets.[12]

Even if the objectives of the immediate invasion were narrow, it was still ominous. The word "Munich" haunted Truman's generation—a reference to concessions made to Hitler in 1938 that were widely thought to have encouraged further aggression. Munich meant that the Soviets would become more adventurist if they were not faced down. Truman felt a keen need to regain the global initiative, and taking a stand in Korea would demonstrate to European and other allies that the United States was out in front. A show of force might even scare Kim Il Sung into backing down immediately. Truman was also mindful of domestic politics. The Republican strategy for returning to the White House after an absence of nearly two decades was to paint the Democrats as soft on communism. Truman and the Democratic Party were accused of "losing" China, and if Korea fell too, it could mean defeat in the 1952 elections.

Korea's importance as a symbol of resolve rather than immediate necessity is seen in the American's lack of advance preparation, despite several years of armed clashes between north and south. Army Chief of Staff "Lightning Joe" Lawton Collins once called Korea "a peninsula sticking out of Asia" of little significance. Defensively, it would be taxing to protect from a determined China, and offensively it would be a bottleneck if invading Asia was contemplated. American plans to maintain a presence in East Asia put little emphasis on the mainland and instead concentrated forces on offshore islands that were easier to defend and already tied to the "Great Crescent" of American power stretching from Taiwan, to the Philippines, and up through Japan.[13] The White House had no intention of committing so much to Korea that the Great Crescent would be weakened. If the Soviets themselves entered the war in force, the Americans anticipated withdrawing to Japan.[14] Korea was a show of imperial resolve. Willingness to fight even in Korea would send the message that the United States could be counted on anywhere. Korea itself was not without strategic importance—it might eventually provide resources and labor to the hub economy of Japan—but it did lack military importance in the big picture.

Much has been made of the US army being unprepared to fight in Korea. It is true that the first American troops were hastily assembled and ill-prepared. But most regions of the world did not have aircraft carrier Japan off their coast, hosting four American divisions. The "Communists picked the worst place in the world," according to Chief of Staff Collins, Korea was the "one place to which we could move troops quickly."[15]

Like Washington, the Kremlin wanted to use Korea in the global competition, but without risking much. Stalin's caution can be seen in several ways. He warned Kim Il Sung not to expect Soviet ground troops.[16] Soviet submarines nearby at Port Arthur and Vladivostock did not attack American ships, even when they might have tipped the balance in the siege of Pusan. And when China entered the war, Stalin refused Soviet air cover. An official Army history of Korea concluded that both sides tried to "localize the war politically and militarily."[17] This was part of the recipe for stalemate that eventually entangled the POWs.

The North Korean invasion advanced so rapidly that only American troops from Japan could stop it. On June 30, two days after the fall of Seoul, President Truman sent in the infantry. The United Nations sanctioned the effort and a variety of countries sent troops, though Americans dominated the United Nations Command (UNC). Reflecting a policy of limits, Truman referred to it as a "police action" and declined to ask Congress for a declaration of war. The first ground troops hurried to block the valley roads, but the KPA kept rolling over them. Barely a month into the conflict, the victor of World War II had been pushed so far down the peninsula it could smell the ocean. Walton Walker, the general on the scene, motivated his officers by invoking Dunkirk and Bataan—places where armies with their backs to the sea met disaster. At the village of No Gun Ri, commanders followed panicky official instructions and ordered GIs to massacre columns of South Korean refugees for fear of infiltrators.[18] The Americans retreated toward the port at Pusan at the bottom of the peninsula. At the nadir, the perimeter around Pusan was just 80 miles. But as distances shortened, reinforcements could reach threatened points on the line more quickly. Pushed tightly into a corner, the army became solid as a doorstop.

The Pusan perimeter held long enough for General Douglas MacArthur to launch an amphibious landing at Inchon on the west side of the peninsula on September 15, 1950. His troops cut across Korea to the eastern coast, blocking the KPA's supplies. At the same time, United Nations forces broke out of Pusan and began pushing from the south. The KPA fell apart. Exposed to air attack while on the run, thousands died in the scramble back to the Parallel. Out of an original invasion force of 90,000, only 25,000 to 30,000, in small groups, are thought to have slipped past the gauntlet. During this time a large number of communist prisoners were taken. Many were North Korean veterans, but quite a few were South Koreans who had been hastily impressed into the KPA.

Smashing the invasion so handily created a choice. Like dogs and bears, armies want to chase anything that runs. The rout gave President Truman and his advisers a chance to go beyond containment and actually push communism back. Truman decided to allow MacArthur to invade and occupy the north. "Rollback" was a major change in objective; in a sense, crossing the 38th Parallel was the start of a new war. Conquering the North might seem to go beyond the principle of limited war, but it was done on the assumption that China would not intervene. To avoid provocation, MacArthur was told to stay well south of the Yalu River that separated China from Korea. To the Chinese, protecting North Korea was vital to their southern border, and soon after MacArthur bisected the Parallel they were expecting to intervene. The Chinese were indebted to the many Koreans who died in China's civil war, and they intended to protect the solidarity and prestige of the communist movement.[19] The Korean peninsula was a traditional route for Japanese invasions of Manchuria, where 80 percent of Chinese industry was located. Aggressive western troops on the border were considered a fundamental threat to Beijing. A poem written by a soldier was used for inspiration:

> The American imperialist is a ball of fire,
> It will burn China after burning through Korea;
> China the neighbor rushes to put out the fire,
> China can be saved by helping Korea.[20]

Both MacArthur and officials in Washington proceeded to ignore warning after warning from China as they approached the border, even as Mao Zedong led a national mobilization for war. On October 19, 1950, UN troops conquered the capital, Pyongyang. As UN troops quickly advanced, they became spread out from other units. Their vulnerability to a counterattack was not appreciated even after Chinese soldiers began appearing in battle at the beginning of November. Then on November 25, the main contingent of Chinese stormed into the war. UN forces were surrounded and sliced up by 300,000 Chinese. Disaster now apparent, UN troops had to reverse direction and break through to the south, or east to the sea. GIs who thought they would be home for Christmas were now fighting for their lives. This was also when the largest contingent of Americans became prisoners. The Chinese reported capturing more than 3,000 in their first weeks of fighting.[21]

Back in the United States, the scope of the defeat emerged slowly due to censorship. An Associated Press reporter had to travel to Tokyo to reveal that "correspondents are not permitted to use the word 'retreat,'" and stories often had lead paragraphs scissored out. Military censors were especially prickly about reports on GI morale.[22] American readers did receive a map's-eye view of events. The urgent movement of reinforcements and the number of miles the Chinese advanced were reported, as were the locations of key battles, which kept moving southward. With headlines like "Half of Trapped GI Force Escapes," about a surrounded regiment having to sneak through enemy lines, readers could fill in many of the censored lines. Casualty figures were downplayed, but adjectives still described "staggering" blows and "blasted" regiments.[23] Battles were fought in multiples of ten below zero Fahrenheit. In early January 1951, headlines read "Seoul Abandoned to Red Armies; City Afire," then "Reds Now Half Way to Pusan Beachhead," which sounded like a repeat of the beginning of the war.[24] Once AP reporter Don Whitehead got back to New York, he could write that "the bleak, bloody story of Korea is approaching an end." According to Whitehead, many officers and "most war correspondents" were certain that evacuation from the peninsula was "inevitable."[25] The retreat erased the hopes raised by Inchon.

By early February 1951, the danger of defeat faded as the Chinese phalanx was ground down by superior UN firepower and taut supply lines. Along the Chichon-ni road, artillery and tanks wiped out a 2,000-person detachment of Chinese, while suffering 15 dead and wounded.[26] Months of effort, astounding casualties, and supply shortages had exhausted the Chinese troops. Half of the soldiers also had a shortage of toes, which had turned black and fallen off from frostbite.[27] Chinese troops began deserting in significant groups, especially those impressed from nationalist forces defeated in the Chinese civil war. This influx became part of the UN side of the POW quandary. The UN troops were able to re-retake Seoul and return to the general area of the 38th Parallel. Seoul changed hands four times, a measure of the desperation of the fighting. A new Chinese offensive in spring 1951 progressed for a time, but was turned around by the end of May. The collapse of the spring offensive resulted in an especially large number of POWs. China lost 90,000 troops in the last week of the campaign, 10,000 to capture.[28] Mao and his advisers concluded that they could not win the war outright, although Chinese generals remember the war as a success because it prevented an American invasion.[29] They had hoped to win the South, but would settle for saving the North.

By summer 1951, neither side believed it had a sensible chance of winning, which changed the character of the war for good. Expectation of a negotiated settlement meant that facts on the ground would shape peace talks, so jockeying for advantage and narrow attacks to adjust an armistice line became the rule. This meant that keeping territory already won would require elaborate fortifications of cement bunkers and networks of tunnels. The Chinese dug hundreds of miles of tunnels, which they called a Great Wall underground.[30] Once they were below the bombs, the UN lost some of its edge. Offensives against UN firepower had always entailed great sacrifice, but the underground Great Wall also made UN offensives exceptionally costly. In May 1951, Washington gave up on using "military means" to unify Korea, codified in the secret planning document NSC-48/5.[31] The last major UNC attempt to shift boundary lines began in late summer of 1951. The US Army 2nd Division suffered 3,000 casualties to take three small hills in the area known as the Iron Triangle. Nearby, an attack on Heartbreak Ridge cost 5,600 killed or wounded. After weeks of effort and thousands of casualties, the enemy simply backed up to the next line of hills. This dulled the American command's appetite for major ground offensives. UN Commander Matthew Ridgway decreed that all assaults of battalion size and larger had to be approved by the Far East Command.[32] The UNC began relying more on aerial bombardment for the remainder of the war. The largely static trench lines were especially grueling and demoralizing for the combatants. Dimming war aims made the conflict difficult to understand and support. The initial goals were to save the Seoul regime and, after Inchon, to reunite the peninsula. The stalemate removed these motives and offered no clear replacements.

Forced by circumstance, the parties began armistice negotiations on July 10, 1951. According to the army history of Korea, the advent of talks created a "disinclination on both sides to disturb the status quo radically."[33] With their allies saved from destruction, each side signaled its intention not to broaden the war. Washington declined to attack rich targets in Manchuria and removed nuclear weapons stationed on Guam.[34] Stalin nearly abandoned Kim Il Sung after Inchon, continuing to send munitions only when China provided the manpower.[35] The military stalemate shaped the remaining course of the Korean War. Most conflicts end with a victor dictating terms, but in a negotiated settlement, every last detail—including exchange of POWs—could be contested and paralyze the peace talks. Both sides still had fight left in them and were not so desperate for peace that they would swallow a poisonous truce. Negotiations extended the conflict into the political arena, where the parties tried to push an armistice to their benefit. Shifting gears into political warfare was natural for both contenders, since they had so much to tell the world about the respective merits of their societies. The Americans were enamored by psyops and the Chinese were experienced revolutionary agitators. In the game of propaganda, POWs would be used to keep score. This not only prolonged captivity, but it also made prisoners more conspicuous than in any previous conflict.

For Americans, the unsettling course of the war fed their Cold War preoccupation with weakness. The superpower not only failed to occupy North Korea, it was nearly pushed into the sea twice. If a high-tech behemoth could not prevail against peasant soldiers, then there must be something wrong. Korea put POWs front and center so that collaborators were readily available for morality tales.

# 2

# The Middle Passage

*Life-Changing Horrors in the First Year of Captivity*

We buried them naked.
—Bill Smith

One of the first things to know about Korean captivity is that 38 percent of 7,190 American POWs died. The Pacific theater in World War II was the closest comparison to Korea; there, a third of prisoners died at the hands of the Japanese. In contrast, 99 percent of American POWs in Europe survived.[1] The phrase "middle passage" refers to the trip across the Atlantic that took African slaves to the Americas. West Africans were transformed from individuals into chattel as they spent weeks chained below deck. Many POWs went through a comparable life-changing trial. For those captured during winter, mortality was higher than the Atlantic passage, for there was no profit motive protecting the commodity. Most prisoners were captured early in the war and suffered through the worst of it. From armed and dangerous warriors, they became utterly dependent on the captor and survived at his whim. They had to focus on the basics of survival: safety, warmth, and food, in that order. Those at home found it difficult to understand why the duty of revealing only name, rank, and serial number was not always fulfilled in captivity. According to military researchers, not one returnee claimed to have stuck to it.[2] Prisoners resisted constantly, but not in overt ways that courted disastrous consequences. Getting historical perspective on the POWs' cold welcome begins with the ordeal the prisoners experienced.

After President Truman entered the war, Task Force Smith was hastily loaded onto six transport planes and was the first American battalion in action. Few troopers had experienced combat, and their equipment was dated. With light weapons that were veterans of World War II and soldiers who were not, Smith headed out to block the full resolve of North Korea. The Korean Peoples Army was proceeding down the road from the capital to the port of Pusan in the southeast, so Task Force Smith set up the first roadblock near Osan. Soon a column of T-34 tanks came within range, but the GIs were dismayed to see their 2.36" bazooka rounds bounce off. The tanks hardly paused as they swept past, killing soldiers. The Americans were overwhelmed and forced to leave equipment and wounded behind. The story repeated itself further south as the troops tried to delay the invasion.

It was in this early series of defeats that the first batches of American prisoners were taken. By the end of July, nearly 900 GIs were held. Later in the summer, a group was forced to parade through the streets of captured Seoul holding banners denouncing the United States. Some were required to read statements at a rally.[3] American prisoners were taken in waves corresponding with enemy offensives. More than 4,000 were captured from November 1950 through February 1951, following Chinese entry. After the stalemate began in summer 1951, fewer than a dozen Americans were usually captured per month. Ninety-percent of American captures and 99 percent of deaths occurred in the first year.[4] POWs were guarded first by the North Koreans, then the Chinese— two quite distinct phases. The KPA made few preparations for prisoners, and the first year was marked by chaotic death marches through the snow to camps that were little more than marks on a map. No clothing was issued or permanent facilities arranged, no organization into squads, and little food was provided. When the Chinese entered the war, they began taking over POW custody and setting up a camp system that provided adequate shelter and calories by summer 1951.

Being taken prisoner was always bewildering, but it was especially so in Korea. The war began unexpectedly and the first troops were yanked out of occupation duty in Japan and given leaflets informing them they were going to a place called Korea to fight communism. It was called a "police action," leading many soldiers to expect light occupation duty such as directing traffic. "I thought we were going to patrol the streets or something," recalled Charles Harrison of Virginia. "But I gets there and seen the blood pouring from the backs of those trucks."[5] By late summer 1950, the North Koreans had grouped 751 prisoners in ad hoc facilities around the capital of Pyongyang. With time the plight of the prisoners might have improved, but any chance for this ended after the amphibious invasion at Inchon. As the UN invasion force approached from the south, the bedraggled prisoners were kept on the move. Their evacuation was led by a notorious North Korean officer nicknamed the Tiger, who announced his authority by shooting a senior POW in the head. Since there was limited transportation, the wounded often had to rely on others to carry them. Guards sometimes helped themselves to prisoners' boots and coats. Marchers went as long as 72 hours without food. Only 500 of the Tiger group were left a few months later.[6]

Veteran memoirs are full of accounts of another danger: the US Air Force, which attacked all structures and anything that moved. A freed corporal reported seeing three fellow prisoners killed by jets in fall 1950. William M. Allen was in a hut with other prisoners when an air strike sent napalm "running down the walls." They rushed for the door, but "there wasn't enough room so we took the whole wall out and ran in every direction.... All of us had our hair and beards burned off. Even my eyebrows were gone." Decades later airplanes still brought back the memory.[7] Friendly fire deaths were inadvertent; others were not. As UN forces advanced, the KPA executed prisoners liable to be retaken. At Hill 303 in August 1950, 45 prisoners were found shot in the head, hands tied with communications wire. Glenn Reynolds recalled that "it was the most gruesome sight I've ever seen. These young guys were seventeen, eighteen, nineteen years old." In late October, 68 prisoners were murdered in the Sunchon railroad tunnel.[8] For many Americans, the first impressions of Korean War captivity came from these atrocity reports.

Those who survived evacuation were eventually placed in hastily created camps in the far north of Korea along the Yalu River bordering China. By spring 1951, POWs in Camp 5 were hungry enough to eat sprouting weeds. Weed soup was called "high gear" because you had to get into high gear to get it down. Some prisoners had watches and currency that could be traded with civilians while outside on work details. Iowan Teddy Sprouse paid $90 for five eggs.[9] All POWs got lice. For men already run down, an uncontrolled infestation could suck enough blood in a week to finish them off. The only defense was daily primate-style grooming. Bill Smith learned to turn his clothes inside out daily and run a burning stick down the seams to get the eggs. "When a man stopped killing his lice," remembered William Funchess, he "soon turned ash-gray and died."[10] Boiling clothes controlled lice for a time, but real relief came only in the second year when the Chinese began dusting the men with the pesticide DDT. There were also intestinal parasites. Teddy Sprouse went into a delirium after self-treating his worms by swallowing a wad of tobacco. He hallucinated that a friend dangled cabbage in front of his mouth to lure out a procession of worms until he gagged on a large one.[11]

POWs on the march drank whatever water was available and soon had dysentery. The combination of maladies was deadly: "What the dysentery didn't drain out of ya, the lice sucked out of ya," recalled survivor Lloyd Pate. Terminal cases got too weak to go outside to void, then expired in a few hours or days. Sanitation was insufferable in the first year. "Our quarters reeked of infected wounds and dysentery," a medic remembered.[12] The men were debilitated by dehydration and having to constantly get up during the night. This became even more difficult as night blindness set in from Vitamin A deficiency. Arden Rowley was fortunate to keep his night vision, so he guided others to the *benjo*. "I'd lead a train of those guys up to the latrine every night, even had to face them in the right direction so they wouldn't pee on each other."[13]

The causes of mortality changed with the months. During evacuations to the rear, most fatalities were among the wounded. In the first half-year in the camps, dysentery, cholera, pneumonia, and hepatitis took the most lives. Later, prisoners died of an accumulation of maladies including exhaustion, poor resistance to disease, and nutritional deficiencies like pellagra, scurvy, and beriberi. It was not uncommon for POWs to lose 50 percent of their body weight. Some awoke in the morning next to a corpse.[14] Freed prisoners displayed a casual familiarity with death. When debriefed, they rattled off the causes of the death of friends with numbing repetition: dysentery, pneumonia, TB, malnutrition, untreated wounds. "No medical treatment" was constantly reported as a cause of death.[15]

Compounding the ills was the cold. Most were captured in the famously freezing winter of 1950–1951, with temperatures dropping below –30 Fahrenheit. Bill Smith recalled, "you could throw a cup of water and it would freeze by the time it hit the ground." The cold made fingers too numb to catch lice, calories too limited to fight infection, bodies too exhausted to carry the wounded, and minds disengaged from the necessities of survival. Getting a drink required squandering energy on melting ice. Burial was another exhausting trial. Given the frozen ground, graves were often little more than a thin pile of rocks. "We buried them naked," Bill Smith remembered. "We needed their clothes."[16]

Prison camps could bring out the best in individuals, but also the worst. Richard Bassett recalled the stealing: "If you hung any clothes out to dry, you either had to stay right there or get a buddy to stand guard so your clothes would not get up and walk off." Hunger and scarcity created ferocious trading that made some racketeers comparatively comfortable. A British officer imprisoned with Americans at Chongsong wrote that "those on the verge of death paid up to ten dollars for a spoonful of sugar."[17] Another contributor to mortality was using food for gambling and loan sharking. Missionary Larry Zellers observed men so hungry that they would trade two meals tomorrow for one extra today, sending them into a fatal spiral. At camp An-Dong, Zellers spotted men cruising the mess hall looking for people who owed food, then "rush to take a seat next to his debtor victim." Some skilled gamblers won more food than they could eat. Zellers believed that such practices contributed to many deaths among the Tiger group.[18]

Informers were a constant danger. Like incarceration anywhere, the captors wanted news. While still under North Korean jurisdiction, Larry Zellers concluded that informing was "the chief weapon of the Communists in dividing the prisoners." The most insidious effect of informing was not getting caught for something, but making prisoners fear each other. "Every person you meet must be considered someone who can hurt you," Zeller recalled.[19] Decaying cohesion during the hungry times made it easier for the Chinese to inject new loyalties later on.

When China took charge of imprisonment, it used a series of transit camps as gathering points. These temporary camps were nearly as deadly as the North Korean ones.[20] Army researchers estimate the death rate at "the Valley" south of Pyoktong at 50 to 70 percent until it closed in January 1951. In fall 1950, about 800 of 2,000 who passed through "Death Valley" northeast of Anju-Sinanju had died. Conditions were slightly better in 1951 at the transit points GIs called "Mining Camp" and "Bean Camp." They were used throughout the year, with mortality of 25 percent.[21] The hub of the established facilities was Camp 5, an evacuated village on the Yalu River near Pyoktong. More camps spread out for 50 miles along the Yalu. In January 1951, columns of prisoners from closed facilities or the transit camps began arriving. Camp 5 did not start out with many supplies and the inmates arrived in desperate condition; 1,000 out of 5,000 perished.[22]

Prisoners had mixed experiences when first seized by the Chinese People's Liberation Army (PLA). Freshly captured prisoners were often congratulated on escaping from the mercenary army of Wall Street. PLA doctrine stressed undermining the enemy by appealing to his foot soldiers. While this was not always followed, it often cushioned the arrival of captives, especially if a PLA officer was present. Captives of the Chinese retained more watches and fountain pens than those caught by the North Koreans, but there was still pilferage, especially of boots. Arden Rowley had his boots forcibly exchanged for a thin pair of canvas shoes. William Allen's clodhoppers were luckily too big for Chinese feet. Like those seized by North Koreans, recent captives of the Chinese often faced fatal marches over hundreds of miles in bitter cold. After Robert Jones walked for weeks to Death Valley, he picked scabs off his wounds "for meat to keep me going."[23]

Despite hunger and the brutality of forced marches, POW memoirs uniformly preferred the Chinese to the North Korean. "As strange as it sounds, it was better for us," wrote William Allen. Without the Chinese, "there would not be a prisoner alive." Archie Edwards of Arcola, Illinois went so far as to say that "none of the Chinese guards were ever mean unless you got out of line, broke the rules. If you were under the Koreans, it was the meanest outfit in the world. Starving you to death, kicking you."[24] Once the camps were functioning well in 1951, "it was like moving from under a bridge into the Ritz Carleton Hotel," recalled Wilbert Estabrook. "All of a sudden we got rice, we got a sugar ration, tobacco ration. We had meat, fish and things like that." They were also given some athletic equipment and allowed to run religious services.[25] Eventually there was mail service, though it was manipulated.

The permanent camps held a peak of 13,000 UN POWs—a challenge to care for, especially since supplies moved only at night. By summer 1951 bare necessities were provided, crowding eased, inoculations made, and an annual allocation of two suits of clothes began. Some nutritional deficiencies continued and medical care was always rudimentary, but the captives now had the basic means of survival. By end of summer 1951 the death rate was almost zero, although transit from the battlefield could still be deadly. In the compounds around Pyoktong there were only two deaths after October 1951, both accidents.[26] Of course, part of the reason mortality declined was that all the weakest prisoners had already died, but there was still a dramatic change in conditions. Improved diet allowed prisoners to regain most of the weight they lost during the starving times. Arden Rowley was 175 lbs. at capture, dropped to 120, but was back to 150 upon release. Although the latter part of captivity met basic needs, the worst periods get the most attention. Rowley said it "irks me" that some prisoners "give people the idea that they were skin and bones" at repatriation. According to him, prisoners who were still emaciated upon release had other health problems.[27]

Many POWs were suspicious of how long it took for conditions to improve. Some suspected that the horrendous experience of the first year was designed to break them down and produce finks and collaborators. Former POWs have said that food got better after armistice talks began so that they would be well at repatriation. However, the improvement is also consistent with bad logistics that got better. Inadequate support crippled the Chinese army; air attacks and lengthening distances left even Chinese troops without food. A document captured in November 1950 described soldiers so hungry they were "unable to maintain the physical strength for combat" or evacuate the wounded. Chinese generals recollected that their supply problems were never solved.[28] For POWs, a big improvement came simply from the thawing of the Yalu River in spring 1951. The ice had been thick enough to support a 60-ton tank, but once it melted they started getting barge loads of vegetables. The Hinkle-Wolff study commissioned by the CIA concluded that "what appeared to be calculated brutality...was probably the result of lack of facilities, the breakdown of supply and communication" and the indifference of common soldiers.[29] The Chinese political objective of winning over prisoners is relevant. The officers in charge of reeducation were separate from the guards and intent on persuasion. The political operatives believed, correctly, that bad treatment bred resentment. Good treatment of captives was a part of well-established Maoist military doctrine known as the "lenient policy." It was designed to recruit captives into the red army and was used full-scale in the Chinese civil war.

Starvation would attract informants, but not adherents. In fact, the earliest systematic indoctrination effort was accompanied by improved conditions. The temporary facility near Kanggye, dubbed "Peaceful Valley" by the POWs, held only 300 or so soldiers for a few months beginning in December 1950 and was thought to be an indoctrination pilot project. Peaceful Valley had better food and a mortality rate of 10 percent, mainly wounded. Some graduates were sent around to explain the Chinese leniency policy to fresh captures. Nineteen were loaded with propaganda pamphlets and released at the front. The fact that one group of prisoners did receive adequate food during the worst period suggests that when the Chinese wanted to capture minds, they fed them first. This was apparent to Arkansas resident James Colbert, a survivor of the deadly Tiger March conducted by North Koreans. Once he reached Camp 3, "the Chinese gave us all the rice we could eat. They wanted to fatten us up so they could teach us to be Communists."[30] Since the chaos of war can cause hunger, proving that POWs were starved on purpose would require archival evidence of Chinese planning. Unless such documents surface, it is apparent that malnutrition was due to disastrous logistics and prioritizing combat troops. Food was still manipulated for reward and punishment, but not to the point of famine.

Despite improvements, the deaths of the first year reminded survivors that they were at the mercy of their captors. It was a population where the worst human behavior was already established. Informing and collaboration emerged well before political indoctrination began under the Chinese. A postwar analyst who went through the piles of debriefings guessed that 10 percent of prisoners informed on their fellows at least once.[31] Fighting, stealing, and mistrust encouraged every man to be for himself, and led many to turn to the enemy. Richard Bassett concluded that "the roots of what happened could be found in that first terrible winter of starvation and death." Prisoners had gone through too much to feel secure about what might happen next. Ex-prisoners told CIA researchers that "uncertainty is the most unbearable aspect of the whole experience."[32] In a dangerous, unpredictable world, it was not wise to antagonize the bosses.

The need for medical care was a strong inducement to cultivate the captors. Frank Noel, an incarcerated AP photographer, reported that in his camp the price for getting an aspirin was a signature on a propaganda peace petition. Cpl. Kenyon Wagner of Detroit stated that before he was given medication for tuberculosis, he complied with a request to write an article about the quality of health care in the camps. A military study after the war found that POWs who resisted the Chinese tended to arrive home in worse physical condition.[33] Although instructors who scrupulously followed the lenient policy would not have condoned medical extortion, sick POWs often felt it was in their best interest to cooperate.

The prisoners remained in a state of uncertainty. With information filtered and mail opened, captives did not have consistent news of the world. Some information came from the trickle of new prisoners, but for the most part Chinese political officers controlled what came in. Officers were segregated from enlisted men and natural leaders who arose were quickly transferred. This was a simple measure, but it kept prisoners off-balance. Residents were divided into barracks and work details with appointed overseers. The captors cultivated dependence in their charges not just for food, shelter, and clothing, but in order to isolate prisoners from prior influences. After the war, a social scientist recommended that American penitentiaries adopt Chinese methods. Dr. Edgar Schein told a seminar of prison wardens that they should create "social disorganization" among inmates to separate them from old influences. For example, "tricking men into written statements" and then reading them to others would teach inmates to "trust no one."[34]

Once the dying was over, prisoners could worry about how to pass the time. One method was smoking the marijuana that grew in abundance, which may have been pointed out by Turkish prisoners. Rolling weed quickly became a favored use of communist newsprint. Morris Wills stated that the marijuana was smoked socially as the men lounged: "Almost everyone enjoyed it and kept doing it." After the camps were picked clean, GIs began bringing leaf back from wood details. The Chinese were ambivalent toward the drug, usually ignoring it, sometimes seizing it, other times using it as a reward. Sgt. Donald L. Slagle reported that it was tolerated in Camp 5, while Morris Wills described a crackdown in Camp 1 in spring 1952 that reduced him to "smoking stems."[35] After the war, cannabis use was cited as yet another example of the delinquency of servicemen in Korea.

The chief concern of every prisoner was going home. The invasion of the South had been defeated by the United States. The invasion of the North had been defeated by the Chinese. What was left to fight over? Unbeknownst to them, a brewing military stalemate would affect them in two ways: It would turn them into propaganda objects, and double the length of captivity. This emerged out of the unique circumstances of limited war.

# Andersonville East

## Communist Prisoners Are Pressured to Defect

The biggest flap of the whole war started on Koje.
—General Mark Clark, discussing a United Nations POW camp

Tucked away in the National Archives in Washington, DC is a faded, cloth register with the handwritten title, "Report of Boards of Officers, POW Division." The ledger is a guide to the investigation files documenting deaths and injuries of prisoners in US/UN custody in Korea. One-line summations describe 279 case folders. Within the terse language of an index can be glimpsed a scene of remarkable savagery. A selection of entries:

Fourteen deaths, killed by other PWs 10 Jun 52
One death and 8 injuries, NK POWs shouting 12 Sep 52
Thirty-nine deaths, and seventeen injuries, disturbance 24 Oct 52
One death, POWs singing NK songs, concussion grenades used 24 Oct 52
Fifty-six deaths and ninety-six injuries, attacks to UN command personnel
    2 Aug 52
PW proceeding from tent to kitchen in violation. Refused challenge by guard
    & was shot fatally 4 Jan 53
PW died from injuries received when falling from jeep & assaulting
    interrogator 7 Jan 53[1]

The first half of the index included the names of casualties, but individuality fell away as cases multiplied. The figure for the total number of killings in UN custody is hard to confirm, but the Board of Officers documented 500 violent deaths. The Ridgway headquarters revealed that by the end of 1951, 6,600 had died of all causes, although the worst violence came after 1951.[2] General Mark Clark acknowledged that hundreds died in factional fighting. In late 1952 North Korean General Nam blamed the United States for 3,000 casualties.[3]

Whatever the precise number, the ferocity is reminiscent of another prison camp, Andersonville, during the American Civil War, which was also racked by violence and predation. Epidemics and hunger made mortality far worse in Andersonville, but there was a similarity in gang murders and resource wars. As a rule, United Nation Command (UNC)-held prisoners in Korea got more and better food than their counterparts fed by the Chinese, their medical care was much better, and a Swiss Red Cross representative praised the warm winter clothing, same as GIs got.[4] These advantages were eclipsed, however, by the endemic violence. Individuals were at far greater risk in a United Nations Command camp than if held by the Chinese after summer 1951.

The violence stemmed largely from a UNC psychological warfare operation. Like the GIs being fed Marxism with their millet, the Chinese and North Korean prisoners were subjects of the Cold War competition for minds. Some of the POWs were alienated from their communist governments to begin with, and they were used to coerce others to denounce their home regimes. When the psychological operation evolved into a demand that prisoners defect and not return to their families, the compounds burst into civil war. The wider war was also affected. The defection campaign led to an 18-month impasse at peace negotiations, prolonging the trial of American prisoners as well.

During the first three months of the war American commanders were more worried about becoming prisoners themselves than the few enemy they had caught. But after the North Korean army scattered following Inchon, the UNC began capturing droves—more than 100,000 Koreans in October 1950 alone. Captives continued to be taken throughout the drive to the Yalu, quickly filling the makeshift camps in Pusan, Pyongyang, and Inchon. Ninety percent of the UNC catch was taken during the first year of the war. The entry of the Chinese created another source of captives once Mao's spring 1951 offensives faltered, dropping thousands more into UNC hands.

Managing the flood of prisoners was difficult. UN forces were outnumbered, and all hands were needed at the front. When it became clear that the war would not end anytime soon, the UNC searched for a way to secure prisoners with as few guards as possible. A prison island would make escapes difficult, so in spring 1951 the UNC moved thousands of enemy personnel to Koje-do, 20 miles southwest of the Pusan nerve center. (The suffix "do," pronounced "doe," means "island.") By the time Koje facilities were finished, more than 150,000 prisoners were deposited into four sprawling enclosures. A peak of 170,000 was reached in summer 1952. There were 21,000 Chinese and the rest were Koreans of both latitudes, but mostly northern. Each enclosure was subdivided into eight or so crowded compounds of five to eight thousand inmates. To reduce the amount of farmland appropriated from island farmers, barracks straddled ridges and harsh, rocky ground. Prisoners were initially segregated by country, later by political label.[5]

The many prisoners and few guards presented the biggest challenge in controlling Koje-do. For much of the time, barracks held five times the number they were built for. Managing them was hampered both by a shortage of guards and their low quality. "All castoffs were channeled into this assignment," complained an officer.[6] A contingent of South Korean guards filled out the ranks, but camp authorities had difficulty communicating with them and considered their abilities below even the American dregs. Army doctrine prefers a ratio of 1:20 guards to prisoners, but in fall 1951, it was 1:33. The proportion of Americans to prisoners was 1:188. General Mark Clark recalled that much of the time, "we didn't even know exactly how many prisoners were on the island." Identification and fingerprinting were not finished until the war was almost over.[7] Prisoners switched identities during work details, delivered messages to other compounds, and generally ran circles around the guards. There was also trading with villagers, which became a conduit for messages and orders from the North.

Given the ratio of guards, the interiors of the camps were self-run. As is often the case in prisons, a harsh, stratified social order developed as cliques competed for supporters, supplies, and prey. The governance of prison communities was taken over by what began as inmate police gangs, but came to rule all aspects of a compound. While the US Army provided enough supplies for POWs, it could not guarantee fair distribution, so gangs became centered on the control of goods. A postwar analysis considered them to be essentially "private armies." The chief, or "hancho," distributed food, assigned desirable work details to cronies, and decided who got comfortable quarters or slept in a cold draft.[8] The inmate gangs were organizing themselves even before Koje-do opened. A South Korean named Se Hee Oh was captured in fall 1950 after having been press-ganged by the KPA. Upon arrival at a camp in Pusan, he and the other new POWs were greeted with a demonstration of authority by inmate guards: "Wading into our midst they began beating us indiscriminately with their weapons. They were extremely violent, cracking heads and backs with hard blows." Oh observed that "they had been trained in crowd control and were masters at the brutality used in the process. They slept, ate and fraternized together."[9] Once on Koje-do, Se Hee Oh managed to head up the kitchen in Compound 65, but was displaced by gangsters from the Inchon area who wanted "the ultimate power position in a prison camp," control of food. There were five different levels of food service in C-65, with access determined by proximity to power. The inner circle enjoyed wine tasting parties, while the bottom rung got scrapings. Clothing was also jealously held. As winter approached, crates of overcoats, socks, and other warm gear arrived. US Army issue tended not to fit East Asians, so the hancho and his favorites got dibs on the smaller sizes. Everyone else dressed in baggy trousers, looking like "bearded, Oriental Charlie Chaplins," according to Oh.[10]

The American command saw the POWs as a resource as well as a burden and began thinking about how to use them. The defense establishment had always hoped that communism's weakness was the resentment of its own people. Encouraging flight by Soviets and East Europeans became a favorite tactic in the 1940s, and in early 1951 the National Security Council resolved to "encourage and induce" as many defections as possible. The Voice of America once played the train song "Casey Jones" in the background of a story about a Czech engineer who drove a locomotive across the border.[11] The offer of a stunning $100,000 for pilots escaping in Soviet MIGs netted three jets, two Poles, and a Chinese.[12] The thousands captured in Korea were a jackpot, the first opportunity to test en masse popular acceptance of communism.

Prisoners taken in Korea offered especially tantalizing possibilities. About two-thirds of the Chinese were actually former soldiers of Chiang Kai-shek's Kuomintang (KMT), the conservative nationalist party that lost the civil war to the communists and retreated to the island of Taiwan (Formosa). Thousands of former KMT soldiers had been retrained in Maoism and absorbed into the Peoples Liberation Army and later sent to the Korean front.[13] After capture by UN troops many reverted, although the number has been exaggerated. Ambassador to South Korea John J. Muccio reviewed interrogation data and suggested that some prisoners criticized Bejing to "secure preferential treatment," noting they had actually fought quite effectively. The Korean soldiers also offered opportunities. The North Korean army had replenished its ranks on the move with 50,000 captured southern soldiers and thousands more civilians, many of whom were later recaptured by the UNC.[14] Between those born in the south and those estranged from Kim Il-sung, many Korean prisoners were receptive to anticommunism. In September 1950, the Joint Chiefs of Staff ordered a pilot program to investigate "exploitation" of POWs for "psychological warfare purposes." Prisoners might be used for propaganda, as spies, or as a conspicuous stream of defectors. Results were judged promising, and in mid-1951 the program was expanded to all POWs. As new prisoners were processed they were scrutinized for receptivity, especially former officers of the KMT. "They selected the traitors and defectors," in the view of a Chinese colonel. "These Chinese turncoats, I have to say, were worse than the American and South Korean guards."[15] They were recruited to help take physical control of as many barracks as possible and turn the prisoners against their governments.

The psyops program adapted for Koje-do followed two distinct tracks: propaganda and force. The 704th Detachment of the Army's Counterintelligence Corp (CIC) worked with agents in the barracks, while indoctrination was run by the Civil Information and Education (CIE) section of the Far Eastern Command, fresh from occupation duty in Japan.[16] Both the CIC and CIE had their own chain of authority to the Far East Command, to the aggravation of the guard officers. The head of CIE's field operations described its objective as persuading prisoners that they would be "better off socially, politically, and economically under a democratic rather than totalitarian regime."[17] A former officer, Monta L. Osborne, was chosen to head the enterprise, in part because he had worked with the anticommunist Chiang Kai-shek.[18] When initially conceived, the psy-warriors could not have realized how much their program would impact the course of the war.

The enormity of the project dwarfed the initial 20 CIE officers who arrived at Koje-do in May 1951.[19] Only nine were designated as instructors, and their background in education was spotty. Asked why one member was assigned to CIE, an officer scratched his head, gazed at the soldier's file, and noted that he once coached grade-school basketball; "somebody must have" seen that, he surmised.[20] Americans did a limited amount of the teaching through POW translators, but depended mainly on personnel sent by Taiwan and Seoul. At least 23 Chinese teachers were secretly hired from Taiwan by the CIE, and another 100 came from South Korea.[21] The CIE hid the source of its operatives, telling even inspectors from Washington that "there is no contact" between prisoners and Taiwan.[22] Several years after the war, an American officer's book about Koje-do gave a dissembling impression that there were no instructors from the KMT, even though Col. Kenneth K. Hansen was the Far East Command's chief of psychological warfare at the time and in charge of it all.[23]

Koje-do was often shrouded from the outside world, sometimes even from the Red Cross. An exception was made, however, for Christian missionaries who held huge meetings in select compounds. A Christian writer accompanying New York's Cardinal Francis Spellman on a tour of Koje-do witnessed nine or ten thousand POWs listening to a sermon in Chinese by the Rev. Earle J. Woodberry. The writer believed that Woodberry and Korean preachers were largely responsible for "the refusal of thousands of POWs" to accept repatriation. An exaggeration, but it does illustrate the effort to win recruits. Also active was an American chaplain from the Eighth Army, Col. Wu Boli.[24]

The CIE attracted prisoners through a variety of educational programs. CIE head John Benben recalled that vocational training was especially popular, followed by reading classes among the many illiterates, especially among the Chinese. The core of the lesson plan, however, was ideological: to give them an "understanding of the events that led to the present world conditions." Participants spent about 25 hours a week in CIE classes, and 80 percent attended at some point.[25] Indoctrination of POWs was also assisted by lectures by South Korean "educators, businessmen, diplomats, and government officials."[26]

The CIE in Tokyo sent over 353 educational films and crates of bound material that had been used in the American occupation. Much of the material was produced for US public schools, including the pamphlets *Our Friends, the*

POWs on Koje-do using US Army soap for sculpture, February 1952. Camp activities encouraged defection from communism. Cpl. Elmo J. Shingleton, Army Signal Corp.

*Policemen* and *Having a Good Time with Others.* Films included *Folk Songs of the South, Meet Your Federal Government, Crime of Korea,* and *Hookworm.* While the titles might seem inappropriate, even comical, they were a break from monotony and did provide a glimpse of America. More tantalizing were the Sears and Montgomery Wards catalogues that were passed around.[27] Most popular were Hollywood films, including *High Noon* and *Young Mr. Lincoln.* Being as large as a city, Koje-do also had its own radio station broadcasting over loudspeakers. Content from South Korean stations and the United Nations blared "morning, noon, and night." The importance of entertainment was "a distinct third" to indoctrination, according to a psyops officer.[28]

Dependent on outsiders for translation, the CIE officers barely knew what was said in classrooms, much less controlled them. A massive postwar analysis was done by social scientists at George Washington University's Human Resources Research Office (HumRRO), it concluded that lack of linguistic skills was "the most significant deficiency" in the program, for "almost none could speak Korean" and few knew Japanese or Chinese. In and of itself, the CIE propaganda had limited effect on its captive audience; it was abstract and removed from the lives of men who were primarily agrarian. HumRRO analysts concluded that the teaching "could not break loose from its Western origin." Since culturally unspecific propaganda left a light impression, the real persuasion came from the operatives from Seoul and Taiwan. These individuals took instructions from their own governments. HumRRO considered them agents "both in the classrooms and out."[29]

Initially, inmate gangs were most concerned with issues of possession, power, and prestige, and did not necessarily take sides in the capitalist/communist ideological battle. Arguments over private or communal ownership had little relevance when the captors owned everything anyway. Few gang leaders were "animated principally and from the beginning" by ideology, according to HumRRO. But as time went on, barracks bosses either got political or were pushed aside. In cooperation with the CIC, agents from Taiwan and South Korea posed as prisoners and took control of many compounds. Chiang Kai-shek sent 75 agents specifically to take control of Chinese barracks, according to Ambassador Muccio.[30] They set up brotherhoods and secret societies in the compounds. The Republic of Korea's National Police and the Pao Mi Chu security bureau in Taiwan helped identify right-thinking prisoners who could be promoted to compound leadership. The Anti-Communist Youth League (ACYL), which had branches throughout South Korea, expanded into the compounds on Koje-do.[31] With help from the guards, they arranged the arrest and segregation of committed communists and systematically promoted friendly gang leaders. In Korean Compound 83, camp authorities chose a new police chief on the recommendation of Lt. Pak, an anticommunist prisoner and influential advisor to the administration. Pak's people identified the red "plotters" in the compound, who were quickly arrested.[32] Similarly, in C-65 "it was the [inmate] guards who wielded the real power in the camp," recalled Se Hee Oh. Called Section Police, they wore armbands and numbered about 100 in his compound. C-65 was commanded by a major from the South Korean military. "I never learned how he happened to become a prisoner of the US Army," wrote Oh.[33] In Korean barracks hanchos tended to be from the south, even though northerners were more numerous and commonly of higher rank. Southerners were more likely to have been press-ganged and hostile to the regime of Kim Il-sung, which got them "preferential treatment" from camp authorities.[34] Taiwan and Seoul steadily gained influence; they not only knew the prisoners, they also knew what the camp command did and did not know, since they often provided the translations. Confined to the periphery, the Americans had only blunt means of influence. They could turn supplies on and off, arrest and segregate troublemakers, and open fire. But aiming these tools depended on intelligence filtered through foreign personnel. American authorities could not enter some compounds after dark, and the more hostile ones not at all, except in force. Ambassador Muccio visited Koje-do after a rash of fighting and found that discipline within the grounds was "no concern of camp command" unless it threatened UN personnel. This left the inmates to run city-sized facilities. "What went on within those compounds was never known or understood by the US military," Muccio recalled.[35] The UNC delegated control to its allies, then lost it altogether.

While resource battles embittered the atmosphere, the worst polarization was over repatriation. For prisoners, getting released was more important than anything except immediate survival, and the Americans held the keys to the gates. American psy-warriors invited talk of defection, and the instructors hired from Taiwan and Seoul were "vigorous propagandists" for not going home.[36] Repatriation turned ideological debates into a life and death issue. Prisoners who wanted to go home would have to fight the nonrepatriation faction, and vice versa. The political competition in the yards enlarged the constituency for nonrepatriation. For committed anticommunists whose treason in the camps became public, avoiding repatriation was a necessity, and they became desperate advocates for defection. Once an open movement against repatriation started, it gained a momentum that the American authorities could not control. While the United States did not promise asylum from the start, it may as well have because creation of a pro-UN constituency had much the same effect. Most prisoners were apolitical, wanted to go home, and would be difficult to turn around. By being open to defection, Washington set the context, providing an opportunity for committed anticommunist prisoners to stake out political turf and begin working on the rest. An ideological program in the camps guaranteed that repatriation would become an armistice issue, if for no other reason than because a portion of prisoners would demand it.

One technique nonrepatriation activists used extensively was petition drives. Petitions demanded things like induction into the South Korean army or simply for the right not to go home. They were often signed with a bloody thumbprint. HumRRO researchers concluded that the petitions represented "political control by highly motivated leaders."[37] The central direction can be seen in the often identical wording of petitions in different compounds.[38] Petitions were also a public announcement that the signers were in the nonrepatriation faction. While a POW might sign out of fear, not sentiment, once that public step was taken his self-interest changed. Since apparent alignment with anticommunists might have serious repercussions back home, it created new militants for nonrepatriation where there were none before.

Another body of information about conditions on Koje-do came from two communist journalists, Wilfred Burchett and Alan Winnington, who published *Koje Unscreened* in April 1953. With wide access to North Korean and Chinese sources, the book obtained substantial insider information that had trickled out of the camps. *Koje Unscreened* adds detail to events documented in other sources. The authors identified Compound 72 leaders as Taiwan Ministry of National Defense officers Chang Hsing-teng and Chang Chi-the. They reported that 100 officers from Taiwan were brought in to be barracks bosses. American CIC and Kuomintang interrogators scoured incoming prisoners for former members of the KMT. The KMT set up secret societies in the camps, which later emerged openly as the Oppose Communism Resist Russia Association (OCRRA), taking control in many compounds. Once strong enough, OCRRA or its Korean counterpart, the Anti-Communist Youth League, opened up storefront headquarters and, significantly, put the names of members on posters. According to the authors, unwilling POWs were systematically compelled to reject repatriation with beatings, starvation, or deadly doses of hard labor. *Koje Unscreened* did acknowledge, in a roundabout way, that many prisoners willingly joined the anticommunist groups, though the authors insisted on labeling all of them agents.[39]

Once China and North Korea sensed that mass defections were in the works, they aggressively sought a presence on Koje-do. The UN command was certain that a number of hearty enemy operatives got captured on purpose so that they could penetrate the island. These men of force and ability ensured that loyal compounds would have exceptionally capable leadership. The pro-communist, pro-repatriation network was resilient, ruthless, and centrally coordinated. The Korean Se Hee Oh watched an attempted takeover in C-65. The anticommunist inmate trustees were relaxing when they were set upon with clubs and improvised blades. Republic of Korea (ROK) guards had to rescue them. The inmate trustees then went on a rampage to catch any closet reds. "The suspect's mat location was noted during the day, making for a quick in-and-out snatch of the POW suspected of Red sympathies," said Oh. Se Hee Oh himself fiercely opposed the "mad dog" communists, but that did not protect him after he spoke out against the better food and privileges enjoyed by the trustees: "My body was a mass of bruises...the pain was a solid ache, my lips were so badly bruised I could not eat."[40]

It is important to note the chronology of violence in the camps. Historian Allan R. Millet found that in March 1951, Koje inmates "still seemed docile and cooperative," requiring few guards. The first major group outburst occurred in June 1951 when three North Koreans were shot dead after stoning guards in C-76. Bloodshed began building, both between prisoners and against guards, as defection became an issue. Ambassador Muccio found that a violent reaction to anticommunist barracks takeovers was well underway by January 1952. Larger spasms of killings followed after partial repatriation was formally introduced into truce talks. The defection issue transformed the camps into a war zone. The POW factions armed themselves with tent-pole spears, barbed wire flails, firebombs, and knives made from the metal reinforcement in combat

Civil war in the camps, July 1952. Homemade weapons seized from Chinese Compound 72 on Koje-do, including fake wooden guns, spears, and barbed wire flails. C-ration tins were used for the grenades, spearheads came from the metal supports in boots or steel drums. Dimitri Boria, Army Signal Corp.

boots.[41] Skull-cracking stones "as big as grapefruit" littered the terrain. In March 1952, in one of many rock fights, opposing Korean compounds 92 (north) and 93 (south) let loose at each other. ROK guards objected to being in the crossfire by killing 12 in C-92. The penalty for throwing a rock at a soldier was to be shot on the spot. According to one journalist, a guard would be reprimanded, in all seriousness, "only if he had missed or wounded the prisoner."[42]

The violence and polarization on Koje-do were chronicled in the award winning historical novel *War Trash* by Ha Jin. Although a fictional account, the author stated that "most of the events and details" were factual. Extensively researched in Chinese-language sources, the book's apolitical protagonist on

Koje-do wants to go home to his family, but had been forcibly tattooed with "Fuck Communism" on his torso. In one gruesome passage, a KMT officer sliced flesh off a POW who insisted on going home, then ate it before a large audience. "That actually happened," according to Jin, who initially dismissed the story as "Communist propaganda." Ha Jin was also critical of pro-communist barracks bosses who sacrificed prisoners in riots fomented for publicity. Jin's title comes from the American phrase "white trash," and refers to prisoners being the expendable refuse of both sides.[43]

To prevent backsliding, antirepatriation leaders used compulsory tattooing.[44] Once they dominated an enclosure, they systematically inscribed residents with anticommunist slogans. A prisoner considering flight to a red stockade wearing a slogan like "Down with the communist dogs" would have to think twice.[45] KMT symbols or maps of China on the back were common. Former prisoner Zhang Da reported that camp thugs brutalized and tied him, then drilled "Oppose the communists and resist Russia" into his arm. He later sliced it off with a razor. Another common tattoo was "Kill the pig for its hair," a play on Chinese homonyms Mao (hair) and his military commander Zhu (pig).[46] Time-Life journalist John Osborne reported that at Cheju Camp 3, *all* inmates sported Chinese characters announcing "Against communism in China, against Russia."[47] Interestingly, some of the tattoos were in English, suggesting an intended audience outside the camps. A journalist accompanying Cardinal Francis Spellman observed "Anti-Communist" and "Jesus my Savior."[48]

The most important message of the tattoos came simply from their existence. In Chinese and Korean cultures, body marking was considered *bu xiao*, a Confucian concept meaning disrespect of elders. This was a powerful taboo; tattoos defiled the body entrusted to the living by the ancestors. They were also associated with branding criminals and vassals. As a mark of ownership, tattoos reminded prisoners of their condition from the time they woke up until they fell asleep. Violence in the camps was intense enough to overcome Confucian taboo. Tattooing was a regular complaint of China and North Korea in the peace negotiations.

According to a Chinese author, tattooing began first in July 1951 among willing nationalist sympathizers, but by fall it was mandatory.[49] A well-placed observer from India, Lt. Gen. K.S. Thimayya, met with many POWs who "said they had no political beliefs when captured. Several told me they wanted to go home in spite of being tattooed all over their body with such things as 'down with the communist dogs.' "[50] Chinese communist Col. Zhao Zuorui was undercover in a nationalist Compound 72 on tattoo day. A KMT leader he identified as Li Da-an called an assembly to announce compulsory tattooing. Those who objected were beaten by trustees in front of the whole group. According to Zuorui, one prisoner still would not relent. The unit leader chopped off an arm,

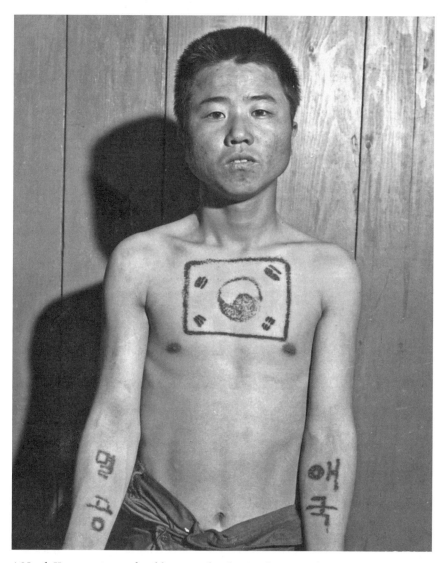

A North Korean prisoner forcibly tattooed with a South Korean flag. Arm on left: "Eradicate North Korean communism;" on right: "Love of South Korean motherland." Koje-do, July 1952. Dimitri Boria, Army Signal Corp.

then tore out his heart and displayed it to the crowd.[51] Forced tattooing demonstrated just how determined Seoul and Taiwan were to thwart "voluntary" repatriation.

Some American officials outside the CIC became troubled as they caught on to the dubiousness of the defections. P. W. Manhard, an assistant to the US Ambassador to South Korea, spent months on the island assisting interrogations of Chinese prisoners. He reported:

SECRET March 14, 1952

Chinese prisoners of war are controlled by a thin veneer of PW trustees not freely elected by the prisoners whom they control, but appointed by US Army camp authorities on the basis of ostensible anti-Communism....These trustees exercise discriminatory control over food, clothing, fuel and access to medical treatment for the mass of Chinese prisoners. With encouragement from Formosan Chinese assigned to PW work by GHQ Tokyo, the trustees have for several months conducted a drive to collect petitions for transfer to Formosa. This propaganda drive is now reaching a climax with use of brutal force to obtain signatures....Trustees have openly announced to fellow prisoners, "It has been officially decided that all who wish to do so will be guaranteed an opportunity to go to Formosa—those who do not wish to fight Communism will remain in the POW camp indefinitely."...Forced, coerced removal to Formosa [is] in direct contradiction of the UNC stand at Panmunjom on voluntary repatriation.[52]

Manhard's account displays one of the great ironies of the Korean War. The novel repatriation policy was said to be voluntary, but actual practice was often the opposite: It prevented many prisoners from going home. Manhard's reports were taken seriously by American ambassador to South Korea, John Muccio, who referred to barracks bosses as "Gestapos." Another State Department functionary reported that the Chinese compounds opposed to going home were "violently totalitarian" and run by "thugs."[53]

While both pro and anticommunist barracks were tightly run, the nonrepatriates had more difficulty controlling the ranks, for they stood in the way of home. Deterring escapes into rival yards was imperative. Ohio native James Jacobs was a guard on Koje-do who caught a prisoner scaling a fence one night. He returned the man to the compound leaders, but next day found his corpse hanging from the fence. HumRRO analysts were clearly embarrassed to report that, "generally speaking, brutality was most evident in the anti-Communist South Korean compounds." They explained this unwelcome finding by claiming that communist compounds were controlled so tightly that violence was not needed. However, it is hard to imagine how communist cadre could out-menace the tearing out of a beating heart. The anticommunist yards were also unique in having internal jails for "PW's suspected of Communist sympathies or other dissident views." HumRRO again attributed this to the communists not needing confinement because of total domination.[54] A more likely explanation is that right-wing jails were needed to cure homesickness and were indulged by the UNC.

A number of influences, then, pushed barracks clans toward political identifi-cations, and once politics were enforced with the brutal methods of resource gangs, the ideological polarization became self-perpetuating and all-defining. The world of Koje-do had conspired in all its detail to pit POWs against each other. While armistice negotiations stopped and started over the next 18 months, developments in the camps grew more intractable. With everything to lose, the infighting was fierce.

The Americans had not yet raised incomplete repatriation as a condition of peace talks, but the communists quickly perceived a plot to humiliate them and kidnap their soldiers, and were sure to reject a formal proposal for voluntary repatriation. When the terms of a prisoner exchange finally came up, there was every possibility that peace talks would collapse. If that hap-pened and the war dragged on, American prisoners would suffer too: They would be captives of both the Chinese and a psyops campaign of their own government. Proposing voluntary repatriation would also raise the stakes on Koje-do. The committed communists would need to prove to the world that voluntary repatriation was a wicked effort to withhold prisoners, and could launch desperate riots and mutinies. The anticommunists would also feel an urgency. They could not know for certain that the Americans would not renege and send them home in order to achieve peace. The more numerous and fiercely disciplined they were, the harder it would be to sell them out. The Koje psyops operation was setting the scene for what General Mark Clark referred to as "the biggest flap of the whole war."[55]

# Welcome, Fellow Peasant

## The Chinese Seek Converts

The policy of good treatment of POWs should be properly carried out, giving them a good impression. Those who were well treated or given medical care on the battlefields were often deeply moved and it became easy for us to reform their thoughts.

—captured Chinese document

In December 1950, a man named Arden Rowley found himself shivering in the North Korean cold. Rowley was in a combat engineering battalion of the 2nd Infantry Division and had helped chase the North Koreans back up the peninsula. He was one of thousands captured when the Chinese stormed into the war. Many died around him in the early, temporary prison camps, but Rowley held on until conditions improved. In the regular, permanent prison camps along the Yalu River, the Chinese provided sufficient food, clothing, and shelter—but in return, they wanted the prisoners to accept the gift of light: revolutionary thought. This was the leniency policy. Each platoon was assigned an instructor to supervise the POWs during long, daily studies of revolutionary politics.

Reeducation of prisoners had worked well during the Chinese civil war, and an experienced cadre of political operatives were sent to Korea. They were joined by several hundred young Chinese recruited right out of university.[1] Western prisoners, however, proved less impressionable than soldiers of the defeated Kuomintang (KMT). Arden Rowley saw firsthand how hard it was for captors to make friends with those they kept caged. In a memoir, Rowley wrote that guards (not political instructors) had seized one Harold J. Addington for an infraction of camp rules, trussed him up, and suspended him in the air. The agile Addington wriggled free and ran like hell into a crowd of prisoners, who protectively bunched around him in a face-off. The guards began setting up machine guns, while the political officers raced over to see what was happening to their prized pupils. Rowley wrote:

The Chinese instructors were devastated by what was happening. Here they had spent months telling us that Communism was the greatest and bragging to us about their lenient policy toward us, and all of a sudden they were faced with the most blatant incident of torture. We continued to form a tight group around Harold as we talked and negotiated with them. They told us that if we did not turn Harold over to them the machine gunners would most assuredly open fire.... Our [instructors] were standing nearby with tears running down their cheeks.[2]

The Chinese wept because they were believers. They considered American GIs to be humble laborers forced to fight against fellow workers. The Chinese were eager to explain that poor peasants in Asia could not possibly threaten the American homeland, so GIs were really there to serve their masters in Washington and Wall Street. POWs thus had two distinct groups of Chinese to cope with: the guards, and the political cadre. Armed soldiers stayed on the periphery to keep order and prevent escapes. "You didn't even talk to the guards," recalled Rowley. The political officers were a different breed. Well educated and familiar with the United States, some spoke excellent English. They were often full members of the Chinese Communist Party with years of success winning adherents to the revolution. After experiencing firsthand the destitution, violence, and oppression of old China, they believed that communist revolution was the only way for the wretched of the earth to rise. The Korean War was an opportunity to work with not just any oppressed group, but with the foot soldiers of the key imperialist power. Any real revolutionary would be thrilled by the prospect of enlightening such a strategic group of workers. The cadres' sincere intent to win hearts and minds was a counterweight to the universal tendency of guards to brutalize inmates. Arden Rowley's political instructors feared that months of progress would be destroyed with a single stupid incident. Actually, only limited numbers of POWs were warming to Marxism, but the Chinese desire to be the respected, politically wise elder brother gave the prisoners some leverage. They extracted a promise that Harold Addington would not be mistreated after they turned him over to the guards. (Addington reported that he was sent to solitary confinement for seven weeks.)[3]

The Chinese' revolutionary fervor is essential to understanding why the prison camps were run as they were. In stories about their captivity, ex-POWs prominently mention hunger, brutality, and close brushes with death. The reports of misery often come to dominate the memory, when actually there were very distinct phases of captivity. To get prisoners to warm to socialism, they had to be treated leniently. A US Army study said that treating opponents as victims of overlords was "so successful" during the Chinese civil war that much of the nationalist army turned against Chiang Kai-shek. This experience informed

Korea. A CIA survey found that "enthusiastic idealism" was "pervasive" among the instructors, who were "patient" in their efforts to explain socialism. Good treatment was supposed to start the moment a soldier was seized. Freshly captured William H. Funchess was "dumbfounded" when a Chinese officer greeted him warmly and said, "We are not mad at you. We are mad at Wall Street."[4] New captives were often given cigarettes. Formally, the Chinese did not even classify them as captured soldiers, rather as civilians illegally pressed into service by Wall Street. Prisoners were not called prisoners by the political cadre, but rather "student" or "comrade." Certainly, early captivity was sometimes as rough as anything dished out by the North Koreans, but the official lenient policy was usually followed in the established camps and often in the field. One captured document told soldiers, "Don't kill or maltreat, don't take personal possessions (especially not combat boots!), treat the wounded. Treat all POWs equally because 'US capitalists are the real enemy and the majority of POWs were laborers who were forced to fight.' " Another read, "Those who were well treated or given medical care on the battlefields were often deeply moved and it became easy for us to reform their thoughts."[5]

Another practice passed down from the Chinese civil war was catch-and-release. In one of the buried little secrets of the war, more than 500 American captives were let go after hurried political instruction. They were given pep talks, and sometimes revolutionary leaflets to pass on to other GIs. In the Chinese civil war, this had been quite effective for persuading soldiers that their own officers were more of a danger than the red army. One group of Americans unilaterally freed by the Chinese in late November 1950 said that they received food and bandages over three weeks of internment and were then walked near to American units and released. Four were released from William Funchess's group. Jack Chapman of Oklahoma knew of a group of 19 that were loaded down with propaganda and dropped off at the front lines.[6] The Chinese were serious about their politics.

A cold-hearted exception to the leniency policy was a group of 78 Air Force flyers subjected to months of deprivation and torture. They were singled out to extract confessions of germ warfare to support a propaganda campaign. Not all were beaten, but the physical and mental pressure on them was relentless. One B-29 copilot reported that he lost part of a hand to frostbite after being left in the cold with bindings cutting off circulation, and another said he fainted from suffocation, only to be awakened by his skin being burned.[7] Another method was to keep a flier awake by badgering him so long it desiccated his mind. The Air Force flyers were isolated in filthy cells that were often too small to stretch out in and always cold. Although it is less recognized, solitary confinement in and of itself is actual torture. Humans are biologically social, and prolonged isolation debilitates brain function. Prisoners of all kinds say that isolation is worse than beatings.[8] Another technique the Chinese applied was "stress positioning," where airmen were forced to hold a particular body position for long periods. A B-29 crew member reported having to stand through 40 hours of questioning, pausing only for latrine breaks.[9] The Hinkle/Wolff CIA study of captivity concluded that "any fixed position which is maintained over a long period of time ultimately produces excruciating pain." The authors specified that stress positions were "a form of physical torture." As prisoners stood endlessly, fluid accumulated in the legs, swelling them double. After about 18 hours, "the skin becomes tense and intensely painful," and expresses watery serum. Circulation declines, and victims eventually suffer kidney failure. Decades later, stress positioning was defended by the second Bush administration.[10]

Marine pilot Col. Frank H. Schwable said that it was "hard for anyone to understand" what he went through in an isolated valley. Guards interrupted his sleep every night for months. "I could lie down only when told, and was kept just sitting and sitting for weeks on end, the result of which was that my back became strained to a point where it was impossible for me to sit still more than fifteen minutes," he reported. The gathering Korean winter gave him something to think about. Cold eventually frostbit his knuckles and he was certain he would not survive the winter. At a point of physical collapse, Schwable was told—and believed—that he would die without confessing to germ warfare, and finally began signing statements. Once released into the regular prisoner population, witnesses reported seeing Schwable hallucinating and shadow boxing with invisible opponents.[11] Thirty-eight fliers eventually confessed to using bacteriological weapons in Korea. All recanted after repatriation.

While brutality did occur, it was not a constant in the regular permanent camps. When it did happen, it was generally inflicted by guards, not political instructors. The US Army concluded that "extensive research has disclosed that systematic, physical torture was not employed in connection with interrogation or indoctrination. For the most part, physical punishment resulted from offenses such as attempts to escape, stealing, and infractions of camp regulations." Not one POW is known to have died during a Chinese interrogation. Violence would poison classroom indoctrination. "They were interested in turning us into little commies," explained Arden Rowley. Torture stimulates solidarity among victims and is a lavish use of energy. As for physical assaults, a think tank contracted by the Army concluded that "three-fourths of all returning PW's received no mistreatment in Korea, and 94 percent experienced no incidents considered by them to be war crimes or atrocities."[12] (The ratio was undoubtedly different among those who did not make it back.) Though violence was more a possibility hovering in the background rather than a routine occurrence, prisoners were still a population under great stress. Ultimately, they were still trapped, held against their will at gunpoint, and for most the kind words of the leniency policy rang

hollow. While the instructors believed in the strategy of leniency, they still had
to keep control of classrooms made up of enemy soldiers. Violence was not a
pedagogical method, but instructors could and did resort to harsh punishments
if a prisoner was disruptive. Infantryman Bill Smith reported:

> We was having a lecture one time, and one of the guys said according to
> the Geneva Convention, we're supposed to get mail. And the guy who
> was doing the instructions up there said "you don't get mail for the sim-
> ple reason that the planes come over, they bomb everything, they even
> bomb the little dog on the road." And I just shifted kind of like this and
> said "yeah, he was probably pulling the 105 Howitzer." Unbeknownst
> to me the guy behind me was educated at Harvard and he knew every
> word I said. He grabbed me up like that, turned me around, spit in my
> face. And I kicked him. Reflexes. Shouldn't have done it but that's what
> happened. He took me up to the instructor and says, "I could have you
> shot. I should have you shot. Get down on your knees, and pray to me
> that I don't have you shot." I just backed up and said "shoot me, I pray
> to no man." Two of my buddies, very fortunately, ran up, threw me on
> the ground and dragged me out, said "he's beeokey," which in Chinese
> means sick. "Beeoky, beeokey, beeokey." That morning about two or
> three o'clock, they came and got me, took me in a room, pitch dark, and
> I stayed there for four months. Each day I got a bowl of cracked corn
> and millet and a bowl of water. The only daylight I saw was when they
> opened the door to feed me, and the only human I was in contact with
> was the Chinese guards at the door. After four months, when I got out
> of there, I couldn't hardly walk. That's when I was blind, I couldn't see,
> and it took me, oh, two weeks to get back to moving normally. I hadn't
> heard any voices or anything for so long. Everything seemed so strange.
> It was like almost learning a new language. Because you know, you're
> there and you're trying to keep your mind busy and yet you don't know
> where you are, but you know you don't wanna be there, but you have
> no control over it.[13]

Although violence was selective, the lore of Korean captivity is of relentless
atrocity. This is partly understandable; the men suffered terribly the first year
and the subsequent months of boredom were less noteworthy. But for some,
the actual war crimes were not enough. For example, a published collection of
reminiscences contains one man's extraordinary tale from an indoctrination session. The informant claimed that his close friend refused to sing the communist
"Internationale" and kept belting out "God Bless America" instead. He was taken
outside and cut in half with a machine gun. This event appears nowhere else

in the historical record, despite being a memorably poetic atrocity committed before hundreds of witnesses. It diverged from the patterns of violence and also bucked Chinese segregation of races into different companies—the storyteller was white, the victim and bosom buddy was black. Repatriates queried by this author had never heard of it and frankly doubted it.[14]

As it had done in China, the PLA put people into three categories: backward, middle, and advanced. The backward would never accept socialism and were segregated, the majority was in the middle and might be won over, and the advanced could be mobilized to appeal to the middle. In the camps, the backward, recalcitrant prisoners were the "Reactionaries." POWs who accepted Chinese politics became known as "Progressives," or just "Pros." The Chinese expected officers and the rich to be the most reactionary, but everyone was invited to progress. Required biographies helped identify who might be most alienated from American society, and prisoners showing promise were given special attention. Private Roger Herdon had lost his right hand and a tutor painstakingly held his left hand and traced out sentences. According to Herdon, the first words he was able to write since being wounded were "American imperialism, American monopoly."[15]

Significantly, the captors separated the officers, leaving the enlisted men adrift. "We were all the same rank," remembered Lloyd Pate. No one could tell anyone what to do. "Who the heck is going to enforce any type of discipline with a bunch of privates, PFCs, and a few corporals thrown in there?"[16] This helped the Chinese assert political leadership and reduced repercussions to GIs who accepted it.

Probably the most corrosive of military community was the snitching. Informing began during the hungry times when it could mean survival, but once a person started, the captors owned him. The Chinese guards inherited snitches from the North Koreans and developed more as well. News of escape plans was especially valuable, but the Chinese also wanted to know who was encouraging resistance to indoctrination or stealing food. Teddy Sprouse said that he and his friends anticipated a chance to requisition some potatoes, so they dug a secret hole in their hut, smuggling out dirt by the handful. Soon after filling their cache with spuds, they were dragged before a punishment hearing. They never identified the snitch. Larry Zellers recalled that "even if there is only a handful of informers in the entire group, you don't know who they are." This suspicion poisoned relations among POWs. An Army summation after the war concluded that "fear and suspicion" of informants was the biggest barrier to solidarity. "There was a rat in every squad," according to Lloyd Pate. "They'd start switching people around, and you'd wind up with a rat."[17]

Through close supervision and removal of officers, the captors tried to make the prisoners more receptive. In spring 1951, indoctrination began in earnest.

Each company of 200 POWs was assigned an English-speaking instructor who supervised lecture and study. He controlled daily activity, who worked, who did not. He determined whether the prisoner's lot was "pleasant or difficult." The possibility of early release for good students was also dangled in front of some POWs. This was enticing, since they knew of the prisoners freed at the front. The education program was insulated from other parts of the Chinese army, with military interrogations conducted by a separate branch. Serious intelligence gathering usually involved transporting a POW to Pyoktong, which was rarely done with nonofficers.[18] Typical days consisted of two hours of lecture to a large group, then breaking into squads for another four hours of supervised discussion. In groups, prisoners had to go over material until everyone could repeat the proper answer to a question. Much of the reason for cooperating was simply to get it overwith so they could go to lunch. Sgt. Walter McCollum from Louisiana explained, "You have to understand that having to listen to an extra hour of that [lecturing] could be pretty stiff punishment. Sometimes it made you want to scream, hearing it over and over again. But the men learned to answer right." Pupils were routinely required to write "cognitions"—that is, short summaries of what they had learned that day. A squad monitor appointed by the captors was responsible for collecting the assignments and making sure that everyone understood the lesson. Monitors suffered the sharpest scrutiny. They had an "infallible" way of getting them all written: "We didn't eat until my report was in," according to one prisoner. Rewards were possible for writing correct theme papers. In Sgt. McCollum's class, it was "first prize, two packs of ready-rolled cigarettes. Second prize, a cup of peanuts. Third prize, an apple....They got a lot of essays written."[19]

PLA instruction was notable for the extent that it used public scrutiny to challenge individual beliefs. Students were required to deliver answers out loud and have them checked for soundness by the group. Like a dreadful parochial school, if they did not recite a lesson correctly, they repeated it until it was. Individuals were under group pressure to get it right so everyone could be dismissed. A British soldier recalled one study session where they were shown photos of war crimes, then asked to discuss and respond. They concluded there was no proof of who committed the crimes. Wrong answer. The political officer, known as "Maggot," then harangued and argued for two full hours. Finally, no one disagreed.[20] Few prisoners saw much significance in parroting political statements. They were not providing military information or finking, and they were a long way from home in a very odd environment. In a frozen hut somewhere in Asia, what was the point of delaying lunch by defending Rockefeller to instructors who would never change? POWs were very aware that they were usually agreeing just to get along, and maintained a separate mental place for their own thoughts.

Chinese political trainers also used personal autobiographies and extensive public confessions to draw out intimate details. Prisoners often had to rewrite their personal histories over and over again until satisfactory. Violators of various regulations might be required to give a confession to a class, or the whole camp. William Funchess was spotted stealing corn from a field while on a work detail. He claimed that he then apologized to an assembly for "getting caught." Classes also included criticism sessions where prisoners were required to admit their sins, or identify them in others. Criticism sessions could last until everyone had spoken. POWs digging for something—anything—to say sometimes fell back on trivialities such as frequency of tooth brushing, but checking for aberrant doctrine was the main purpose. The utterances of each POW were subject to endless rounds of criticism, which exposed the building blocks of thought, allowing correctives to be applied at each and every deviation. They were under constant pressure to say the right thing. "Repetition, harassment, and humiliation were the principal coercive techniques" of indoctrination, concluded a US Army study.[21] Prisoners became hyperalert to what views were expected of them and could give the appearance of a thorough conversion, right down to the class-struggle terminology in "brainwashed" radio transmissions.

Since the entire group was responsible for learning a lesson, the prisoners took it upon themselves to reform the more stubborn. Collective scrutiny became more important as the instructors figured out that most students were just mouthing the words. Political officers began insisting that statements and essays had to demonstrate genuine belief, not contrived agreement. A British prisoner remembered, "there was no way of evading the forced study, and hostility paid no dividend." If they did not learn the political line, lunch was delayed or reduced by half: "The educators held the whip hand."[22]

Although the Maoist rhetoric often sounded odd to American ears, the Chinese still managed to persuade many that the United States had used biological weapons. Beginning in early 1952, a road show went from camp to camp with lectures by American officers and exhibits of germ war technology. What prisoners found most plausible from the "B-bomb" or "BW" talks were the detailed technical descriptions of weapons and delivery methods by Air Force personnel, sometimes underscored by displays of emotion. One former POW reported that the presentations were "very convincing," especially the testimony of an Air Force officer: "He was almost crying.... I myself was getting pretty well convinced." The germ warfare charges briefly muffled POW resistance to indoctrination and complicated the contempt they felt for it.[23]

There were other cracks for the Chinese to work at. Unlike the World War II mobilization, many of the soldiers dropped into Korea had little time to adopt the crusade as their own, which eased the task of indoctrination. When a journalist was asked by a GI what the war was about, the reporter responded, "Didn't

After the hunger. Four American POWs in Camp 5, Pyoktong, North Korea, winter 1952.
Imprisoned AP photographer Frank Noel received film and a camera through Wilfred
Burchett. The Chinese supervised the shoot, but the photos do show the prisoners
were no longer starving. Left to right: Jerry Oakley, Albany, OR; Clayton Rogers, Little
Rock AR; Charles Davis, Mount Vernon, IL; and Roland Hamilton, Middletown, OH.
Associated Press.

your officers tell you?" "Naw," the soldier replied, "we don't talk of such things
with Bob....What's Communism anyway?" One of the brass's biggest difficulties in selling the war was its distance from American shores. Unlike the previous conflict, there was no bombing of a Pearl Harbor or sinking of American
ships in the North Atlantic. Most soldiers had not heard of Korea and anticipated a short police action. Some were reservists who had fought in the previous
war and were resentful of being called up again, especially ahead of undrafted
younger men. As it became clear that it was a real war, a cascade of young men
joined the National Guard, began college, or joined the Air Force—anything to
stay out of the infantry. Director of the draft Gen. Lewis B. Hershey complained
that "everyone wants out; no one wants in." General Hershey may have heard the
popular saying among draftees: "There are two things we gotta avoid, Korea and
gonorrhea."[24] Much of the American public stopped seeing the point of the war,
so it is unsurprising that those taking the biggest risks were often disenchanted
as well. It was harder for POWs to counter Chinese arguments if they could not
fall back on a certainty that the war was right. The sour little war lacked the rai-
ments of satisfaction and necessity that could justify the sacrifice. The length

of captivity also fed feelings of abandonment, which was unsettlingly close to the Chinese claim that GIs were cannon fodder.

One accusation the prisoners knew was true was that bombs were killing civilians. Marching north, the captives had seen entire villages blown off the map, which the Chinese kept reminding them of. This was an argument that went beyond politics, because even if the North was to blame for the war, no one could deny the human cost of the American air war. Dovetailing on the death and destruction, the Chinese demanded to know why the POWs were so far from home, sticking their noses in an Asian civil war. When challenged in detail, prisoners could not always give a good explanation why peasant infantry in East Asia was a danger to Americans. A less-effective propaganda claim was that the war was started by a South Korean invasion of the North. But opposing "war" generically gave the Chinese more mileage. Lectures also tried to link economic troubles in the United States to the rule of big business. Emphasizing the power of corporations over domestic life made it more plausible that Wall Street was also responsible for the war. Descriptions of land reform underway in China were offered in contrast to "the Twilight of World Capitalism."[25]

Camp newspapers carried both political doctrine and human interest stories. They had much the feel of a high school yearbook, earnest content expressed with undeveloped skill. Photos of athletic contests shared space with articles like "Why Do We Have Slums?" by Cpl. James F. Friday.[26] Even Lloyd Pate, celebrated after the war as an inveterate resistor, says that he wrote an article for Camp 5's newspaper entitled "The Importance of Personal Hygiene." There was a fuzzy line between collaboration and journalism. Len Maffioli, a Marine gunnery sergeant, said he wrote "harmless articles of gibberish" for two cigarettes per article.[27] However, he was critical of authors who complimented the captors excessively. He would no doubt include the Central Committee of US-British War Prisoners Peace Organizations in Korea, which printed the article "POWs Hold Grand Peace Rally." It reported on the "overwhelming success" of a POW rally in support of a speech by North Korean commander Nam Il. Camp 10 residents provided the content for *Out of Their Own Mouths: Revelations and Confessions Written by American Soldiers of Torture, Rape, Arson, Looting and Cold-Blooded Murder*. One of the most celebrated events was the Inter Camp Olympics held in 1952, which was popularized in camps and international forums. The event demonstrated the Chinese leniency policy, with politics more implied than stated. These elaborate events featured races, high jumping, swimming, and parades of healthy bodies. Prisoners from scattered camps came together for the big event, allowing friends to catch up. In Eastern Europe, communist media regularly featured statements from POWs. Common themes were the good treatment of captives and the barbarity of Wall Street's armies. A private from Texas was quoted as saying that he had "only one complaint, and that is against Uncle Sam's air force." An officer from New England strained credulity by saying that "we have been treated better than we deserve."[28]

While a prison camp is an inherently coercive place, Army social scientists concluded after the war that collaboration was not usually due to being back-roomed by burly guards and insidious interrogators. Only 3 percent of those later categorized as "participators" reported that they were ever isolated and given the treatment. Among the hearty band of resistors, however, 37 percent felt that they "suffered great pressure."[29] In other words, assisting the enemy was not usually the result of prolonged torment culminating in "cracking." The inclination to aid the enemy seems to have been a character trait that some GIs brought with them, rather than a function of indoctrination or trauma. Sgt. Lloyd Pate wrote, "A lot of people think these men were brainwashed, but it just isn't so." According to Pate, collaboration began before the indoctrination classes started: "Back in the States in the Army these men were brown-nosers, bullies and show-offs. All the Chinks had to do in Korea was give them a chance to show their true colors." Repatriates often remarked that such-and-such collaborator cared nothing for the politics, he just wanted privileges. Psychiatrist Robert J. Lifton studied collaboration for the Army and concluded that "anxiety and desire for material advantages" were the chief motives for turning to the enemy.[30] Some participators were said to have simply continued doing what they always had—submitting to whoever the boss happened to be. Collaborators sought the security and community of the more powerful clan. When their traditional authority figures were removed from the scene, they began bowing to whatever new ones appeared. Giving orders not to assist the enemy was of limited use on personalities that obeyed whichever boss was present. Such character traits were set well before youths entered basic training and were not easily amenable to patriotic campaigns at home calling on boys to be men. One study suggested that collaborators tended to be loners who had "lost their identification with the society" they came from, but were welcomed into the Chinese family. Former POW Lloyd Pate believed collaborators lacked independence: "They always had someone they could run to and now the Chinese were their guardians." Several studies, including a massive review by the Defense Advisory Committee on Prisoners of War, concluded that although some became believers, most collaborators were unmoved by communist doctrine.[31] Age was also an issue. A variety of sources remarked that younger prisoners were more receptive to the Chinese.[32] While certain personalities and backgrounds were prone to collaborate, material rewards were also at play. Perks included more medical care, softer quarters, choice work assignments, clothing, food, tobacco, and money.[33] But these payoffs were actually very modest, not enough for anyone who valued peers more than bosses.

After the war, there was much concern about prisoners who "went red." While the number was exaggerated, many prisoners were influenced by some of the

Chinese arguments—particularly germ warfare, the pointlessness of Americans fighting so far from home, and the feeling of being left to rot in prison camps while leaders quibbled. Others became Progressives to curry favor with authority and get rewards, and a few joined study classes simply for something to do. Still, there were a limited number who were genuinely attracted either to Marxism itself, or at least had a vague sympathy for the Chinese perspective. Postwar discourse at home very rarely considered the possibility that Marxism made sense to some. With few exceptions, political transformations were explained by brainwashing, effeminacy, or craven opportunism. But some of the Progressives were drawn by the same things that have always attracted young people to the class struggle: They saw injustice and sought explanation and a plan to address it.

Judging by the 21 who went to live in China after the war, the most successful indoctrination was of young POWs from hardscrabble backgrounds. An author who researched their backgrounds reported that 18 of them grew up in poverty, and most were under 21 at capture. Reporter Virginia Pasley believed they refused repatriation because of the psychological scars of poverty and broken homes, but from the Chinese point of view, disaffected working-class youths were the most desirable and familiar population to work with. The 21 individuals were certainly aware of class privilege in the United States. They had often struggled from job to job in an unsettled economy, that was why they enlisted in the military. Men who had grappled with unpredictable job opportunities were attracted to the promise of a managed economy. Morris Wills liked the "orderly planned way" of socialism described by the Chinese. Another one of the 21, Clarence Adams, got a college education, married, and had a family, and stayed until 1966. Adams was especially moved by the Chinese commitment to racial equality. As an African American growing up in Memphis, Tennessee, he could not attend classes with his neighbors and had to trek to an inferior school in another part of town. At a media appearance at the end of the war, Adams explained why he chose China: "My family and millions of other Negroes have suffered under the brutal attacks of white supremacists and the cruel slave laws of the southern states." His daughter recalled that Adams went to China for education and opportunity. After returning to the United States in 1966, Adams and his wife eventually opened a chop suey shop where he worked into his seventies.[34]

Back in the United States, shortwave radio broadcasts were the first sign that prisoners were being used for politics. These broadcasts were diligently monitored by the Army's G-2 intelligence division and a box in the National Archives contains a parade of GIs calling home. In a transcript from May 1951, Sgt. Richard K. Artesani said, "Dear Folks: I am getting along all right. The food is very good.... Most important thing at this time the withdrawal of all foreign troops from Korea...GIs not interested in war 5,000 miles away...love to all...Avoid another world war." The political content was often perfunctory; the POWs were torn between participating in enemy broadcasts and letting their families know they were alive.[35]

American POWs became a staple in international propaganda. As on Koje-do, prisoners were an ideological resource in the Cold War. The real test for the Chinese was whether they could keep students engaged month after month. While communist cadre had great success converting captured soldiers during their civil war, Americans were another matter. Mainland Chinese citizens were there for the duration—they had to adapt to the new regime, but the POWs were preoccupied with going home to their own world. Making socialism in Yunan relevant to Arkansas would be a great challenge. But the Chinese could keep trying since the GIs would remain guests for a long time, thanks to the peace talks heading for stalemate.

# 5

# Prisoners of Limited War Languish as Propaganda Becomes a Substitute for Victory

There is no substitute for victory.
—General Douglas MacArthur

Prisoners in Korea, whether they were in the north along the Yalu River, or in the south on Koje-do, shared two traits. They were away from the front, but they were still war material. Armies commonly use captives for labor, intelligence, or tactical propaganda against active soldiers, but these were prisoners of a Cold War that was about ideology and world opinion as much as terrain. Circumstances would soon make Korean War POWs more important than any before or since. In the summer of 1951, both China and the United States had met their primary goals of saving allies from destruction, but neither could unite Korea at a cost worth considering. Both sides preferred stalemate to a dangerous escalation beyond the Korean peninsula, so in July they entered armistice negotiations. Pronouncements and negotiating stances were crafted with an eye for international consumption. Both sides used prisoners to tell stories about the other's perfidy.

The major powers involved in Korea saw themselves at heads of a collision of civilizations. American foreign policymakers wanted to distinguish the justness and effectiveness of their social system and demonstrate that they could persevere anywhere they chose. In Beijing, the heirs of the Middle Kingdom also had millennialist aspirations to be the center of human history. Mao and his comrades wanted to show to the Third World their strength against western imperialism, and also to surpass the leadership of the Russian Bolsheviks. The Soviets sought to bleed the West and maintain their revolutionary credentials. As military objectives faded, two campaigns dominated the clash of publicity: germ warfare and voluntary repatriation. The Chinese relentlessly publicized POWs forced to admit germ warfare atrocities, while the United States announced that

prisoners on Koje-do were defecting from their communist governments. This
continued for 18 months.

When armistice talks first began, it was assumed the war was all but over.
*U.S. News* ran a two-years premature postmortem titled "Who Won the War?"
(Answer: Russia, kind of.)[1] Armistice negotiators did not appreciate how the
new situation would discourage a settlement. The Chinese delegates did not
bring winter clothing, and their counterparts had similar expectations. Most
matters were resolved by October 24, 1951, when a new border was agreed to
based on the battle line at armistice rather than the 38th Parallel. The biggest
agenda item remaining was how to deliver each side's prisoners; lesser issues
to be resolved en route were whether forward airfields could be expanded in
the North and Soviet participation in an armistice supervisory committee.
American negotiators initially offered a one-for-one deal where one communist
POW would be exchanged for each UN captive until all 12,000 allied soldiers
were back, to be followed by the assumed balance of more than 100,000 communist prisoners. This would insure that all UN prisoners came back and slow
the enemy's recovery of ten divisions worth of potential soldiers. It was expected
that this opening position would be rejected; the JCS said to push it at first "for
purposes of negotiation," but to backtrack if talks were collapsing. They anticipated bargaining down to a final position of all-for-all, with both sides starting
and completing release at the same time.[2] The UNC lost interest in one-for-one
after partial repatriation blew up the talks.

US peace negotiators knew little of the explosiveness of Koje-do and it took
some months before the defection campaign emerged as an issue. As the team
led by Admiral C. Turner Joy worked to end the shooting war, another branch
of the military was busy with psyops. General Robert A. McClure, head of Army
psychological warfare, was enthused by the constituency of stay-behinds and
success in preliminary indoctrination efforts. In July 1951, on the eve of negotiations beginning and with the defection campaign already in motion, McClure
suggested making an open declaration of the principle of voluntary repatriation. Encouraging defectors from Eastern Europe was already a favorite psyops
technique, so extending the program to Korea was natural. "Inducements to surrender will be meaningless," McClure warned, if Koje-do prisoners were forcibly delivered to uncertain fates.[3] Dragging them home by their shackles would
be ugly and might dissuade East Germans or Poles from defecting. McClure
considered communist regimes to come from a mold, so a tradition of grant-
ing asylum in Korea might make future armies melt away before attacking—
the ultimate triumph of psyops. Back in the executive branch, an enthusiastic
Psychological Strategy Board (PSB) memo described asylum for POWs as a way
to drain the enemy and avoid losing "more American lives," which might even
outweigh the GIs expected to be withheld in retaliation.[4] The Joint Chiefs of

Staff was intrigued. Chairman General Omar Bradley noted that leaflets offering safety had induced some POWs to surrender and forcing them home would be a "violation" of that promise. But Bradley also saw an ideological principle beyond the battlefield surrender tactic. Voluntary repatriation would be of "great value," Bradley wrote to the Secretary of Defense, in exposing "the despotic totalitarian" nature of the enemy.[5] Communism's legitimacy came from representing the humble of the earth, which would suffer if peasants and laborers refused to go home. This would take psychological warfare to the global level.

Despite Bradley and McClures' interest, incomplete repatriation was poorly received because it could prolong negotiations and provoke retaliation against American prisoners. Many officials felt no obligation to men who had been shooting at GIs a short time earlier. A complete exchange also conformed to international law. Geneva Convention III, Article 118 mandated that POWs be "released and repatriated without delay" after the end of fighting. This 1949 amendment was in response to the Soviet Union withholding thousands of German and Japanese slave laborers for many years after World War II. Led by the United States, Geneva representatives tried to prevent retention of prisoners in future wars. Delegates from Austria and the USSR proposed exceptions to prompt and complete return, but these were voted down, led by the Americans.[6] There was to be no wiggle room in the return of prisoners. If an invidious captor claimed that POWs did not *want* to go home, there was an article blocking that, too. Article 7 added that "prisoners of war may in no circumstances renounce in part or in entirety the rights secured to them by the present Convention."[7] This was interpreted to mean that prisoners could not reject going home, since it would be too easy for a captor to compel them to do so. The 1949 Conventions therefore specifically addressed the possibility of POWs saying, or being represented to say, that they did not want to go home and explicitly rejected it. It was known at Geneva that some World War II prisoners had violently objected to being returned to the Soviet Union, but no provision was made for them.

The organization most opposed to McClure's idea was the State Department. In a parlay with the Pentagon, State Department legal advisor Raymund Yingling pointed out that the United States was "the initiator" of Geneva's prompt return clause. Retaining prisoners like the Soviets did could be "very embarrassing." Questioned whether State wanted prisoners to be forced home, Yingling replied that "we would not accept" an enemy claim that GI's "did not want to come home."[8] In a different meeting, State Policy Planning Staff member Charles Stelle did not believe that forced repatriation would discourage defections anywhere else because motivations were "always local."[9] East Berlin guards would desert based on what was happening in East Berlin, not old rumors from East Asia. Incomplete repatriation was being sidetracked even as agitation for it on Koje-do picked up. In August 1951, Secretary of State Dean Acheson shot down the idea in a note to the Secretary of Defense. Acheson, an attorney by training, wrote that partial repatriation contradicted Geneva and that "strictly" following international law was the best way to get all Americans home. The negotiating team at Panmunjom was instructed accordingly, but that did not put an end to it.[10] Secretary of Defense George C. Marshall knew President Truman had feelings on the issue and got the National Security Council's Psychological Strategy Board (PSB) to study nonforcible repatriation anew. The PSB considered the matter and recommended a compromise drawing on Acheson's earlier views. Geneva required immediate repatriation, but said nothing about releasing POWs early. Why not simply parole favored prisoners ahead of time? They could stay in South Korea or go to Formosa. Releasing "small numbers" would respect international law and present the opposition with a fait accompli.[11] Once out, prisoners could not be put back no matter how much blood the enemy invested. President Truman personally favored nonforcible repatriation, for he remembered that five million Soviets had ended up in US and British prison camps after World War II, and Moscow wanted every single one back. Most were soldiers who at some point had surrendered to the Nazis and then switched sides to escape the fatal prison camps, or for political reasons. Many joined an anti-Bolshevik division of defectors and were eventually recaptured wearing Wehrmacht uniforms. They were terrified of returning to Stalinist Russia and objected mightily, but received little sympathy. Washington still valued relations with Moscow and Supreme Allied Commander General Dwight D. Eisenhower considered them traitors. Ugly scenes ensued as POWs were forced aboard ships back to Russia. At Fort Dix, New Jersey, rioting Soviet prisoners were fired on by guards. Three committed suicide, and nooses hanging from barracks rafters suggested that more had planned to. Subsequent returnees were calmed by tranquilizers slipped into their breakfasts. Despite reports of arrests as soon as they stepped off the boat in the USSR, Washington and London continued sending them home.[12] It was on President Truman's watch that prisoners had tied the nooses to the rafters, and he did not want a repeat. The president's humanitarian commitment was not unqualified nor was he fixed in his position, especially if the entire truce hinged on it. If the United States dropped partial repatriation, according to a summation of his view, it should get "some major concession" for it.[13] Truman could not have known how long voluntary repatriation would protract the war and may not have appreciated how many defections were coerced.

Prodded by the president's view, the State Department developed a new legal rationale that could plausibly get past the context and plain-language reading of Geneva. State reasoned that the Conventions did not specifically allow using force to compel repatriation, therefore, it was not authorized. That left a dilemma, since POWs were supposed to be returned post-haste, but violence could not be used. The contradiction could be resolved only through interpretation, which should side with individual rights—the general goal of Geneva.[14] This was inventive legal reasoning, but Article 7 still specified that prisoners could not renounce their right to return. But the president was intent and nonforcible repatriation was adopted. At a JCS meeting, General Omar Bradley asked the State Department if the communists were correct in charging that the United States was breaking the Geneva Conventions. State's Alexis Johnson replied, "Well, we have rationalized our position in a way so that we can at least say that it is in accordance with the Geneva Convention."[15]

The northerners had expected that setting an armistice line would be one of the most intractable issues, but that was settled in late November, 1951. In December, they reached the sedately named "Item 4," the terms of returning prisoners of war. American delegates opened by requesting an exchange of prisoner rosters, a seemingly minor detail. The northern alliance was versed in events on Koje-do and anticipated trouble, so they demanded that agreement be reached first on the terms of an exchange. Why swap lists if it was not yet established that there would be an exchange? When UN negotiators stalled on this, communist delegates pointedly demanded to know if some prisoners might not be coming back. No such guarantee was forthcoming, so they held on to the rosters for weeks and stonewalled Red Cross inspections of their camps.[16] The sides traded demands and rejections for the remainder of the month, then on January 2, 1952, lead negotiator Admiral C. Turner Joy officially proposed that prisoners should not be forcibly returned. The communist delegates reacted harshly, saying it was "shameful" and "barbarous" to engage in "trade of slaves." The American negotiators replied creatively that voluntary repatriation was simply a variant of the same principle "advanced and advocated by your side." Tens-of-thousands of captured South Korean soldiers served in northern ranks, supposedly willingly. If they really had not been dragooned, then they must have had a choice, just as prisoners of the UNC were choosing the South. This was clever debating, but the opposition was unmoved. UNC negotiators never tried seriously to get back South Koreans serving in the KPA.[17]

The Americans remained undecided what final form nonforcible repatriation should take—either unilateral parole, or insisting that a peace agreement include it. Although the PSB favored simply letting them go, others wanted to force public concessions out of the enemy. Lead negotiator Admiral Turner Joy, of two minds on the issue, demanded either dropping the whole business before American prestige became committed, or "standing firm for our principle" and quit negotiating until the enemy capitulated. In February 1952, Joy told the Pentagon that a furtive parole was insufficient. Getting the communists to accept a humiliating armistice would show that they were really ready to stop fighting. Joy also worried about retaliation, arguing that allied POWs had a better chance of all coming home if the bombing of North Korea continued until the enemy gave in.[18]

The UNC retained the option of early release throughout the war and some officials continued to lobby for it, but a number of factors went against it. For one, battlefield conditions encouraged a hard line. Now that the dangerously unpredictable phase of the war was over, American commanders were confident. Field positions were largely static, but the enemy was faring worse under the UNC's superior bombardment. The State Department's Charles Bohlen advised "no great urgency" in seeking an armistice. Touring the front, he felt that the balance of force suggested "stringing" negotiations along "even in endless debate."[19] This concurred with policy set in NSC-48/5 in May 1951, which directed that UN forces "continue to inflict heavy losses on the Chinese." NSC-48/5 was a strategic overview of East Asia, and it provided a rationale for not hurrying a ceasefire: "A settlement will permit the withdrawal of Chinese forces from Korea for use elsewhere and will put an end to Chinese losses in Korea."[20] The UN had a huge advantage in logistics, with supplies offloaded in bulk at deep-water ports and transported by the truckload across roads safe from air attack. The other side moved only at night over paths stretching all the way to China. UN advantages in artillery, air, and mobility meant that the enemy would always lose more troops. Since communism was treated as monolithic, draining the enemy in one theater would help elsewhere. At a State Department–Pentagon summit in September 1952, Chief of Naval Operations Admiral W. M. Fechteler argued against any softening on repatriation. "We are inflicting severe damage," he said, especially by killing experienced pilots. The State Department suggested attaining a quick ceasefire by returning prisoners who wanted to go home and leaving resolution of the defectors until after the war. Defense argued against this, proposing instead a "unilateral indefinite recess" in talks "while at the same time intensifying the military pressure."[21]

Continuing the war also helped expand the American defense budget. Leaders including Truman, Acheson, Marshall, and Ridgway worried that peace might reduce domestic support for the vast military buildup advocated in the document NSC-68. NSC-68 envisioned permanent mobilization for a clash of civilizations, with a quadrupled defense budget and energetic diplomacy to confront communism anywhere, anytime. The Korean War also drowned out American public fears that a big military would create a "garrison state," a then-powerful buzz-phrase referring to trading freedom for security. Korea did bring acceptance of, or at least acquiescence to, permanent mobilization. Budget constraints had originally shelved NSC-68 in 1950, but "Korea saved us," Secretary of State Acheson wrote.[22] Traditionally after a war, the United States had demobilized and retained only small peacetime forces, but a war-sized military has endured ever since 1953.

In February 1952, American officials reached consensus on the form of voluntary repatriation, which went even further than Acheson or McClure's original ideas. The UNC would demand that the principle of voluntary repatriation be a condition of peace and written into the armistice. Not only would the enemy not get back all his soldiers, he would have to agree to it publicly. An idea for enticing defectors had evolved into a strategic element of negotiations—or, as historian Rosemary Foot put it, in a phrase delicious enough to name a book, "a substitute for victory." This was a play on General Douglas MacArthur's famous proclamation that victory had no substitute. In Foot's formulation, moral victory on repatriation became a replacement for triumph on the battlefield. Credit for winning the first Korean War—saving the South—had been eclipsed by losing the war for the North. Voluntary repatriation would be a humiliating political defeat for the enemy and demonstrate American commitment to individual rights and dignity. The Voice of America soon announced that "three-fourths" of Chinese prisoners rejected communism.[23] Having failed to conquer an East Asian peninsula, the substitute victory would have to do. Thus, numerous factors coincided with Truman's objection to forced repatriation. He was only partially responsible for the policy; psychological warfare operatives on Koje-do produced the defectors and created the option for the president. His sentiment synergized with a dwindling desire for a quick end to the war. Together, they overrode objections to extending the war and its sacrifices.

As the war progressed, officials were heartened by wider advances in defense. NATO grew by three million troops, enrolled Turkey and Greece, and West German rearmament commenced.[24] Taiwan received security guarantees, involvement in Vietnam expanded, and the Southeast Asian Treaty Organization was formed. Defense pacts were signed with Japan, Australia, and New Zealand. Japan's economy revived on war orders, making it an eight-cylinder engine of capitalist growth in East Asia and a solid ally. The hydrogen bomb was adopted.[25] Certainly there were other factors behind these developments, but the Korean War accelerated them. Voluntary repatriation was not a conspiracy to boost defense by protracting the war. In the diplomatic traffic reproduced in the series *Foreign Relations of the United States*, officials consistently favored a truce as soon as they could get one that would not force prisoners home. The expressed priorities were protecting nonrepatriates and gaining moral and political advantage in the Cold War. The security buildup was welcomed, but it appears to have followed rather than preceded President Truman's decision. It functioned as an enabler, meaning that there was little downside to extending the war. Officials did consider ways to make nonforcible repatriation more palatable to the communists, such as making it de facto rather publicly requiring it in the armistice, but the benefits of the complete package and the punishing air war always led the Americans to hold out. While compassion and moral leadership were the official rationale for voluntary repatriation, the defense buildup may have become the point in the cunning mind of Secretary of State Dean Acheson and others. Either way, prisoners became more central to the war as benefits ramified and growing investment put credibility on the line.

For his part, Mao Zedong also felt little rush to end the war. The Great Wall underground created a rough strategic parity versus the well-armed enemy. The Chinese leadership returned to their civil war doctrine of protracted war, trying to create "insurmountable contradictions" for the imperialists at home and abroad. To the northerners, voluntary repatriation was transparent kidnapping, and no self-respecting power would stand for it.[26] At the end of 1951, Mao and Stalin agreed that the Americans were stalling, but since UN allies were impatient to end hostilities, Washington would have to deal. Therefore it was important not to appear eager for "a rapid end to the negotiations."[27] Feeling militarily confident, the northern alliance turned to blunting the American psychological warfare campaign. If the world was convinced that POWs really were refusing repatriation, then the northern alliance would be blamed for prolonging the war by demanding all of them back. It was essential to prove what the northerners already believed, namely that "brigands from Taiwan" and Seoul were behind the trouble. Shortly after voluntary repatriation was officially proposed at Panmunjom, a huge riot swept the camps. Northern loyalists attacked guards and repatriation refuseniks. Authorities responded with sustained gunfire, killing 69 prisoners and wounding 142. An American guard was also killed.[28] For the remainder of the war, communist negotiators at Panmunjom said that violence in the camps proved that the imperialists were kidnapping the sons of the red flag.

The Koje rebellions were just one response to the American psychological warfare campaign. The quest for a substitute victory also impacted American GIs held captive, for they were used in what the Chinese also called the "political battle." The introduction of voluntary repatriation made it unlikely that peace talks would succeed soon. This protracted the political struggle, so the communist side needed a durable theme for demonstrating the UNC's malevolence. In March 1952, a few weeks after voluntary repatriation was formally proposed, China blared the charge that the US Air Force had spread disease among civilians by releasing infected insects. Persuading the world of American war crimes became China's highest publicity priority. *Newsweek* reported that there was a "worldwide epidemic" of unlikely stories about "bugs, ants, grasshoppers and spiders" raining from the sky.[29] To make the accusation credible China invited scientists, journalists, and clergy to come inspect the evidence. Beijing kept stirring the pot with periodic revelations throughout the war. *Time* magazine claimed that one-third of the Chinese media was devoted to the issue and that in Europe, "US denials are swamped by 'eye-witness' reports." *Fortune* magazine referred to germ warfare as "the Lie That Won." At first, Washington brushed off the charges. For eight weeks, China let American officials deny germ warfare, then sprang a trap: public confessions by two American flyers. In recorded statements, Lieutenants John Quinn and Kenneth L. Enoch gave their names and serial numbers and went on to denounce "inhuman Wall Street capitalism" for forcing them to scatter microbes to the four winds.[30] Enoch and Quinn's coerced testimony was part of China's retort to voluntary repatriation, making the flyers collateral damage to the substitute victory. Forced confessions followed from 36 more airmen. Weaponized microbes were the antecedent for demonstrating a series of inventive crimes. The Moscow newspaper *Pravda* claimed that "cannibalistic American imperialism" planned to use pathogens to slash world population by 700 million. Radio Beijing reported that American bombers made "reprisal attacks" on POW camps in the "wild hope of wiping out key witnesses and evidence."[31]

The Air Force confessions made an impression at home. While infantry grunts had made embarrassing broadcasts in awkward jargon, the germ testimony came from "mature, trained Air Force and Marine officers"—the men most expected to give only name, rank, and service number. This required explanation, and a debate began over how much individuals should endure in captivity. In these early moments there were some suggestions that the men were weak, but the more common presumption was that some inexorable force had broken them. Torture was one explanation; another was drugs. When an American civilian released from China reported he had been injected with "truth medicine," the *Times* "raised immediate speculation" about the authenticity of the Air Force confessions.[32] The most entrancing explanation came from a brand-new term, "brainwashing." Brainwashing provided a reason why good officers such as Enoch and Quinn cooperated with the enemy, and it fed the folklore growing around POWs.

It has been debated for decades whether or not there were any real bacteriological attacks amidst the ocean of propaganda. Chinese medical authorities certainly believed they were under attack, and mobilized a vast public health response. One comprehensive 1998 study argued that new evidence confirmed that insect vectors were used to spread exotic diseases.[33] However, there has been a dearth of evidence from the American side. Beyond the Air Force confessions, all of them recanted, no one has ever admitted any participation whatsoever, whether incubating flies, loading odd bombs, making damage assessments, or training front-line GIs to cope with the hazard. The dearth of any uncompromised evidence from American sources means that if bacteriological attacks did occur, they were limited and experimental. But that brings a problem of too many confessions. Only 224 fliers were held in prison camps, but 38 confessed to germ attacks. If 38 out of 224 fliers were conducting germ warfare, then one-fifth of an air war bigger than World War II was devoted just to dropping bugs. Under the theorem that huge secrets cannot be kept for long, 38 is a preposterous number of confessions. The Chinese certainly had motive for a hoax: diverting attention from the threat of partial repatriation. Still, the United States is known to have been working on bacteriological weapons, and a desperate war would be an obvious chance to test them. The Americans certainly had the stomach for it, considering the sustained conventional bombing of civilians. General Ridgway had actually asked for permission to use poison gas, though it was denied.[34] International observers traveled to Korea and saw live, out-of-season insects in the field. Significantly, they were supposedly delivered with canisters resembling those used in Japan's germ attacks on China in the Second World War. The Japanese program and its scientists were taken over by the United States.[35] Experimental germ attacks are thus entirely plausible. Their actual existence, however, is contradicted by documents surfacing from the archives of the old Soviet Union. In one cable to the Kremlin, Politburo member Lavrentiy Beria detailed an audacious hoax: a pathogen charade organized mainly by China. Soviet officers helped create "false regions of infection" for international inspectors. Beria even claimed that condemned criminals were infected to provide appropriate victims for the foreign investigators.[36] Following the death of Stalin, the Kremlin sought to wind down the war and considered the biological campaign a hindrance. In May 1953, they sent a grumpy message to Mao Zedong saying that "the accusations against the Americans were fictitious," and asking him to stop it.[37] Potemkin contamination zones explain why no reliable American reports ever emerged and also create a steep hill for germ war evidence to climb. It is unlikely that the United States used any bacterial weapons in Korea.

During the first months after reaching "Item 4-POWs," neither side knew the scope of nonrepatriation. The UNC delegates had not given nor possed a good estimate of how many prisoners did not want to return. In breathing spaces between mutual denunciations, delegates got around to the question of numbers. The northerners kept up their demand for return of all prisoners, but they also began making allowance for special cases, such as southerners captured wearing uniforms of North Korea, and a modest number of turncoats who worked for the UNC on Koje-do. If those who stayed could be portrayed as enemies of the people and spies, then what the UNC called voluntary repatriation could be recast as security against infiltrators.

By 1952 there were nearly 170,000 POWs, mostly on Koje-do. Of them, 21,000 were Chinese, 100,000 North Korean, and 49,000 South Korean.[38] Most of the South Koreans were conscripts or captives vacuumed up earlier by the KPA. From the start, communist negotiators were told not to expect back most South

Koreans. They were housed separately and 38,000 were reclassified as civilian internees (CIs) and released unilaterally in 1952, leaving 132,000 total. At the end of March 1952, American negotiators suggested that perhaps 116,000 of the 132,000 eligible prisoners might accept repatriation. China and North Korea accepted that figure as a discussion starter. To Admiral Joy, head of the UN delegation, success seemed in sight. He wrote in his diary that the communists appeared willing to accept "moderate adjustments" to the 116,000 figure, so long as they got back most Chinese.[39] Although the northerners were signaling cooperation, they were acutely mistrustful. They knew of the shenanigans on Koje-do and would need firm numbers before signing an armistice. For talks to go forward, the contentious prisoners of Koje-do would have to be polled.

The UNC launched Operation Scatter in April 1952. It was designed to find out where each prisoner wanted to go after the war, then reduce strife by segregating them by repatriation choice. General Ridgway told the Pentagon that the operation would resolve truce negotiations by finding as many POWs to go home as possible.[40] Scatter also revealed the trajectory of American policy. A defection drive had been launched by psyops, but it was too successful and kept peace out of reach. Screening the prisoners would remedy this by identifying as many as possible to go home and satisfy negotiators. After this brief interregnum, however, policy would revert to the enforcers sent by Taiwan and Seoul for the rest of the war. But as of April 1952, Admiral C. Turner Joy and his team wanted the talks to succeed and believed they hinged on returning enough prisoners. A dose of reality, however, was injected by Koje commandant Francis T. Dodd. Out of 132,000 prisoners, Dodd guessed that only 85,000 would go home without compulsion, an unlikely figure sure to be rejected. Taking Dodd's warning to heart, Admiral Joy recommended that "minimum standards" be used to classify prisoner as repatriates. He tried to remove the clandestine operatives from Koje-do, but that was at cross-purposes with the substitute victory.[41] Nonetheless, screening rules encouraged going home. To avoid it, POWs had to say not just that they did not want to return, but that they would "violently resist." Screeners were supposed to terminate the interview if a prisoner desired repatriation.[42] To address the tattooing and petition signing, Joy's team got pledges of safe passage from the Chinese and North Korean representatives. Despite the intentions of the Joy team, they were going against months of activity by psyops, Taiwan, and Seoul. A poll reliable enough to support an armistice would have to carefully protect the privacy of respondents. Just the logistics of polling 132,000 heads and segregating them by loyalty was formidable. Since the UNC controlled only the perimeter wire, cooperation from the barracks bosses would be necessary through seven delicate days.

On April 5, 1952 loudspeakers on Koje-do began blaring the news of the impending screening. For two days, the amnesty promises from Chinese and

North Korean commanders were repeated, along with UN instructions on polling. Announcements were made in Korean, Chinese, and English, so even guards were filled in. Residents heard this message from their homelands:

> We wholeheartedly welcome the return of all of our captured personnel to the arms of the motherland; we have further guaranteed, in an agreement reached with the other side, that all captured personnel shall, after their repatriation, rejoin their families to participate in peaceful construction and live a peaceful life.... This reasonable position of ours definitely will not undergo any change on account of the fact that a number of our captured persons...have had their arms tattooed or have written certain documents or committed other similar acts. We are deeply aware that such acts have certainly not been done out of their own volition and that they should not be held responsible for these acts.[43]

A UNC statement told POWs to think carefully about their families, warning there was "no guarantee whatever" that refuseniks would end up where they wanted.[44] There was no promise of asylum or prompt release. The UNC pledged only that nonrepatriates would be separated from other prisoners.

While the public address system told listeners to be candid, the crackling audio reassurances could not compete with prisoners' daily environment. As UNC guards prepared for trouble, prisoner cliques got ready to make it. Loyalists to China and North Korea believed there was a plot to hold them hostage after the war, and prepared to disrupt the screening. The Chinese nationalists and adherents of South Korea directed their attention not to the authorities, but their fellow incarcerates. In Chinese compound 92, Admiral Joy was told, bosses held a mock screening in anticipation of the real one. At roll call, all who wanted to go home were asked to step forward. They were "beaten black and blue or killed." CIE official John Benben reported that "throughout the processing, fights took place during the night, screams charged with torture broke above the night's din, and injured crawled to the gate on all fours, many to drop exhausted before reaching it." Some darted over barbed-wire fences to different barracks, while others were "pulled down and dragged away." Benben blamed violence on communists, but also specified that the compound he described was controlled by anticommunists. The pro-repatriation barracks opposed the screening altogether and blocked entrances. Since the authorities could not safely enter these zones, tens of thousands were not polled at all until tanks arrived in June.[45]

The UNC was unprepared to create a safe environment for questioning. It would have required a huge commitment of manpower to police nearly every square yard of Koje-do, and administrators lacked personnel even to use neutrals as screeners. In the Korean compounds, polls were taken by the Korean

Screening tents on Koje-do, June 1952. Chinese and North Korean POWs were asked if they would violently resist returning home after the war. Most compounds voted in blocks—nearly all prisoners were for or against repatriation. US Army Signal Corp.

instructors of the CIE. (Korean screeners objected to the wording of the survey questions, which they felt pressured POWs to return.) Authorities had no effective means of supervising what the screeners actually said. For the less numerous Chinese compounds, Mandarin or Cantonese speakers from the US Army were used, but in both places prisoners wanting to go home had to reveal themselves to personnel strongly identified with their captors and nationalist bosses.[46] Homesick POWs trapped in antirepatriation zones could not be sure the screeners would not reveal them. They were promised separation and could visually confirm that repatriates exited through one door, defectors another. But it might be a trick, and even if it was not, the compounds of their former tormentors were just a stone's throw away—a dire distance on rocky Koje. Barracks bosses did everything they could to get around the safeguards built into Operation Scatter. Using their control of the interior, they embargoed information, interfering with loudspeaker announcements and printed bulletins. Many prisoners did not understand that the screening could determine if they were repatriated after the war. Hanchos told them the survey was to identify committed communists for execution. "Physical terror" continued "before and even during polling process," according to the US ambassador to South Korea, who inspected Koje-do.[47] Even POWs who understood the process could not be certain they would stay safe for months to come in a treacherous environment. Like the defectors, there was no guarantee whatever that residents would make it home.

As early reports from the canvassing came in, Admiral Joy regretted telling his adversaries to expect back 116,000 soldiers. Only 38,591 openly choose repatriation. About 47,000 had not yet been polled because their compounds blocked it, but these were still pitiful numbers, especially among the Chinese, where only about a third were coming home. Admiral Joy's group shuddered at this figure. China was the senior negotiating partner and aspired to be the guiding force of international revolution; it had much to lose and great capacity to obstruct peace. To make the figures a little less outrageous, the UNC made an executive decision to add most unscreened prisoners to the group going home, which is how they arrived at a figure of 70,000.[48] While the obstreperousness of red barracks suggested most wanted repatriation, the decision was made with little regard for any who secretly did not want to. Results were so surprising that Joy became convinced that thousands more wanted to screen north, especially after speaking with eyewitnesses. His April 12, 1952 diary revealed,

> I interviewed at my house Lieuts. Wu and May (our Chinese interpreters)…. The picture Wu and May gave us was not pretty. It seems that the compounds with pro nationalist leaders were completely dominated by those leaders, to such an extent that the results of the screening were by no means indicative of the POWs real choice…. Wu and May gave as an example a labor battalion compound which was not so dominated. In this compound of 1,500 POWs 85% elected to be repatriated. Wu and May [believed] that the majority of the POWs were too terrified to frankly express their real choice. All they could say in answer to the questions was "Taiwan" repeated over and over again.

To lift the fear, prisoners would need to be free of hanchos for six weeks of reorientation, but the interpreters thought this could boost repatriation to 85 percent.[49] Similarly, senior linguist Aoa Meisling reported that compounds 72 and 86, holding two-thirds of the Chinese, were controlled by Taiwan loyalists using "violent systematic terrorism and physical punishment of those choosing 'against going Taiwan.'" Later that month, Sabin Chase, head of State's Far East Research, went to Koje-do to see for himself. He met with a sample of prisoners and concluded that the screening reflected local conditions in the camps (i.e., terror), not genuine desires. It was "impossible," another State official concluded, "to tell who really doesn't want to be returned as opposed to who has been coerced."[50] The end result was clear in the data. Army researchers Bradbury and Meyers noted that POWs voted in blocks according to "the size and vigor" of political cliques. One enclosure promised violent resistance, another elected overwhelmingly to go home. Most prisoners were rather apolitical, or, as Bradbury and Meyers put it, "ideology was not significant" to them. The "vast majority obeyed their leaders."[51] Given a choice, the apolitical could be expected to follow their longing for home.

Some of the most interesting (and overlooked) data came from the surveys of hospitalized POWs. Two different diaries, those of Admiral Joy and on-the-spot medical worker Stanley Weintraub, reported the results of in-patient screenings. Ill and injured prisoners were canvassed in their wards in the 1st POW Field Hospital located on the mainland at Pusan. The 1st was a single hospital in name only; it consisted of acres of huts and tents and accepted a stream of injured and ill patients from Koje or fresh off the battle-field. Weintraub was a 23-year-old army administrator in a hospital with 7,000 beds, surely the largest in the world at the time. With thousands of walking or semiambulatory patients, it was run much like any concentration camp, with multiple compounds separated by barbed wire. It also relied on companies of healthy POWs for the endless tasks of upkeep, who lived in adjacent stockades.[52] The 1st Field Hospital suffered some of the same turmoil as Koje-do; Weintraub named a memoir *War in the Wards*. When repatriation interviews began some compounds blocked them altogether, while others opposed repatriation. Most interesting, however, were the units that were peaceful, yet screened north. These clearly were not dominated by communist militants since they allowed screening. As on Koje, disciplined cadre tried to block gates, succeeding in ward compounds 1, 2, 3, and 6, according to Weintraub. On April 16, angry, menacing patients, "some dragging plaster-encased limbs," congregated in C-3 and sang the North Korean army anthem. Anticommunists, on the other hand, were in charge of C-5, which rejected repatriation.[53] Processing of laborers in C-7, however, went "smoothly, interrogation rapid," indicating communist cadre had little sway, but it was not controlled by anti-communist hanchos because 75 percent (1,700) screened north. Weintraub thought C-4's 1,600 patients and numerous orderlies were firmly against repatriation, but was surprised when 75 percent went north. This suggests C-4 anticommunists shaped outward appearances, but did not yet own the residents. Two brothers shook hands in a fond farewell before exiting through separate doors. Weintraub usually did not record where inmates were born, so many of those who screened south may well have come from the numerous southerners present, making the rate of North Korean defections lower than 25 percent. (This was strongly true of C-10; see Table 5.1.) Weintraub himself blamed turmoil on "insanely fanatical" communists. He reported that 60 anticommunists fled from red-dominated C-2 and several were murdered in C-3, but his numbers from pacific wards complicate his statements.[54] Admiral Joy's diary included the outcome in C-10. Out of nearly 2,000 North Koreans, almost 1,900 screened north. Of the Chinese, 288 out of 296 chose repatriation—97 percent—vastly different from Koje-do.[55] Again, C-10 was not violently communist, since it allowed screening. The turnout made Joy optimistic that a more reasonable total might be delivered to Panmunjom.

*Table 5.1* **Screening Results, Hospital Compound 10**

|  | *Total* | *Rejected Repatriation* | *Chose China or North Korea* |
|---|---|---|---|
| Chinese | 296 | 8 | 288 |
| North Koreans | 1,965 | 92 | 1,873 |
| South Koreans* | 866 | 524 | 342 |
| Total | 3,127 | 624 | 2,503 |

*Captured from North Korean army.

There are good reasons to take the hospital screening as more representative than Koje-do's. For statistical reliability, a sample size of 7,000 from peaceful compounds was none too shabby. The hospital also served as a natural randomizer of data, since sickness and injury know no ideology. Residency was temporary and fluid, making it harder for political cliques to dominate wards. Wounded prisoners from the front had not been exposed to island pressures at all. The peaceful wards had what a good pollster would want: size, randomness, and little political danger. The 1,500-man labor battalion mentioned by the Koje interpreters could be added, since it was also peaceful, yet chose China. When left to themselves, POWs wanted overwhelmingly to go back to their families. This is consistent with the interpreters' observation of widespread violence. It is common sense that most soldiers would go home—especially when, as found by Bradbury and Meyers, political sentiments rarely dictated life decisions.[56] That so many chose to stay anyway is explained by the simplest and most conspicuous factor on Koje-do: They were forced. Similarly, any anticommunist POWs stuck in loyalist barracks suffered a similar misfortune. The UNC screening figures were the worst available; guesses would have been better than incorrect data carrying the appearance of thoroughness.

The large number of refuseniks was simply not believed by many in the UNC. Suspicion there was "something phony" went right to "the top of the Far East command " in Tokyo, according to a Time-Life journalist.[57] At a stunned meeting of the Joint Chiefs of Staff, General Collins wondered if "there is any way to reduce that number" to smooth an armistice. General Ridgway tried running a few of the POWs through the screening tents again, but with no changes in the circumstances, there were no changes in the results. A flummoxed Admiral Joy resisted bringing the troublesome figures to the truce tent and lobbied for a comprehensive rescreening.[58] Some way, somehow, they had to find more POWs to send home, which the hospital results backed up. But this sentiment went against the psychological warfare that had been entrenching itself for a year onto an island that Americans did not control. When ambassador to South Korea John Muccio went to Koje-do to investigate, he concluded that repolling would not change the numbers much since guards lacked "internal control" of the yards. In the clipped sentences of telegrams, Muccio wrote: "If repolling Chi POW's contemplated, recommend separate detention all previous POW's leaders." General Ridgway initially warmed to the idea of a rescreening after meeting with Joy's interpreters, but General Van Fleet, commander of the 8th Army, argued it would take weeks to build new facilities and separate POWs from enforcers, and it still might not work. The 70,000 number was not so far from what camp commandant Dodd had predicted; coming up with a few thousand more returnees would not make things "materially different," Ridgway concluded. It would still be below the 132,000 their opposites wanted and the 116,000 they expected.[59] Culling the barracks a second time might gain nothing while inviting substantial political risk. If a recount did as intended and found many more repatriates, it would suggest that there really had been duress. Charles Bohlen of the State Department told the JCS this would help the communists "throw doubt on the whole process." A second survey would also be at cross-purposes with a presidential policy that considered antirepatriates as freedom fighters. There was no rescreening. The JCS fell back on the thought that they were just postponing a second poll until after the war when an armistice would likely have neutrals do it.[60]

On April 19, negotiators brought the ominous numbers to the morning session. Admiral Joy tried to reduce the sting, explaining that the total was reached with "carefully considered and painstaking" effort. Incredulous Chinese and North Korean delegates asked for an immediate recess, then returned to say that if the UNC wanted an agreement, it must "reconsider fundamentally this estimated figure. I repeat, this figure absolutely by no means can be a basis for further discussion."[61] The UNC's surprise at the survey results soon began wearing off and it got ready to take full advantage of the psyops windfall. In June, after tanks crushed mutinous units, the aborted screening was restarted and when it finished, the UNC's final roster of repatriates reached 83,000.[62] This was remarkably close to General Dodd's 85,000 estimate; he had probably just added up the populations of pro- and anti-barracks. Nevertheless, the space beneath an acceptable number of repatriates had narrowed, and there was also movement by the Chinese. Word from Premier Zhou Enlai via India was that 100,000 might be acceptable, as long as it included all the Chinese, minus a few spies.[63] The sides had come within 17,000 POWs apart. An increase in repatriation by that amount could likely have been accomplished with a limited rescreening. If the estimate that 85 percent of the Chinese wanted to go home was close, then much of the gap could have been closed by them alone. Whatever might have happened, the fact that the United States did not follow up on it demonstrates the growing attachment to the substitute victory.

The practicalities of a fair rescreening would have been formidable. Penitentiaries are far more controlled environments, yet predation is endemic. The most important step would have been the most difficult: removing the entrenched gang leaders and agents of Seoul and Taiwan, possibly requiring violence resembling the forced repatriation the UNC wanted to avoid. Effective policing of the compounds would have required guards to control every nook and cranny where individuals might be attacked. It would have meant not just blanket surveillance, but all the caretaking activities would have to be done or directly supervised by UN personnel. Guards would have to hand out the firewood lest someone create a fuel cartel. Each meal would have to be watched to ensure that everyone received rations. Achieving control in depth might have required tens-of-thousands more guards, according to Col. Kenneth Hansen of the psyops brass.[64] UNC armies were already stretched thin against superior numbers near the 38th Parallel. Guard details had always been stingy, which was part of why Koje got out of control. An honest effort to bring peace to the camps might also have required replacing ROK guards, who were the majority. Controlling enclosures would require a familiarity with individuals and how they fit into camp society. Troublemakers would have to be quickly identified and isolated. A proper informer network would require bilingual agent handlers with the cunning and meanness of character required for intelligence work—traits not always found in the same people, particularly the recruiting pool of retired missionaries. The delicate work of intelligence was not achievable simply with more guards; it would require commitment and inspired administration. The only thing more difficult than an honest rescreening was what the United States did instead: double the length of a major war.

There were many smaller steps that could have reduced coercion and probably attain a minimum acceptable to the other side. First would be removing as many key leaders and agents as possible before the gangs could rouse resistance, followed by banning inmate-run jails. Seizing space inside a fence line would allow prisoners to approach and request transfer out of threatening barracks. A fundamental step would have been to establish that the UNC, not gang leaders, was the ultimate authority. The most important measure not taken was giving early parole to special friends. There were quite a few prisoners who had proven their commitment to the UN side; keeping them imprisoned was pivotal in preventing many more prisoners from going home. There was nothing preventing their release—38,000 South Koreans captured in KPA uniforms were returned to their home villages in late summer 1952. General Mark Clark continued lobbying for early parole as late as March 1953, although he understood that the "political implications" were outside his purview.[65] Unilateral freedom might provoke withholding of UN prisoners, but that could and did happen anyway. The fact that the UNC did not take even the first steps to enhance freedom of choice is some of the strongest evidence of the substitute victory becoming paramount. But putting it first made it unsafe for thousands of prisoners to express their choice—the opposite of repatriating voluntarily.

The decision not to rescreen marked a step into dreamland. Although key figures knew the survey was compromised, the realization vanished from discussion after summer 1952 and the number of refuseniks was treated as solid for the duration.[66] It was a feat of amnesia for both bureaucracy and individual conscience. Forgetfulness allowed officials with misgivings to believe they were prolonging the war rather than force earnest men back to gulags and firing squads. This thinking guided UN allies as well for the remainder of the war.

The substitute victory caused collateral damage beyond Koje-do. It plainly extended the trials of all prisoners and soldiers, but mention of Korean civilians is in order. The UNC understood that the enemy would have to be pressured into leaving prisoners behind. With battle lines static, the North was systematically bombed town by town. "If we stay firm" on nonforcible repatriation, Secretary of Defense Robert Lovett explained to the cabinet, "we can tear them up by air. . . . We can make it a most unpopular affair for the North Koreans."[67] There were few restrictions on ground targets. In June 1952, the Joint Chiefs targeted the North Korean power grid and cut electricity 90 percent.[68] Modern warfare depends on civilian production, and anything remotely related to the war effort was fair game, something the POWs witnessed. Walking north after capture, William Allen recalled that "everywhere we marched we saw total devastation. The air force must have bombed their targets over and over again." Conley Clark, a career infantryman, was disturbed by a fellow POW who strafed civilians. "There's no such thing as innocent civilians," the pilot retorted, "they are all enemy."[69] General William Dean, the highest-ranking POW, was held separately by the KPA throughout the war and nearly every North Korean he met had lost a relative in the bombing. Virtually no structures remained above ground in the cities of Hwangju, Kunu-ri, Sariwo, and Sinanju, according to Air Force records.[70] Conley Clark described riding across open countryside, then seeing a pile of bricks appear, then more piles: "Gradually, there appeared foundations of buildings, and an occasional remnant of wall, marking the location and dimension of what must have been a large city." Decision-makers saw civilians as a strategic target, not incidental casualties. UN Commander in Chief Mark Clark urged the JCS in September 1952 not to budge in negotiations while civilian mood was "bordering on panic." The heavy bombing was emptying towns, "undermining morale of the people of North Korea and their ability to wage and support a war."[71] With voluntary repatriation as a measure of success, the Truman and then Eisenhower administrations kept escalating the bombing of the civil society that was broadly associated with the war. In May 1953, with signs of real concessions imminent, the United States assaulted North Korea's irrigation system just after farmers' seasonal transplanting of rice seedlings. Planes burst five dams, releasing biblical floods. The Toksan irrigation dam north of the capital Pyongyang released a three-square-mile lake that "scooped clean 27 miles of valley," according to an Air Force assessment. It was a strategic attack on the civilian food system, a portion of which fed troops. Historians Halliday and Cumings noted that comparable flooding was inflicted by the Nazis on the Netherlands in 1944, which was judged a war crime at Nuremberg.[72] Intensification of the air war was part and parcel of POW political warfare.

Compared to awesome displays of power, the lives of individual prisoners barely registered. In the big picture, was repatriation an issue at all? Washington felt it was bleeding the enemy while strengthening itself, and the communists believed that holding off a superpower was enhancing their credibility and might fragment the UN allies. Would not both sides have continued the war under one pretext or another for as long as they benefitted? Although many factors allowed POWs to become the deal breaker, it was still the axis around which other issues turned. In opening talks, both sides considered the conflict virtually over. They were close to agreement in early 1952, but could not settle on the number of prisoners to be repatriated. It is likely that if the United States had not demanded or the northerners not refused incomplete repatriation, the war would have been settled much sooner. Armistice negotiations stalled when it came up and concluded as soon as it was settled. The operative rationale for American decision-makers was that there could be no armistice until the enemy gave in on POWs. The Army history of the Korean War recognized repatriation as the lynchpin of the later part of the war. In his classic *Truce Tent and Fighting Front*, Walter G. Hermes wrote that "the UNC had kept faith with the nonrepatriate prisoners and won a psychological victory." It had also made "no forcible repatriation" a part of international law:

> Yet the humanitarian approach in protecting nonrepatriates had been expensive. To safeguard their rights had cost over 125,000 UNC casualties during the fifteen month period while the enemy lost well over a quarter of a million men.... Viewed from this angle, the precedence given the 50,000 nonrepatriates and the 12,000-odd prisoners held by the enemy over the hundreds of thousands of soldiers at the front raised a complicated question.[73]

Just weeks after the war ended, Secretary of State John Dulles told delegates of the Pacific ANZUS alliance that "two principles were at stake in the Korean war," stopping aggression and "political asylum" for POWs.[74] Since fighting continued over the right to refuse repatriation, the success of the latter part of the war can be judged on how well that right was respected. The result will be the subject of the chapter after next, but first, a return to the Chinese-run camps.

# 6

# The Failure of Chinese Indoctrination

That political crap.
—GIs' description of Chinese
education classes

The Chinese were boring. The daily two-hour talks prisoners had to listen to were dry, doctrinaire, and in reruns. Only a limited number of presentations had been prepared and POWs soon became "so confounded fed-up" with hearing the same lectures day after day, and then having to repeat discussions about them as well.[1] As GIs fought nodding out, they would have been bemused to learn that attending the talks would make them politically suspect at home. It was widely accepted in the United States that the communists were distressingly successful at tearing down Americanism. A variety of evidence supported this, such as 91 percent of prisoners conceding to write autobiographies, which the Chinese inspected for openings. Signing propaganda petitions was common, although only 5 percent wrote or circulated them. One fourth made recordings for broadcast, though they were often just greetings to loved ones with limited political content.[2] Some critics at home claimed that one in seven POWs assisted the enemy, while others cited an astounding ratio of 1:2.[3] The mythology of collaboration rested on the belief that the prisoners were soft, did not resist enough or escape enough, and that their minds were bent to the Chinese will. How and why this publicity campaign occurred will be discussed later, but since it relied on the idea of prisoner weakness, it is important to establish what did and did not occur in the camps. This chapter demonstrates that with limited exceptions, Chinese indoctrination was not successful. Prisoners shrugged it off as soon as their minders were out of earshot. The collaboration that did occur provoked outrage beyond its scale largely because it seemed new. But comparison with other wars shows that assistance to the enemy was not unusual, though little noted. The lack of historical perspective contributed to an emotional overreaction.

Like inmates everywhere, GIs learned how small even a populous prison camp could be compared to having had the run of the world. Barracks mates looked the same, smelled the same, and kept the same irritating habits. Variety in diet consisted of getting rice rather than cracked corn, bits of pork instead of fish. The dreariness of camp routine was compounded by not knowing when it would end. There was no regular mail for the first half of the war, and after that letters were rationed. Information was carefully managed and there was limited news about the course of the war. Endless rumors, however, careened from barracks to barracks. Some guys were "going around just making up rumors" for sport, remembered Bill Smith.[4] The most exciting tales were about an end to the war, but there were so many it was hard to believe when it finally came.

When the pupils arrived at the first indoctrination classes, they were still shaken by the middle passage and took pains not to offend the instructors. They responded very cautiously in Chinese-led discussions and sullenly repeated the political verses they were taught. On the surface, prisoners could appear well-schooled in Chinese views. But as any teacher can attest, students can mouth back all kinds of things without a lick of it sinking in, and these pupils were more insolent than most. They responded like any students who are force-fed information. They were quietly contemptuous, unmotivated, and participated just enough for the instructor to stop bothering them. Naturally, there were a few who were interested, or trying to curry favor with the teacher, but the curriculum had little influence outside the contrived atmosphere of Chinese reform school. An Army information pamphlet concluded after the war that "the overwhelming majority of the prisoners did not accept the indoctrination to any degree."[5]

Ignoring ideological arguments was especially easy for the GIs who were cynical and apolitical to start with. An astute Pentagon analyst noted that the same resistance the boys had showed to civics class at home served them well in prison camp. "The almost universal way of referring to Communist indoctrination...was 'all that political crap.' It was 'crap' not only because it was Communist, but because it was political," wrote analyst Harvey Strassman. This same attitude was the "bane" of Army Information and Education Officers, he added. The US military itself largely dropped political indoctrination after it concluded that unit cohesiveness—professional soldiers' commitment to each other—was the best combat motivator.[6] The Chinese could hardly be expected to do better than America's home ideologues.

The political cadre made extensive use of English language material, but with the exception of the New York *Daily Worker*, few of the periodicals were in current American vernacular. A fair number of books were available later in captivity, but they were largely the high classics of either English literature or Marxism—dry fare for many of the POWs. Camp libraries drew heavily from

Chinese or East European sources, and no matter how earnest the translations were (or maybe because they were earnest), the words sounded odd to American ears. Pentagon analyst Albert D. Biderman noted how ignorant the captors were of American popular culture. The Chinese attempted to provide entertainment, but the themes of their books and films could not match Hollywood. GIs were not charmed by the "boy meets girl, boy chucks girl for tractor" genre of socialist realism. Biderman found that some of the heavy-handed propaganda offended viewers, such as a film depicting nuns and priests mowing down women and children.[7]

Despite the challenges, Chinese political officers were intent on using good treatment to win prisoners over. But to get genuine converts, they had to enter into dialog with the GIs, which created space for opposition. Guards could still maintain control brutally, but it became apparent that violence was kept apart from the indoctrination sessions. As prisoners came to the realization that "they were not going to kill any of us," attentiveness in class fell.[8] It began slowly, first as simple emotional detachment, or zoning out. In the camps this was referred to as "playing it cool." The men became "aloof, unresponsive, minimally communicative, and noncommittal on everything," according to a postwar social scientist. As one repatriate explained, "it was easy to beat their propaganda. All I did was play dumb, act dumb all the time and ignore their lectures. Every time a guy came around to argue with me, I just said 'yeah, yeah, you're right; everything you say is true.' "[9] A few made the mental leap into contemplating the world of Chinese peasant revolution, but as time went on, most began evading their lessons more actively, like Nick Tosques:

> The afternoon was study time. We'd study about how Mao Tsetung and his bunch got rid of Chiang Kai-shek and all the capitalists in China. How capitalism was no good. How the working man was exploited. How communism was the only way to go.... It was pounded and pounded into us. Everyday. Everyday. Capitalism no, communism yes. Like most of the others I went along with it. Yeah, yeah, yeah. You're right, you're right. But in the back of our minds all we're thinking about is home. About getting back, going to work, and buying what the hell we wanted....After each study session we'd be sent back to our huts to discuss communism, but what we'd do, we'd put one guy on watch and then we'd talk about anything *but* communism. What kind of work did you do at home? What kind of car did you drive? Did you have any girlfriends?[10]

Student delinquency increased after armistice negotiators exchanged rosters at the end of 1951 and identified who they held. Mail service commenced and GIs immediately wrote home. The first day they got letters back from their families was momentous: "Everybody was running around hollering," remembered Arden Rowley. "At that point, we realized 'my family knows I'm here.'" It was immensely reassuring that their country knew they were alive and expected them home. "The lectures really went downhill" after that. "Guys would sit there and play grab-ass, or make up little games to play," according to Rowley, "and every once and a while say, 'ahh, that's a bunch of bullshit' to the instructors up on the stage." "The lectures became a circus."[11]

The Chinese also faced huge racial and cultural obstacles to winning genuine converts. The hatred of the Japanese during World War II was still fresh, when propaganda posters portrayed them as simian. The book *War Without Mercy* described how WWII soldiers had not seen themselves as protecting a political ideology or an Open Door economic policy; rather, it was a primal battle to see which race could survive in the Pacific.[12] POWs in the Korean War still commonly lumped East Asians together, and there was a stark division between the keepers and the kept. The jailors were invariably Asian, and few of the Americans were. No matter how enticing the Chinese tried to make the leniency policy, prisoners felt trapped by an alien race in a strange land. "Chink" was not just a subhuman species—POWs used it as a ubiquitous adjective as in "the chink commies," "chink indoctrination," "the chink brass," and "the chink instructor."[13]

Ironically, the revolutionaries of the PLA chose to put black prisoners in separate companies. As an oppressed nationality, African Americans were expected to be more receptive to socialist ideas and were given more attention. However, the separation felt all too familiar. "They told us there wasn't any segregation in Communist countries," recalled one veteran, but then they "put all the Negroes all together in Camp 5." The Chinese said racial friction among POWs was the reason for separating them.[14] After the war, segregationists in the United States liked to claim that African Americans were especially prone to collaboration. This association was reinforced by credulous newspaper stories suggesting that the Ku Klux Klan appeared in the camps, courageously resisting collaboration. Pfc. James R. Dunn of Anderson, SC, claimed that collaborators would "get a little note, signed KKK, telling them they'd better straighten out. We never did hurt 'em bad, but a few got dumped into a latrine." After the war, a *Washington Daily News* article praised such activity: "Instead of breaking, Corp. Gray helped organize the 'KKK,' a secret anti-Red group."[15] Although journalists were told the KKK targeted all collaborators, not just African Americans, the choice of name insured that readers could not help but associate treason with color. It is not clear that the KKK actually had a real presence in the camps. Arden Rowley, for one, never heard of it until coming home. Newspapers may have imagined an underground resistance out of a few incidents, assisted by the imaginations of GI storytellers. After the war, the supposedly disproportionate collaboration of African Americans came under scrutiny. However, even though African Americans "received the greatest brunt" of indoctrination efforts, it is not at all clear that they responded differently than whites. A military study did conclude that "only 2.7% Negroes resisted against an over-all 5% average."[16] But with a couple hundred African American prisoners at most, the sample size was not statistically significant. More importantly, a sound comparison could not be made, since the races had different experiences under the Chinese.

Perhaps the strongest barrier to indoctrination was that prisoners remembered what their lives used to be like. At home, they had the best movies in the world and they owned or could realistically aspire to having hot water, electricity, cars, TVs, and myriad consumer goods. Even the poorest prisoners could see that the guards lived austere lives. The Chinese instructors reacted to tales of American bounty with either disbelief or a furtive fascination. Chinese denunciations of racial oppression and a perplexing war did sometimes resonate with the POWs. But that did not cause many to identify with revolutionary peasant movements in the Third World. The GIs' exposure to communism was in a prison camp, and almost none wanted it.

To relieve boredom and the stifling political conformity, POWs became mischievousness. A favorite trick was to mispronounce political slogans in ways the Chinese ear could not catch. Arden Rowley wrote that the Chinese could persuade them to sing revolutionary songs by delaying a meal ("we literally had to sing for our supper"), but they could not block a secret code of mauled phrases. The verse "dong fang hong tai yung son" became "who flung dung at Mao Tse Tung." The line from the communist Internationale "arise ye wretched of the earth" became "arise ye red shit of the earth." When two prisoners were caught filching onions from Korean farmers, they had to make a ritual self-criticism in front of other prisoners. "We have stolen these onions from the Korean people, we are sorry we did it," they said, "and promise not to get caught again." Eventually, POWs became bold enough to flatly refuse to write self-criticisms. Rowley was finally judged irredeemable and transferred to a "reactionary" company with no regular political classes at all. His new company was isolated from other prisoners and left alone. "I really enjoyed the volleyball and got pretty good at it," he recalled.[17] In memories of Camp 5, one common tale of impudence was that of "Rotorhead" Thornton, a helicopter crewman and camp clown who rode an imaginary motorcycle. He grasped invisible handlebars, kick-started his mount, and roared around like a four-year-old. He once stopped to fix a flat tire, then accused the Chinese of stealing his tool kit.[18] According to legend, Rotorhead reported his bike stolen and demanded a replacement. The camp commandant supposedly declined, explaining that then he would have to get one for everybody.[19] Another often repeated story was about a germ warfare exhibit that contained specimens of microbe-carrying insects. A trickster snatched one up and gulped it down. In different tellings it was a spider, a fly, and an unfortunate ant walking past. In another version the prisoner ate not an insect but a strip of aluminum foil supposedly used to spread bacteria.[20] The foil would be another joke on the Chinese, since the prisoners knew the metal ribbons were dropped by American planes to jam radar. Camp 5 inmates devoted a whole week to goofing and messing with their captors. During "crazy week," 300 men all reportedly went to the latrine at 2 a.m.; others walked silly, cut off half a mustache, or played basketball without a ball. William Funchess plowed a field, shouting commands "gee" and "haw" to an invisible mule.[21] Wilbert Estabrook recalled, "It became quite apparent that we could get by with a lot of foolishness, that it wouldn't end in your dying."[22] Sgt. Lloyd Pate was designated a "reactionary" and spent time in solitary. Despite being fingered as a troublemaker, he was surprised by how far he could go. Pate claimed that he once verbally unloaded on a tiresome instructor, who barely responded. "I don't know why they let us get away with it," he later wondered. If he had been the guard and spoken to like that, "you can bet there would have been hell to pay."[23]

The prisoners moved from insolence to outright resistance. Jack Chapman of Oklahoma recalled the day they refused to march in a May Day parade. About 200 were lined up on a road, but when it was time to move out, the first row of men sat down. "As soon as the guards get those up, the next ten sit down. And this continued and it ended up we didn't march. We really got lectured for it. I forget what they called us—warmongers, that's right." Chapman reported that on another occasion the library somehow caught fire and burned to the ground while prisoners dragged their feet bringing water.[24]

The Chinese realized their charges were not accepting socialism like the nationalist soldiers captured during their civil war. Some of the strongest evidence that indoctrination lacked traction was that it was thoroughly revamped. Instructor Wu Henian recalled trying to teach the scientifically inevitable decline of capitalism, but "socialist theory was unacceptable to almost all POWs." The revered Chinese premier Zhou Enlai himself advised teachers to take a new approach. According to Wu, "we changed by telling them that such a war was unnecessary, was dirty.... Some POWs began to think the American government should not be in such a war."[25] By the spring of 1952, even the watered-down indoctrination classes were in trouble. In Camp 4, a company of 400 prisoners went on strike and refused to attend classes at all. The strike succeeded after two days, according to postwar testimony. Mandatory attendance ended throughout the camps, although some prisoners continued voluntarily. After the war, a lot of ink was spilled over prisoners' alleged easy acceptance of communism, but the trajectory of the indoctrination classes shows that most prisoners were truculent. Incidentally, not until mandatory instruction ended were the Progressives clearly delineated as a group.[26] Previously, everyone had to recite lessons in class, but those who continued studying after compulsory attendance ended quickly got a reputation. But for the most part, the Progressives continued to circulate in their regular companies and the camps never became violently polarized.

Despite much talk of it afterwards, one thing that did not occur in Korea was brainwashing. In the common definition of brainwashing, the subject loses free will because thoughts and memories are erased and replaced. While force can get anyone to do anything, the brainwashed choose to do so because they have been so conditioned. Prisoners in Korea were hectored and pressured, but their thoughts remained their own. Sometime after the war, most of the scientific community concluded that no brainwashing occurred, if defined as a deep, lasting transformation of beliefs. The CIA Hinkle-Wolff study concluded that even in extreme cases such as the germ war pilots, the methods were traditional: isolation, humiliation, endless interrogation, sleep deprivation, stress positions—torture methods "known to police systems all over the world." Even the voluntary Progressives generally returned to their old beliefs soon after release. A 1956 Army training manual on interrogation concluded that there was not one "conclusively documented case of the actual 'brainwashing' of an American prisoner of war in Korea." Scientists failed to communicate this to the public, complained one researcher, leaving the field open to "pseudo-scientific speculation."[27]

Of course, brainwashing can be defined into existence by using it as the label for the actual Chinese indoctrination program. If that was brainwashing, then the condition was rare, temporary, and less than profound. Psychiatrist Robert J. Lifton studied repatriates and concluded that "virtually all prisoners" gravitated back to their old belief patterns after returning to their home milieu.[28] Since a characteristic of many collaborators was a craving for the favor of authority, they snapped back after returning to the authority of the US Army. Even most of the stay-behinds who remained in the "brainwashed" environment in China eventually relapsed. The 23 defectors almost immediately became 21, and all but a few eventually returned to the United States. There is a condition that might usefully be called brainwashing which is most apparent in religious cults, abusive marriages, and the kidnapping of Patricia Hearst by a violent radical sect.[29] But these cases required lavish use of labor, time, and isolation, which are impractical for a mass of POWs.

One of the most inaccurate claims about collaboration in Korea was that it was unprecedented. Postwar pundits claimed that Korea constituted "something new in history," but this thesis was never tested against data from other wars.[30] There was significant collaboration in previous conflicts, it simply was not dwelt on. More than 8,000 prisoners on both sides of the Civil War did more than just aid and comfort the enemy—they switched sides. In the 1846 invasion of Mexico, Irish Catholic deserters formed a battalion in the Mexican army, St. Patrick's Brigade. The Vietnam War saw the gamut of cooperation with captors. Nine servicemen were indicted, but the charges were quickly quashed by higher-ups, undoubtedly to avoid repeating the ignominy of Korea.[31] A closer comparison to Korea would be the Pacific theater during World War II. Gavan Daws' volume *Prisoners of the Japanese* demonstrated that Korea was fully anticipated in the Pacific, both in collaboration and the breakdown of community during starvation. Loan sharking of food, informing, radio broadcasts—all were features of Japanese custody. American officers were persuaded to enforce no-escape pledges. Prisoners poaching food from storerooms had to be careful of "white mice," the WWII term for informers. According to Daws, GIs began acting more like convicts that soldiers: "A pair of socks or a towel stolen at one end of camp would set off catchup thefts all the way to the other."[32]

Unlike the Chinese, the Japanese did not seek ideological converts. They readily compelled English speaking captives to broadcast propaganda, but it was tactical, not ideological. Japanese propaganda tried to sap the "fighting spirit" of enemy troops with complaints about poor medical care or combat fatigue.[33] The American-produced Tokyo Rose broadcasts purred homesickness to the boys, not political paeans to the Greater East Asian Co-Prosperity Sphere.[34] With the exception of a short-lived shortwave program beamed at African Americans on the West Coast, broadcasts were not meant for the American mainland, nor did they promote an ideology like communism that threatened the domestic order.[35] The Japanese could have churned out ideological rhetoric just like the Chinese a few years later, but that was not their purpose, so Pacific collaboration remained out of sight. There were certainly enough cases of misconduct in World War II to support a national scandal, but those prisoners came home to a different mood. Collaboration was briefly noted, then drowned out by the celebration of victory and respect for victims of the Bataan death march. Although the public took little notice of Pacific collaboration, the Pentagon did. Misconduct was extensive enough that a new crime was added to the Code of Military Justice: Article 105, Misconduct as a Prisoner.[36] The 1950s polemics against Korea ex-POWs presumed a heroic past where warriors never wavered, but such a time never existed. Korea was distinctive not for aid to the enemy, but its conspicuousness.

The extent of collaboration depends on its definition. Arden Rowley served as a squad monitor collecting essays for the Chinese and checking them over. Some would consider that aid to the enemy—and if so, virtually all were guilty, even though, in the case of Rowley, the Chinese gave up on him. Ex-POW Tony Ryan complained of the wide definition of misconduct:

> You're guilty of something just because you survived. . . . There had been so much talk about POWs giving in to the Chinese, we were all under suspicion when we came home. You could tell that people were looking

at you....To them, collaboration meant giving anything more than name, rank, and number....We had to write what the Chinese called "self-criticisms." Hell, they were a joke to us, and they kept the guards off our backs, so we wrote them. Is that collaboration? No way, man![37]

If collaboration meant actually embracing Chinese politics, it was limited to a small minority. If more were affected, it left no tracks. After Korea there was so much attention on collaboration that a simple truth was obscured: how *poorly* Chinese politics actually caught on. Studies of Korean captivity commonly emphasize the extremes of either collaboration or resistance, but for the bulk of prisoners, political education was something to be endured—droning speeches in classrooms that either sweltered or froze.

Interestingly, the conclusion that the prisoners were pushovers transcends Left and Right. In their book affirming germ warfare reports, Endicott and Hagerman touched on the issue of collaboration and attributed its "high incidence" to the lack of "insight and maturity" provided by American culture.[38] On the contrary, the most important explanation for collaboration in Korea is that it needs no explanation. When something as powerful as a state seeks cooperators, it will find them. The POWs responded like human beings, with a mix of resistance, capitulation, and playing it cool. The puzzle about Korea is the stir that came after. But before getting to that, we will finish the story of the other prisoners—the Chinese and North Koreans on Koje-do, whose repatriation problem entangled everyone.

# 7

# The United Nations Command Withholds POWs

Any prisoner who desired repatriation had to do so clandestinely and in fear of his life.

—Neutral Nations Repatriation Commission

On a spring day in May 1952, the American commander of Koje-do prison island ventured out of the office for an appointment. Brigadier General Francis T. Dodd had arrived in February to cope with the rioting against repatriation screening. The latest in a string of commandants, he had to contend not only with the antirepatriation hanchos that answered to Taiwan and Seoul, but also the pro-repatriation activists who had been attacking guards and launching deadly coups on rival barracks. Dodd was going to find out just how deep the trouble went. The prisoners who favored going home had been joined by some especially capable and motivated members thought to have surrendered on purpose. American intelligence officers claimed that the head of Korean resistance was Pak Sang Hyong, a Korean with Soviet citizenship who masqueraded as a private. The agents were controlled by Nam Il, head of the North Korean negotiating team at Panmunjom, ensuring that uprisings were coordinated with the armistice talks. Spectacular opposition to "voluntary" repatriation would show the world that the UNC was coercing prisoners.[1]

Hopeful for dialog, General Dodd and his interpreter headed for a parlay with North Korean leaders of Compound 76. Previously, this steadfast communist yard had fought off screening in a bloody clash with guards. A couple of compound representatives met him at the fence and launched an hour of polemics and repetitious complaints. With translation, Dodd endured every word twice. The droning was probably to dull his alertness. Slowly, more prisoners drifted over to the fence, apparently listening. Then one of the dreary routines of camp life arrived: The "honey bucket" brigade needed to pass

89

through the wire to service the latrines.[2] When the gate opened, General Dodd was suddenly rushed and seized. His interpreter held on to a post long enough to be rescued, but Dodd was dragged off to a prepared cell. Premade banners were unfurled, promising to treat the general well—unless a rescue was attempted. Prisoners of war had captured an American general in his own prison camp.

The Dodd kidnapping showed what high stakes the POW issue had become. Armistice talks had resolved nearly everything except a prisoner exchange. On April 28, 1952, shortly before Dodd was seized, the United Nations Command had made what it said was its final offer: dropping objections to improvement of North Korean airfields after an armistice in return for partial repatriation and exclusion of the USSR from a postwar armistice body. The Soviet exclusion was less controversial and eventually accepted, so all remaining attention shifted to the POWs. This put the northern alliance in a spot. If refuseniks were accepted as credible, then the communists might be blamed for blocking an armistice by demanding their return regardless. The natural retort was that prisoners were actually being coerced into defecting, so China and North Korea needed dramatics. Hence, General Dodd's afternoon appointment.

The kidnapping occurred just as the overall UN command was being handed from Matthew Ridgway to General Mark Clark. Clark had never heard of an island called Koje and had to be told how a formality like prisoners of war had torpedoed negotiations. In the meantime, Dodd's emergency replacement, Brigadier General Charles F. Colson, secured Dodd's release by issuing an embarrassing public statement: "I do admit that there have been instances of bloodshed where many prisoners of war have been killed and wounded by UN Forces.... After Dodd's release, unharmed, there will be no more forcible screening or any rearming of prisoners of war in this camp."[3] Colson's concessions were immediately repudiated by his superiors and both men lost their careers. Colson's admissions were a triumph for the communists; they struck at the heart of the substitute victory's claim of free choice. Prisoners suffered so horribly that they recklessly snatched a general. Previously, the upheaval on Koje-do was little noted in American public discussion. General Clark observed that "great care" had been taken "to make sure the newspapers did not get the story."[4] Now everyone knew that something unusual was going on, reinforced by rebellions in other compounds. Radio Beijing crowed that Colson's admission proved what it had said all along, and Soviet-bloc publicity organs shifted gears from germ war to prisoner abuse.[5] Communist prisoners now joined the reports of American collaboration, germ war confessions, and executions of bound prisoners in making Korean captivity notorious. The American public learned of an Alice in Wonderland camp where the prisoner kept guard and the guard was a prisoner.

Koje-do had attained notoriety, but is also important for evaluating the success of the Korean War. Prolonging the war succeeded in achieving voluntary repatriation. "Our victory in the battle for men's minds" was of more enduring importance than the Inchon victory, wrote one contemporary magazine.[6] If so, then the authenticity of this achievement needs careful consideration. American and other UN troops and prisoners endured 18 additional months of war. The fairness of their sacrifice depends in part on how well Chinese and North Korean prisoner choices were respected.

By spring 1952, riots and kidnappings showed clear intent to disrupt the screening and defection campaign. With armistice negotiations frozen around repatriation, it was imperative for the UNC to get control of Koje-do. Up until then, the number of guards had been kept to a minimum, but in the politicized landscape the prison camps urgently needed troops from the mainland. The command created Operation Breakup to disperse POWs into smaller, manageable compounds on other islands and on the mainland, and to keep pro- and antirepatriation prisoners as far apart as possible. Haydon "Bull" Boatner, a combat general fluent in Chinese, got the assignment. Remarking that "prisoners of war do not negotiate," Boatner quickly demonstrated his presence; red flags were banned and five prisoners killed for passing messages between compounds. The most difficult task was breaking up rebellious compounds. For that, the UNC sent Boatner a battalion of tanks and a full infantry regiment. The tanks came directly off the frontline, traveling 200 miles to reach transport ships.[7] Additional troops came from UN members Canada and Great Britain. In a real sense, the focus of the war had shifted to the prisoner of war camps.

Just before Operation Breakup kicked off in June 1952, Red Cross inspectors were escorted off the island. Shielded from scrutiny and shadowed by tanks, lines of infantry with fixed bayonets began sweeping through opposition compounds. The most resistant was Dodd's C-76. Infantry wore gas masks and tossed tear gas and concussion grenades (no shrapnel, rarely fatal). Many prisoners did not fight, but the hardcore were pushed into a corner against the prongs of wire.[8] By the end of Breakup, 31 prisoners and one American were dead. Hundreds of injured were evacuated to Stanley Weintraub's hospital complex in Pusan. General Boatner moved about half the prisoners off Koje and divided the remainder into compounds of 500 or less.[9] Most pro-repatriation Koreans (the most militant) stayed on Koje, while rightist-controlled barracks were moved to the mainland under ROK guards. The Chinese were put at opposite ends of Cheju-do.

Interestingly, the man the UNC chose to crush the mutiny on Koje-do did not believe that nonrepatriates were staying of free choice. General Boatner disapproved of voluntary repatriation because it lengthened the war and risked retaliation against American POWs. Boatner lamented that "18,000,000 words were recorded" in 575 armistice meetings over two years, mainly about a prisoner exchange.[10] He blamed the CIE program for unrest, especially the Dodd kidnapping, and promptly shut it down (it resumed soon after he left). He also suspended additional defections. "I was afraid we would run short" of the number needed for an armistice, he explained later.[11] If there were any more anticommunist prisoners hidden in Red barracks, they no longer had a way out, but the general had little feeling for POWs who had been shooting at Americans a short time before capture. The suspension did not last beyond his short regime.

Operation Breakup was too big to conceal and reinforced the suggestion that prisoners were resisting coercion. Radio Beijing claimed that 570 Koreans were killed in one compound alone.[12] The actual conditions were not bad enough for the Soviet newspaper *Pravda*, which reported that new flamethrower designs were tested on 800 pro-repatriation prisoners and another 1,400 were shipped out for atomic weapons tests. American allies and their publics began worrying about what the cowboy Americans were up to on that island.[13] Canadians were sufficiently incensed that they fired a general who lent troops to quell the rebellion. The Joint Chiefs of Staff noted that East Bloc propaganda about Koje "falls on receptive ground."[14] In the United States, the scandal of needing a military offensive to subdue purported prisoners added voltage to the term "POW."

The substitute victory—Washington's bid to salvage the war—had been challenged effectively by the enemy. With the dispute now public, it was all the more important for large numbers of POWs to carry through in rejecting repatriation. If the numbers fell well below the announced figures, the substitute victory could become the extra defeat. The number of redefectors ("bugouts," the Americans called them) had to be kept low. With intense international attention, it would take only a few heart-wrenching tales of torture from bugouts to fuse an impression of coercion. The nonrepatriation campaign in the camps had to work.

On the battlefield, the stalemate ground on. American officials liked the idea of peace, but wanted to achieve it with more military pressure and keep their position on prisoners. Similarly, Mao Zedong told his negotiators at Panmunjom to "let the war drag on until the United States is willing to make compromises."[15] They each had strategies for continuing the war. The northern alliance kept improving the underground Great Wall beneath the 38th Parallel. Their troops made short forays out of their strongholds to destroy smaller forces, known as "eating sticky candy bit by bit."[16] In February 1952 General Ridgway indicated that the enemy was "well dug in," and by July troop strength had doubled since the start of talks.[17] Concurrently, the UNC kept up air attacks on military and civilian targets. With both sides set in their positions on prisoners, negotiations broke down altogether in October 1952.

Although stubborn, neither side wanted the war to go on forever, and they eventually became more receptive to ways out. A transformative moment came on March 5, 1953, when Soviet Premier Joseph Stalin died. The new leadership sought comprehensive change, especially reallocation of military resources to the austere civilian economy. They needed normalcy for that, and there was no better way to calm relations than by ending a shooting war. Kremlin leaders pressed to reopen armistice talks at Panmunjom, and by then the Chinese had tired of spending so much blood and half their budget.[18] In late March 1953, Beijing expressed willingness to exchange sick and wounded prisoners and allow refuseniks to be turned over to neutral nations for rescreening in safety. Clear acceptance of any version of partial repatriation was new and held real promise. While still hesitant to resume talks, the United States accepted the sick and wounded trade as a test and pushed things along by threatening a wider war. The medical experiment moved quickly and became known as Little Switch, while the full exchange after the war was Big Switch. In April and early May, Little Switch returned 684 POWs to the UNC, including 149 Americans. Nearly 7,000 went north. It was appropriate that an exchange of stricken prisoners signaled the approach of the end. The fighting had dragged on over POWs, and only the dead and maimed had paid a higher price for the delay. Little Switch also presaged controversies in the United States when reports suggested that GIs were chosen for their friendliness to the captors.

Little Switch revived negotiations over the delicate details of exchanging POWs. The parties soon agreed that typical prisoners would be released directly after an armistice, while defectors would be turned over to a Neutral Nations Repatriation Commission (NNRC) for an "explanation period." Under neutral authority, free of intimidation, prisoners' true desires would be determined. For 90 days, representatives from home, "explainers," would try and persuade prisoners to return. Seven persuaders per 1,000 inmates would be supervised by neutral soldiers. After explanations, remaining nonrepatriates would wait a final 30 days unless an armistice political conference let them out sooner. India agreed to chair the NNRC, and its 190th Infantry Brigade became the Custodial Forces–India (CFI), which took custody of nonrepatriate prisoners of both sides and superintended armistice protocols. The NNRC interpreted the terms of the armistice by majority vote of the five nations making it up. Indian General K. S. Thimayya was the deciding vote in a commission uneasily balanced between east and west, with Sweden and Switzerland in one bloc, Poland and Czechoslovakia in the other. The warring countries made significant concessions to end the war. The PRC and Democratic People's Republic of Korea (DPRK) painfully accepted that many of their soldiers were not coming back and would make scandalous publicity. The United States relinquished possession of the POWs for four months—enough time for the rule of inmate paramilitaries to be challenged. But the denouement was uncertain, and would depend on what happened under Indian custody.

Before the shooting stopped, one last drama entangled peace negotiations and yet again, it concerned prisoners of war. South Korean President Syngman Rhee opposed the explanation period, or even an armistice for that matter. Rhee's troops guarded 35,000 North Korean prisoners in mainland camps. On June 17, 1953, Rhee closed all the compounds he could and scattered the prisoners to protect them from "brainwashing" during the explanation period. ROK soldiers succeeded in guiding 27,000 POWs away from the camps and into the South Korean army.[19] These prisoners lost their one chance at going home—the NNRC explanation period. The largest group of North Koreans denied repatriation came from this group. After political drama with Rhee and a spike in fighting, a final armistice line was agreed upon and on July 27, 1953, the firing stopped. Soon, prisoners were trucked to Munsan-ni near Panmunjom in the demilitarized zone. For those returning to their homelands, the war was over. But thousands of Chinese and North Korean prisoners and a few hundred from the United Nations would have to stay another four months with the NNRC.

Moving to new camps guarded by Indian troops offered an opportunity to break away from gang rule. Tattooed POWs depended on the NNRC to create an atmosphere free of fear to counteract living in a police state so total that it owned the epidermis. But like the Koje screening in 1952, the explanation period was freighted with the weight of previous events. Taiwan and Seoul had had another 15 months to tighten their hold on prisoners, now geographically separated from rivals. Contending Koreans were divided by the ocean and the Chinese groups by the rugged interior of Cheju-do. Apostates were more isolated than ever, unable to flee into different compounds. POWs had had hundreds of hours of introspection to adjust to their situation. Anticommunist bunks were organized right down to five person cells who were responsible for everyone sticking to the program.[20] As long as inmate guards blocked the gates from the inside, there was little chance of going home.

Even with their tools of compulsion, compound strongmen faced a challenging period under the NNRC. At any moment POWs could ask the custodial forces of India for release. For men universally afflicted by barbed wire fever, the 120-day delay alone was incentive not to defect. Ensuring the propaganda triumph, as well as compensation for the added sacrifices of the war, all hinged on what happened outside UNC control. Operatives began preparations to strengthen the defection program. The Chinese camp newspaper *Flash* went from printing once a week to three. The whole population watched a series of skits dramatizing how to foil the explainers. Actors appeared before communist explainers while someone in an Indian turban looked on. Using the advantage of scripting, masterful debaters slashed the air with eloquent ripostes. Camp residents were given calendars numbered backward so they could cross off each day until release to Taiwan or South Korea. Outside help, candidly referred to as

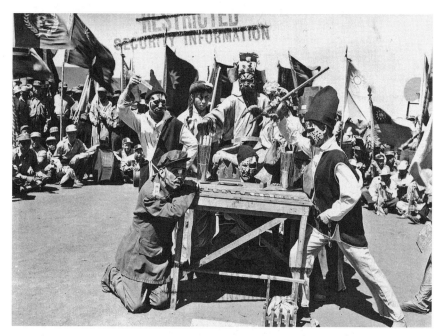

Traditional Chinese spirits in service to propaganda, July 1952. In this skit in an anticommunist compound on Cheju-do, Guan Yu, the god of war, presides over a trial condemning communist leader Mao Zedong. Taiwanese flags fly in the background.
Dimitri Boria, Army Signal Corp.

"propagandists," was brought in. They gave presentations on what to expect and reassured POWs they would not be abandoned to the communists.[21] Chinese prisoners listened to a message from Taiwan's Chiang Kai-shek himself, pledging they would not be sent to "bandit territory," while Syngman Rhee made a simi-lar broadcast.[22] The Chinese received an early welcome of eleven planeloads of gifts and letters from Taiwan. The CIE provided a going-away present for movie nights—a fresh stack of Hollywood features and cartoons.[23]

Risk and expectation weighed on the explanation phase, and concern circu-lated on top floors. In June 1953 the State Department warned the White House to make a contingency plan in case of "large-scale defection" from the "present stand on non-repatriation."[24] The UNC needed the whole defection program to continue on its own, under POW steam. The vocational and literacy programs would be recreated inside Indian barracks. A report to the Psychological Strategy Board documented some of the precautions:

> PsyWar has devoted a major effort to intensify the program of educa-tion and recreation for prisoners of war, during the crucial final phase. This final effort is receiving top command backing.... The goal is to

have the major phases of the program operating throughout the NNRC period, under Prisoner of War instructors and directors. Utmost effort is being exerted to reassure PWs and to assist them in coping with and protecting them from Communist explainers. The objective is to have anti-Communist PWs *remain firm in their decision not to return* to Communist domination, thus bringing about one of the greatest propaganda victories over the Communists [emphasis added].[25]

The reference to "protecting" POWs from explanation sessions derived from amnesia about the defective April 1952 screening and characterized the official mind set. Operatives believed that unarmed northerners, restricted to explanation tents and supervised by Indian soldiers, were the threat to free choice, not inmate trustee squads. Preparations for the months under the NNRC were put in positive terms; POWs who clandestinely favored repatriation were dismissed as "infiltrating agent-agitators." Col. Kenneth Hansen said that refuseniks were being trained to resist brainwashing during the "four or five hours" of explanations for each prisoner. Hansen cited scientific authorities to prove that explanations could have a "hypnotic" hold on the audience. In his book, Col. Hansen of psyops sometimes drifted away from the line that nonrepatriation was voluntary, such as when he accused communists of trying to organize "breakout" attempts from NNRC custody. If free to go, they would not need to escape. When Polish and Czech NNRC representatives wanted leaflets to reaffirm that prisoner choices would be protected, the Chief of Far-East Psychological Operations called it an attempt to "terrorize the prisoners and provoke them to an escape attempt."[26] By defining stratagems for Indian custody as protection, American operatives could overlook the months of coercion. The Chinese and North Koreans were expected to subvert the NNRC and try and force prisoners back. Volunteer repatriation was a new human right achieved at great cost, so unbridled defensive measures were in order.

Most important was making sure that compound hanchos were not separated from their charges. The anticommunist brigades had to retain their dominance over any POWs silently waiting to escape. Prisoners were organized into companies or compounds of up to 500, so when the UNC handed them over to NNRC custodians, it insisted that they remain intact for the duration. India, not knowing what it was in for, went along.[27] Companies would leave together, travel together, and arrive at the new camps in formation. This was harder than it sounds, for it required persuading a reluctant American Navy to cough up more transport ships. The Navy always filled its LST troop ships to 600 capacity, but that would fracture company authority. However, the substitute victory carried weight and the Navy "gave in"; it would be "one compound to an LST."[28] This exemplified the calculation in keeping barracks bosses in control and the "top command backing" the report to the PSB spoke of. Prisoners would not get a minute out of sight.

After sailing compound-by-compound to the west coast of the mainland, prisoners filed onto trains to Munsan-ni, where they reported to a UNC-built $7.7 million prison camp laid out in 500-person yards.[29] The moment of being handed over to India was a vulnerable one for barracks hanchos because of a short gap in authority. The yards were enclosed with two barbed wire fences with an alleyway between. Prisoners entered this passage, then walked clockwise through the wire corridor until they reached a gate into the interior. Situated there was a table where guards matched names against a roster, observed by NNRC executives and delegates from the conflicting states. The passageway was beyond the reach of inmate enforcers, but POWs returned to their control once inside the yard. This was not much of an opening, but some prisoners took it. As an American witness described it, when a prisoner reached the table he would suddenly "cut and run, throw himself on the breast of the nearest Indian officer, and ask for repatriation."[30] These were brave leaps into uncertainty. Nine in the first group made it, but what followed set a pattern for the rest of the explanation period. Major General William S. Lawton, who was in charge of the delivery, warned NNRC executives that if they and the communist observers did not leave, they would be attacked by rioters. They were inside the fence ring and might be trapped; several POWs had already tried to assault the communist representatives. Potential rioters were bunching up inside the compound, no doubt glaring through the wire, so the official delegates decided to scoot, leaving behind just the CFI guards.[31] Now prisoners walking through the corridor saw only guard uniforms and wire, with no civilians to run to. One leak was plugged, with half of the very first group of 500 to go. Soon after, an Indian source leaked to the press that the "batches of 500" from the UNC really should have been broken up.[32] Things had moved a long way since April 1952 when Admiral Joy scraped and scratched for more prisoners to return.

The resilience of compound organizations was kept up with help from the outside. The "instructors" hired by the CIE remained as official observers of the explanation period and were present every day. Fifty Chinese nationalists served as observers and interpreters during the explanations. NNRC chair K. S. Thimayya learned that inmate leaders "came from Formosa and South Korea," and doubted they were "bonafide" prisoners at all.[33] The Indian military developed a chart of the anticommunist organizations. Korean authority rested first with the Anti-Communist Youth League (ACYL) in Seoul, which passed clandestine directives to the POW General Staff, whose control branched down to enclosures, compounds, and finally to tent commanders and bunk cells. The General Staff had intelligence squads, and if they detected a loyal communist or anyone considering repatriation he was "savagely punished" and sometimes murdered. A CFI unit history considered the ACYL a military organization. Each compound was assigned 50 "military police," who "kept severely aloof from the other prisoners and maintained a standing watch both by night and by day."[34] With a ratio of 1:10, there were almost as many inmate guards as Indian.

India had underestimated the challenge. Commanders were shocked by the aggressiveness and coordination of POWs. They soon realized that fences could be scaled in ten seconds and the posts holding them could be rocked flat in minutes, faster if preloosened the previous night. The seven large enclosures with their multiple compounds were line-of-sight, allowing efficient communication by semaphore flags. This allowed "collective opposition," the Custodial Forces–India military history ruefully remarked.[35] In a crisis, the entire population could launch a huge riot. Guards on Koje-do had quad .50 caliber machine guns and tank-born flame throwers to regain control. If the NNRC pressed things too far, it would have no such recourse. CFI guards arrived with light police weapons and had not anticipated using them much. By one guess, it would take twice as many guards as prisoners to get control without a massacre, but the CFI was outnumbered eight to one. The UNC had told India that only three battalions would be needed, but the Indians decided four would be better, then hastily organized a fifth. Still understrength, even the medical staff walked guard stints.[36]

Throughout their expedition, Indian commanders understood that they lacked final authority. As guests in Korea, their safety and effectiveness depended on the cooperation of the armies stationed in the area. Syngmun Rhee forbade all NNRC personnel from stepping foot on South Korean soil, forcing them to ride American planes into the demilitarized zone (DMZ).[37] When considering tough action against the paramilitaries, the NNRC had to consider the response of Syngmun Rhee, who repeatedly threatened attacks. A major newspaper, *The Hindu*, faulted the UNC for failing to "take due note" of Seoul's "threats." An array of American tanks with barrels pointed south made a military assault unlikely, but the CFI was still worried about provocations like shootings of guards.[38] A concerned Prime Minister Jawaharlal Nehru publicly demanded guarantees that the armistice would be properly implemented. The UNC waited four weeks to make a formal reply, stating only that it would prevent any attempt to move prisoners, meaning that Rhee would not be allowed to repeat a mass release. This spoke volumes—as long as POWs stayed behind wire, India was on its own. It undermined the single most effective method of pacifying the barracks: removing paramilitary leaders. Polish and Czech members of the NNRC demanded that the prisoner platoons be broken up and produced a list of leaders for arrest. But this was sure to trigger deadly riots without any backup for the CFI. India decided that under the forbidding circumstances, seizing hanchos was not practical.[39]

Shielded from interference, the barracks bosses continued dominating other prisoners, but still, refuge was only a gate away. Once past the wire, escapees were home free—no hounds would run them to ground. Intimidation had to be close at hand, so the hanchos used their military police as flying squads to prevent anyone from approaching the fences. On December 12, a North Korean from Compound E-38 evaded the paramilitaries and told Indian guards to watch for four compatriots. Later that night, four limp, strangled, and stabbed corpses were dumped by the wire.[40] Author John Toland uncovered the story of Ju Yeong-bok, a North Korean major who wanted to emigrate to a neutral country rather than stay in South Korea. Fingered as a flight risk, he was beaten with a bat until he could not walk. Days later, he waited until dark and ran for the fence. He scrambled over the wire, to the shouts of trustees trying to reach him. "His hands were stained with blood, his clothes were torn into shreds and he had left a trail of red footprints in the snow," according to Toland.[41] There were more bugouts as the CFI established its neutrality. General Shankarrao Thorat ordered that fence climbers not be shot unless it was certain their purpose was not repatriation. The CFI's relations with prisoner organizations deteriorated as the number of "spontaneous repatriates" grew. After NNRC chair Thimayya and his party were cornered and roughed up, the CFI was instructed not to enter compounds at all except in prepared shows of force.[42]

Sixteen explanation tents opened on October 15, 1953, each with guards, a set of persuaders, folding chairs for prisoners, and multiple observers. POWs were first brought to a holding area with room for 250 that was several hundred yards from the interview tents. They then moved in groups of 25 to a waiting area nearby. Prisoners entered the tents alone, but were still with their original units until the last moment. After hearing out the persuaders, they exited through the "north" door home or "south" back to the holding area.[43] The first truckloads arrived chanting "*hui Taiwan.*" It would be a trying day for Chinese explainers. A few prisoners greeted them warmly and immediately went out the north door; more listened passively and then returned to the "lobby," and others screamed bitterly at the explainers. The Indians introduced heavy wooden benches in place of the folding chairs, which took flight too easily. In a Korean tent, one man listened quietly, encouraging the explainers to keep talking. He let them use up an hour on him, then smartly informed them that they had wasted their time and flounced through the south door. Knowing that some prisoners would waver, the activist-minded intended to disrupt the explanations.[44] One POW who did choose repatriation (quickly escorted out by General Thimayya to his automobile) said that he had been warned that the other men would rush anyone who tried to exit the wrong door. They would "create a confusion, make a noise, etc., get hold of him and kill him."[45] Fear adhered to the skin like the crude tattoos. While the CFI did take care of bugouts once they reached the tents, an audience with the explanation panel was a weak balance against several years of terror.

Each prisoner was supposed to hear at least one pitch, but without control of the camps the NNRC could not assure this. One difficulty was that after refuseniks were screened, they were not separated from those who remained. This allowed the most reliable men to report for explanations over and over by switching IDs. The NNRC unanimously wanted to segregate them, which would also provide a chance for reconsideration in new surroundings, but hanchos stridently opposed, backed by American officers.[46] There was also nowhere to put them, since the UNC did not built enough yards for segregation. Despite favoring segregation in principle, a three-nation majority decided not to provoke violence by sending processed prisoners into nonexistent facilities. Men who did not decide on the spot to go home returned to the probing scrutiny of the paramilitaries. Chinese officials protested mightily and then suspended explanations, one of several long delays. Hammers and nails finally got busy and limited segregation began on December 20, a couple days before the scheduled end of explanations.[47]

Segregating prisoners after interviews also required getting them to the tents in the first place, but most units never left their barracks. Compound 50 informed the NNRC: "All of us anti-Communists, except about 60 betrayers who escaped into the hands of the Communists ... refuse to meet the Communist explainers with desperate courage." The UNC refused to tell POWs to cooperate. With few or repeat listeners, the Chinese began recalling groups that had already appeared, stringing sessions out for hours, or halting interviews altogether in protest.[48] An Associated Press sum-up of the process concluded that beneath all the wrangling, "interviews bogged down" when prisoners refused to attend. To finish the explanations, the CFI would have to compel attendance. In one attempt in mid-October, 400 guards surrounded a compound, but prisoners poured into the surrounding yards and angrily pressed against the fences. Some wrapped cloth around their hands to scale the barbwire and mob sentries. Guards would have had to use automatic rifles, so General Thimayya stepped back from a slaughter to consult.[49] Four NNRC nations were divided on armed compulsion, making General Thimayya the tiebreaker. India reasoned that the armistice permitted force against "unlawful" activity, but since "heavy casualties" were expected, it would not do so without unanimity. "Once the NNRC had issued instructions not to use force," the CFI historian concluded, the success of explanations "really passed over to the prisoners themselves." That ended most processing by November 5.[50] With screening largely halted, there was no normal channel for prisoners to return to their families. The CFI managed to free 135 on New Years 1954 when it marched into Chinese Enclosure B for a roster check. This one incident supplied one-third of all Chinese bugouts, made possible by surprise and the CFI establishing its neutrality. Seoul warned that if India kept it up, "we cannot let our anti-Communist prisoners remain." Facing bluster outside and riots certain inside, the roster checks ended as soon as they began.[51]

In the end, the overwhelmed Custodial Forces–India could not provide a safe, unpressured venue for the POWs, although they did provide a fighting chance for escape. Most company commanders refused to allow the prisoners to visit the explanation tents and the NNRC was unable to force them. Less than one-sixth of the North Koreans and barely 2,000 out 14,700 Chinese ever got near the north door.[52] After its job was done, the NNRC concluded that "any prisoner who desired repatriation had to do so clandestinely and in fear of his life."[53] The explanation period failed.

On January 22, 1954, the prisoners became civilians and begin leaving. The NNRC wanted more explanations, but the UNC refused. The CFI began with 14,704 Chinese and 7,900 North Koreans. Of them, 51 died or disappeared. Of the 132,000 prisoners held by the UNC, 82,493 went home immediately after the armistice and 628 joined them via the NNRC. Not repatriated were 14,235 Chinese and 7,604 North Korean veterans of the NNRC, plus 27,000 North Koreans impressed into the ROK army by Syngman Rhee.[54] Of this 48,839 total, some portion had been forced to renounce their homelands. The unceasing violence and intimidation indicate the number was substantial. A more specific estimate can be calculated from the April 1952 screening results of compounds that were not controlled by political militants of either side. As discussed in Chapter 5, the three peaceful Pusan hospital units and the Koje compound held 8,494 POWs. Seventy-nine percent of them (Chinese and Korean) told questioners they wanted to go home. Applying that rate to 132,000 total POWs, perhaps 20,000 were prevented from repatriation. This is a significant underestimate, however, because much of Stanley Weintraub's data did not differentiate between North and South Koreans. The many press-ganged southerners captured in KPA uniforms weighted the results against the North, and most were gone after summer 1952 anyway. We have to use a smaller but still substantial sample to predict a repatriation rate for North Koreans. Admiral Joy included a breakdown of Compound 10, where 1,873 North Koreans screened north and 92 south, for a 95 percent rate. Applying this percentage to the 111,000 North Koreans held in spring 1953, 105,450 wanted to go home, and 76,451 did, suggesting that 28,999 were stranded. C-10 had too few Chinese for its 97 percent repatriation rate to be solid, but Joy's interpreters reported 85 percent in an unpolarized Koje compound of 1,500. This predicts 17,850 going back to China out of 21,345, and with 7,110 actually returning, perhaps 10,740 were denied repatriation.[55] (A lower Chinese rate jibes with their frequent previous membership in the KMT.) There is reason to think these are conservative numbers. Although many refuseniks were dead-set on defecting, they would never have

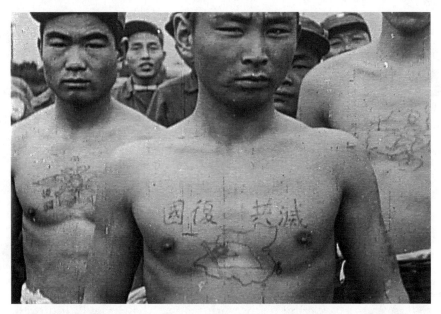

Freed Chinese prisoners on display for the press after landing in Taiwan, early 1954.
Some Chinese soldiers captured during the Korean War refused to return to communism
after the armistice. Others were encouraged to defect with mandatory anticommunist
tattoos. The closer man's tattoo reads "Revive the republic" and "Destroy communism,"
with the flag of Taiwan over a map of China. From the film *Road to Freedom*. National
Archives and Records Administration.

taken that path without a psychological operation in place on Koje-do. Once
they were tattooed and publicly identified with anticommunist organizations, a
certain number committed their minds fully to the cause, but would have happily gone home otherwise. If early parole had been allowed and Taiwan and
Seoul did not control barracks, nonrepatriates would have been a small frac-
tion of prisoners and a hiccup in armistice negotiations. All considered, it seems
sober to estimate that as many as 40,000 or possibly more additional prisoners
would have seen their families if it had been safe. The plain English conclusion is
unavoidable: United Nations forces withheld thousands of prisoners at the end
of the Korean War.

The North Korean regime separated many more people from their loved ones
than the UN did. There were 83,000 captured South Korean soldiers and civilians dragooned into the KPA or labor units.[56] Their repatriation rate was zero.
A trickle managed to slip back to South Korea over the years, including Han
Gil-su, spirited out of a coal mining district in Hamgyong province at the age of
73. Of North Koreans who were withheld, Seoul returned 63 during a political
thaw in 2000.[57]

There is little information in English about Korean prisoners who returned to the North. Regrettably, prisoners repatriated to China were poorly received. They carried a stigma for surrendering in the first place, plus their tattoos were *bu xiao* and revealed their exposure to bourgeois ideology. Many Chinese were reduced in rank or discharged from the military, denied jobs, expelled from the Communist Party, exiled to the countryside, or shunned by their communities and even families. Former prisoners were targeted in periodic political purifications, including Mao's Anti-Rightist Campaign of 1957 and the Cultural Revolution of the 1960s. Communist Party archives contain sad letters appealing for readmission to the party or removal of black marks that blocked jobs, education, and esteem. There was little movement to rehabilitate ex-POWs until 1980. From the North, the CFI received a small number of refuseniks—359 South Koreans, Americans, and other UN nationals—seven of whom changed their minds. Their guards had light duty.[58]

In most accounts of the Forgotten War, peace talks froze for an uncomplicated reason: Thousands of prisoners refused to "return to North Korea and China." Misunderstanding partial repatriation is the rule. T. R. Fehrenbach's influential book *This Kind of War* devoted a chapter to Koje-do without any awareness of the KMT and ROK agents in the camps or the pressure to inflate defections. The "conscience" of officialdom explained policy.[59] An author of similar stature wrote that despite the convolutions, "the issue was very simple": The United States refused forced repatriation.[60] David Halberstam's engaging *Coldest Winter* concentrated on the early part of the war, but did cover the stalemate. However, in 700 pages, he might have explained the truce delay beyond "no one knew how to end it." He was familiar with voluntary repatriation, but only as one in a jumble of threads that negotiators lacked "the political skills" to untangle. Halberstam, whose first calling was journalism, can be partially forgiven since the background he needed from specialized historians was so spotty.[61] The standard understanding of repatriation should be upended. While some prisoners were estranged from their governments, the UN fostered a community of coercion. By creating a defection campaign and handing control over to the ROK and KMT, a deadly atmosphere trapped POWs. The leaders of the anticommunist associations knew their barracks, and it was their judgment that ferocious deterrents were necessary right up through January 22, 1954. Barracks hanchos shrewdly used the punitive reputation of the communist regimes by marking their charges through public lists, parades, and tattoos. For the minority who originally dreaded going back, presumably their own experiences were authoritative, and a crusade was unnecessary. A more balanced approach was the one suggested by Secretary of State Acheson in late 1951: early parole for proven friends. Instead, committed anticommunists stayed in the camps, where they were a counterweight to family love.

The poor treatment of prisoners raises a question: In the middle of a conflict, when making constant trade-offs in lives, how concerned must armies be about the future of POWs after the war? The repatriation problem was only partly the making of Americans, who had limited control inside the wire. An answer comes from officials at the time—those who set the policies and proclaimed them in noble terms. Nonforcible repatriation was based on the "fundamental principle of individual human rights," according to C. H. Peake of the State Department.[62] A key participant, Admiral C. Turner Joy, got religion and told an Armed Forces Day crowd after the war that "the principle of voluntary repatriation symbolized the fundamental difference between the free world and the Communist world." As NSC-68, the mission statement of the Cold War, put it, "the free society values the individual as an end in himself."[63] The pronouncement of a new human right was made by Washington at the time. Officials proclaimed it, fought a war for it, and pressed it on their allies. It is appropriate to judge their adherence to their own principle.

Without doubt, key officials knew that the 1952 screening was compromised by systematic terror, although it soon vanished from deliberations. Not only did the United States not protect free choice, it made sure no one else did either. During the explanation period the UNC could have done right by doing nothing and let the NNRC do its job unhindered. Instead, it pulled the Big Switcheroo, putting the public relations desires of a collective above the individual rights of POWs. Withholding prisoners was eased by slipping into race thinking. In early 1952, Admiral William Fechteler of the JCS referred to even friendly nonrepatriates as "a lot of worthless Chinese" and claimed to speak for more brass.[64] This generationally typical attitude accents a hollow part of voluntary repatriation: Washington fought an extra war for Asians that some functionaries cared little for. Swinging between racial emotions and proclamations of a new human right must have tested their tongues. The captives who were held back are an interesting contrast to reports of abandoned American POWs. Like the Vietnam War, there were recurring assertions of live Americans retained in North Korea, China, or the Soviet Union.[65] The POW/MIA evidence from both wars is controversial and relates to a limited number of individuals, but the withholding of thousands of Chinese and Korean prisoners is well established. Another Vietnam contrast is that its peace agreement forbade partial repatriation of prisoners: "The detaining parties shall not deny or delay their return for any reason."[66]

The genuineness of voluntary repatriation should be prominent in evaluations of the Korean War. It put the war into overtime and cost GI lives, freedom, and alienation at home. What did their extra anguish accomplish? Americans remained behind barbed wire so that Chinese and Koreans could be denied free repatriation. That was not how American leaders liked to think of it, but it is what they did. The undertaking produced waves of complications, including in the reception of returning American POWs.

# PART TWO

# OVER HERE

# 8

# Home to Cheers and Jeers

The homecoming of American prisoners was loaded with anticipation and anxiety. Emotions were primed by the dozens sent home during Little Switch in April 1953, the first solid indicator that the rest might be home soon. Then in August and September, the remaining 3,600 prisoners were released in Big Switch, a definitive end to an unpopular conflict. For American repatriates, the circumstances of war both Cold and limited made their return to society different from past conflicts, beginning with the acrid taste of a battle not won. General Douglas MacArthur (ret.) suggested that the war *could* have been won and Korea reunited. Many agreed with MacArthur's claim that "timidity and fear" shackled the military, feeding doubts about America's place in the world.[1] Korea seemed to suggest a lack of will or ability to face down the Soviets, and the returning POWs were ready examples of irresolution. McCarthyism was at its peak, making wrongheadedness and slander customary. The repatriates' every action in captivity was up for scrutiny, and there were things to find, thanks to the use of prisoners in propaganda. The early glimpses of collaboration were expanded into full portraits of capitulation.

Family and friends welcomed repatriates with little reservation. The closer citizens were to an actual returnee, the less distracted they were by current affairs carping. There was a tension at work, though. Were the repats private citizens, to be returned to roles as sons, fathers, and husbands, or were they the property of Cold War discourse? This was a divide more of psyches than of political factions, for someone was entirely capable of adoring his own son while worrying about the fortitude of a neighbor. But debate still tended to follow this divide, emphasizing either affection for repatriates or worry about a weakened national character. As more stories of misconduct emerged, it became a question of determining guilt: Were the prisoners to blame, or the enemy's mistreatment? This discussion drew on charged images of the admirable son and the repulsive coward. The notoriety of Korea accomplished something unusual: It transformed traditional heroes into shadows. After sacrificing months of freedom for the substitute victory, repatriates were subjects of averted eyes, whispers, and pity, if not outright condemnation. This change takes some explanation, since less than a decade earlier soldiers were undisputed heroes in the victory over fascism.

Concern about collaboration had grown as the war progressed. There were the POWs speaking against the war on shortwave radio and letters reaching the families. Prisoners often added antiwar statements to their letters to expedite release by Chinese censors. Early in 1953, Secretary of Defense C. E. Wilson reported that "virtually all" of the 29,000 letters from POWs carried slogans denouncing "Wall Streeters" or requesting that family members oppose the "useless" war in Korea. Tales of "wonderful treatment" in North Korea were all "in the handwriting of the Americans who are held captive," Wilson complained. The Chinese passed home addresses to publishing houses in Eastern Europe who "bombarded" the families of prisoners with propaganda booklets.[2] Arden Rowley's mother received *United Nations POWs in Korea,* by the Chinese People's Committee for World Peace. When planners sensed the end of the war coming, they feared that the voices of collaborators heard on muffled shortwave broadcasts would become clearer once home. They began thinking about how to reintroduce potentially contaminated GIs back into society and concluded that it must be done cautiously, with careful scrutiny of suspected red dupes. This was apparent during Little Switch.

As Little Switch arrangements progressed in April 1953, defense officials worried that the returnees might have been handpicked to embarrass the United States. According to Air Force chief Millard C. Young, it was "generally recognized" that returning POWs may have been "indoctrinated or brainwashed." His proposal "Problem of Brainwashed U.S. and Other U.N. Prisoners of War" warned that repatriates might denounce the allies and praise the communists.[3] The Psychological Strategy Board issued guidelines for handling Little Switchers. Document D-41 advised treating indoctrinated repatriates as "victims of Communist mental aggression" that should be "whisked away" into an army mental ward. D-41 suggested that family members of mental casualties needed to be handled with as much care as with killed-in-action notifications, with officers trained to "explain this brain-washing problem." The press could be enlisted to prepare the public for "the grim realities of the brain-washing process."⁴ For a week in advance of Little Switch, according to the *Times*, stories circulated in Washington that the communists were using the "brainwash" on POWs. A Department of Defense press release on the eve of Little Switch warned that some American returnees might have been mentally "warped" by the reds. Interestingly, the document stated that such victims "cannot be condemned" for having assisted the enemy. The "brainwash" was still new to most readers, but, drawing on Defense Department sources, the *Times* explained that prolonged questioning, searing lights, and repetition could replace a lifetime of beliefs without physical torture.⁵

News reporters waited for the 149 released Americans when they stopped over in Tokyo, but quickly noticed that some were missing. While still in Tokyo, 20 of the 149 had been tagged as off-limits to the press and segregated. Guarded by military police, they were taken to a far corner of the airport and boarded a separate flight to California. When the 20 landed at Travis Air Force base their plane was surrounded by MPs with machine guns, while an armored car circled in the background. They then boarded a prison plane with barred windows for a final leg. This was supposedly all done on the hush-hush, provoking headlines like "Ex-Captives, Called Dupes of Reds, Flown to California Amid Secrecy."⁶

The ex-POWs were delivered to a sealed psychiatric ward in Valley Forge hospital in Pennsylvania. A terse announcement from the Pentagon explained that they had "succumbed to Communist indoctrination," which *Stars and Stripes* interpreted as "Communist Dupes Destined for High Level Psychiatric Treatment."⁷ At Valley Forge, the men were sequestered with two sets of attendants: psychiatrists and G-2 intelligence officers. For the press, there was little to go on at first. What information trickled out suggested that the men's minds had been overwhelmed by a devious enemy using "brainwashing." *Life* magazine told the country that it was "a story of deep and shocking importance." The enemy had a finely tuned battle plan to "capture the minds of American prisoners and send them back to the U.S. to spread Communist doctrine."⁸ Titled "Valley Forge GIs Tell of their Brainwashing Ordeal," this fearful headline was odd considering the article's conclusion that the ex-POWs' malign beliefs evaporated almost immediately after the hamburger cure—familiar food, comforting surroundings, and a good night's sleep.

Coming from the Pentagon, the suggestion that the repatriates were brainwashed carried extra weight. Significantly, the repatriates were not put in the stockade; delivering the men to a mental ward framed the problem as a medical one. This decision came from high up. The Secretary of Defense's office instructed that they be isolated and "remain in Army repeat Army medical channels."⁹ At a time when the country was particularly impressed by psychiatry and the wisdom of experts, the treatment at Valley Forge gave cachet to the phenomenon of brainwashing. A ranking army psychiatrist present at Valley Forge told *Life* magazine that the men were conditioned "in the same way" as Pavlov's famous drooling dogs. The Chinese "reflex-conditioned our men to give Communist answers.... For a while some of our PWs may inadvertently use phrases like 'Chinese Peoples Volunteers Army' and then catch themselves.... They may even say they saw germ warfare bombs dropped."[10] The army psychiatrist optimistically claimed that the conditioning would wear off, but the portrait he gave was still of exacting, scientific manipulation of minds.

To the Pentagon's embarrassment, the brainwashing story began unraveling as soon as the ex-POWs were able to speak for themselves. Not long after settling into ward CD-10, the repatriates "came solemnly before the press in pairs to deny any Communist taint." It was reported that the boys were "hopping mad" at being called red and were trying to undo the original impression.[11] It seemed that as soon as they were back in the states their condition went away, undermining talk of Pavlov. Pundits and congressmen told a new story: an army hatchet job on good boys. *Newsweek* suggested that the POWs' conversion to Marxism amounted to little more than nodding heads during lectures and quoted a priest who visited them, "I never heard of a real Red taking Holy Communion." Meanwhile, a member of Congress demanded a "Probe in Smear of PWs."[12] *Time* said the original story was one of the Pentagon's "periodic tizzies." An army psychiatrist suggested that the agitated publicity played into the hands of the Chinese, who had warned the prisoners to expect an unfriendly reception.[13] A defensive army spokesman told the *Detroit Press* that it was all started by "the boys" upstairs in "psychological warfare." The press officers did not want to push the red psychiatric angle and "screamed bloody murder," according to this source, "but the matter went all the way up to Mr. Jackson [C. D. Jackson, Eisenhower's psyops advisor] at the White House and we were overruled."[14] The sidelining of public relations officers' opinion showed that the PSB line on mental casualties was being managed attentively. The Valley Forge brainwashing reports were publicized before the returnees were even examined at home; the story was being spun from the top. For his part, C. D. Jackson blamed the Valley Forge sensation on the army for getting "all steamed up" over exaggerated tales from its Far East Command.[15]

For a moment at least, Valley Forge soured some officials on accusing the Soviet bloc of a new crime. The PSB's Horace Craig concluded that there was "a great deal less here than meets the eye" and warned that "we don't want to be stampeded into yelling around in the UN" that the enemy has developed a technique that "isn't even yet a technique." Secretary of the Army Robert Stevens was also having second thoughts after concluding that only five of the Little Switchers had beliefs deemed "security risks." The others collaborated out of opportunism and were returning to their prewar selves.[16] One scathing internal review described the Valley Forge affair as "completely incompetent," with bits of repatriate stories "taken at their face value" and hastily released to the media. An ad hoc Pentagon committee returned the top secret verdict that there was "no evidence of any of them having been subjected to 'brainwashing' techniques," though there was pressure and indoctrination. The best treatment was to return the men as quickly as possible to their previous lives.[17] The segregation of apparent collaborators was not repeated when the rest of the POWs came home. There would be no special ships for traitors that might fuel speculation.[18] Little Switch illustrated how contradictory brainwashing was in the early stages. There was fear of red zombies, but it was balanced by skepticism and sympathy for the soldiers. With some officials pushing it, others downplaying it, there was no consistent handling of the brainwashing story. The association of prisoners with collaboration and brainwashing was there—but not solid.

The rest of the prisoners started being freed the first week of August 1953. They were transported south down to Munsan-ni, where they were greeted by American officers with a smile and a hearty handshake. The pamphlet "What Has Happened Since 1950" caught them up on current events and World Series scores, and another had a drawing of a home with smoke curling out of the chimney. Each repatriate had to sign a statement forbidding "unauthorized disclosures of your experiences."[19] A United Press reporter translated that to mean they must not reflect "on the behavior of United Nations captured personnel," which can be further translated to mean collaboration.[20]

The repatriates returned home on floating laboratories overrun by psychiatrists, criminal investigators, and intelligence agents. A Joint Intelligence Processing Board was needed to coordinate all the experts clamoring to speak with the repatriates.[21] "As soon as we set sail," one returnee recalled, the Counterintelligence Corps began questioning them and kept it up for two weeks. "They wanted to know everything from the day we were captured to the day the Chinese released us." Pfc. Donald M. Elliott remembered, "we were all suspect of no-telling-what," and that most men were questioned three or more times. The Far East Command mandated an hour with a psychiatrist for each.[22] The Army Assistant Chief of Staff for intelligence recalled that "no group of men in Army history has ever been so closely studied as these repatriates were." There were 77 pages of prepared questions, then follow-ups, confirmations, and leads to chase. They took a battery of psychological tests, IQ evaluations, and read Rorschach's inkblots.[23] The accumulated dossiers included reports, "miscellaneous letters, diaries, and photographs," and "all allegations—favorable and unfavorable." Individual files became as thick as phone books; a few reached two feet. This mass of material sustained years of research by social scientists.[24]

Freed on his twenty-second birthday. Pvt. Cordero Ramosi tagged for processing at the 45th Surgical Field Hospital. He was part of Little Switch in April 1953, the early exchange of ill and wounded prisoners. Jack Kanthal, Army Signal Corp.

The returnees had the misfortune of arriving home during McCarthyism, when anticommunist fears had fixated on spies and traitors within America. The first Soviet hydrogen bomb exploded during repatriation, which many thought was designed with stolen plans. The Rosenbergs had been executed for espionage only two months previously. Spy worries made ex-prisoners a natural target of suspicion, for they had run, surrendered, lost the war, and, rumor had it, gotten cozy with the enemy. On September 12 the repatriates shared headlines

Open wide! At a Tokyo military hospital, nurses of the 8059th brace for 3,600 prisoners freed at Big Switch, August 1953. Arnold Siegel, Army Signal Corp.

with comedian Lucille Ball, who had once voted red. "I did it for Grandpa," she explained. If even Lucy had to account for her behavior, so would ex-prisoners.[25] One worried citizen suggested using x-rays and Geiger counters to make sure the repatriates were not smuggling atomic bombs into the country. If it wasn't already obvious that spies and agitators would use repatriation to slip into the United States, there were returnees to confirm it. "P.W.s Say Pro-Red G.I.s Return to Propagandize," warned one newspaper.[26]

Communism was considered an infectious agent, and prisoners had been in close contact with carriers. Fear of political epidemics intertwined with the public health ones. The White House received several telegrams requesting quarantines of the repatriates because they might carry plague planted by the Chinese.[27] The Cold War so saturated newspapers that on a single day *The New York Times* contained 25 such stories. A sample:

> "Wide Crackdown on Reds in Italy"; "U.N. Seat is Asked For 'Purged' China"; "British Curb Writer" [Winnington]; "Poland Softening Her Farm Policies"; "Besieged French Await New Push" [Dienbienphu]; "Formosa Asks Anti-Red Pact"; "Ruble Said to Buy 7C Worth of Food"; "11 Measures to Outlaw the Reds"; "Navy Gives Breakdown On 328 Security Cases."[28]

As the transports laid anchor, suspicion gathered at the docks. Like a teenage couple slinking out of the bushes, the question on everyone's mind was, "Did they do it?" The soldiers getting off the ships seemed to confirm the worst, as they ignored army warnings and freely gave reporters examples of assistance to the enemy, sometimes accompanied by threats to get even. Headlines included "P.W.s Blast G.I.s Who Aided Reds," "Bitter G.I.s Out to 'Get' Informers Among P.W.s," " 'Buying that Red Stuff' Won Favors for P.W.s," and, simply, "The Rats."[29] Readers learned that the compounds contained "Progressive" and "Reactionary" cliques, that everyone had to endure indoctrination, and that some kept talking the talk even when the monitors were not around. The nature of journalism heightened the perception of treason. Shipboard military investigators had the luxury of compiling evidence from multiple sources, cross-checking details, and weeding out uncorroborated rumors. Journalists, on the other hand, filed their copy soon after scribbling down quotes.

It took six weeks to bring all of the POWs home, so there was plenty of time for emotion to build. Back in their hometowns, soldiers felt the stares. "You could tell people were looking at you," Tony Ryan recalled years later. "You're guilty of something just because you survived." Albert Biderman, a careful Air Force researcher, found that returnees were routinely suspect.[30] New Jersey resident Richard Godlewski felt ashamed for having been captured because it went against the expectation "that you fight until the last man dies." When Jack Chapman returned to Oklahoma, he went to a tavern with his uncle to catch up. When the bartender found out where Chapman had been, he said "Oh, he's one of them cowards." Chapman recalled, "Oh, that hurt." From then on, "I didn't tell nobody I had been a prisoner of war."[31]

Negative stories were by no means the only ones. The happy fact that the GIs were home was especially prominent in local newspapers. With nearly 3,600 men returning to 48 states, most daily newspapers in the country had a local homecoming to cover. Many citizens were only two degrees of separation from the family of a returnee and felt personally connected. Suspense built as people scanned the daily roll calls to see if a local boy appeared. Each day's list of returnees was accompanied by human interest stories and national updates on the course of repatriation. Anecdotally, it appears that collaboration reports were bigger on the national wires, while the local papers were more celebratory. Smaller papers regularly asked local boys what they knew about the Progressives—it was on everyone's mind—but may not have focused on it as much. The weight of coverage was patriotic, with stories of endurance and valor. Reporters loved stories that turned collaboration reports on their heads. An often-repeated angle suggested that cases of collaboration were really tricks played on the enemy. One headline read, "City P.W. 'Played Dumb,' Beat Red Propagandists." Cpl. William Hansen said he just sat there and agreed with everything they said until they went away. This explanation for the apparent rash of collusion was welcome. A *New York Times Magazine* article congratulated such dissembling and raised it to a strategic level; it was "deceit for survival, an extension of battlefield tactics." Brig. Gen R. E. Chambers said many Progressives were just "taking measures to survive," but would slough off the indoctrination soon enough.[32]

While some fake Progressives were just getting by, others were said to have actually been undercover agents posing as Progressives. The collaborator-as-secret-agent idea provided the plot for a hastily made movie immediately after the war. Ronald Reagan starred in *Prisoner of War* (MGM, 1954) as a faux progressive. In a nonfiction variation, *Combat Forces Journal* suggested that the enemy had planted the collaboration stories. A soldier who helped process releases at Munsan-ni called this "the Reds' smartest and dirtiest" trick yet. They achieved a "super frame-up" by telling prisoners caught escaping or committing infractions that so-and-so had turned them in, thus "spreading hatred and distrust among our own people."[33] Those festering resentments were now being repeated at home, according to the author. Thus, the earliest stories of collaboration coexisted with contrary reports. The subsequent army consensus that Korea soldiers were weak was not preordained.

Months later the army began prosecuting collaborators, but the immediate reaction in fall of 1953 was to cover it up. Returnees who gave interviews on army turf were required to have a counterintelligence officer present to head them off sensitive issues. They were supposed to remain quiet on leave, too, but many forgot as soon as leather hit land.[34] This appears to have prompted more forceful instructions to men repatriated later in the process. One anonymous soldier related that his officers told him he would "get home okay" as long as he did not talk about the Progressives.[35]

Although the Pentagon at this point was trying to downplay collaboration, some factors predisposed many to believe that an entire generation might have failed in its duty. For one, it was commonly accepted that communists had infil-trated throughout society, and given that premise, it was a short step to start guess-ing who they might be. Any group might attract such speculation, and POWs were highly visible and just back from communist land. Many people saw col-laboration in black and white, which made even minor concessions to the enemy seem like more than they were. If communism was a disease, then a person either had it or did not. Cultural historians see a parallel between anticommunism and the 1950s preoccupation with alien possession.[36] In the movie *Invasion of the Body Snatchers*, a victim might appear normal on the outside, but underneath had transformed into the alien enemy. Similarly, a serviceman in North Korea endors-ing a peace petition or making a radio broadcast displayed the tell-tale signals of having joined the other side. Minor accommodations with the enemy were evi-dence of switching sides, rather than evidence of having been a captive.

There was also a misconception about the process that led to helping the enemy. Cooperation with the foe was usually understood as crossing a Rubicon.

Vulnerable individuals were worn down until they snapped. Once men "broke" they were irretrievably lost to the other side. Thus, even relatively minor coop- eration was understood to be a terminal act of capitulation. This impression was strong enough that the major review of imprisonment after the war, the Secretary of Defense's Advisory Committee on Prisoners of War, felt the need to challenge it. "Virtually all POWs complied with some Communist demands," the committee concluded, but individuals "are seldom if ever stripped of all inde- pendent will," and most continued resisting in some fashion.[37] Prisoners often rediscover their nerve as soon as the immediate pressure is off, or simply when they acclimate and feel less frightened. Years later in Vietnam, a tough clique known as the "Alkies" turned their defiance on and off. In the punishment ward they named "Alkatrez," even the most respected members like Jeremiah Denton and James Stockdale sometimes signed propaganda statements in order to pre- serve their limbs.[38] But this was forgiven by their fellow soldiers, as long as they resumed resistance after recovering. Because of a different climate after Vietnam and shrewder military policy, the ruggedness of the Alkies was unquestioned. In 1953, however, it was commonly believed that broken prisoners could not repair themselves and once they gave in on one thing, a torrent of collaboration would follow. With such a narrow perspective, all that was necessary to condemn a per- son was discovery that they committed *some* infraction, which was easily done when dissecting so many histories.

The men's character was suspect, but close attention inevitably brought out the conditions of imprisonment. Even the most judgmental could not fail to be moved by what many had gone through. There had been earlier reports of bru- tality and summary executions of prisoners, but now there were eyewitnesses telling, for example, of one death march through the snow where only 101 of 162 survived. An Army Signal Corp film sent to local TV stations showed "row upon row of bodies, many with their hands tied behind them.... Ghastly reminders of Communist atrocities in Korea."[39] Early estimates of the death toll were exagger- ated—there were about 12,000 MIAs, and this figure was sometimes conflated with the number taken prisoner. With 3,600 returning, it was thought 8,000 more must have perished in captivity. The real total captured was 7,000, but in October 1953 the US Information Agency widely reported an incongruous 6,113 "mur- dered, tortured and starved," which would not leave enough for nearly 4,000 to come back.[40] But mortality was high by any count, and the public realized the manner of death was often slow. There was finally an update on the Air Force fly- ers who claimed to have participated in biological warfare. Americans had been dismayed to learn of their confessions, but now there were explanations. The article "P.W. Flyers Reveal Torture by Reds" reported that returnees revealed "a pattern of deliberately planned and brutally executed mistreatment and torture of American pilots and airmen." One recalcitrant flyer was reportedly chained to a stake and broiled to death in the sun. A subheadline reported that the men "Tell of Red Rope and Water Torture" (a reference to waterboarding).[41] Early on, mistreatment was offered as an explanation for why some soldiers assisted the enemy. Although there was potential for sentiment to turn on the repatriates, in late summer 1953, stories of torture and bravery abounded.

An influential moment came at the end of Big Switch. Rumors that some Americans might defect came home with the earliest repatriates. It was logical that some might not come back—voluntary repatriation was a public relations calamity for the communists, so some turnabout could be expected. One early military guess was that 200 Americans might stay.[42] Nothing was known, however, until the very end of the prisoner exchange. In the last week of September 1953, 23 American soldiers announced that they were going to live in China. The men went on Beijing Radio and said that camp authorities had tried to get them to go home, but "unfortunately under present day conditions in America the voice of those who speak for peace and freedom are rapidly being silenced.... The real traitors are those who try to trick the American people into another war they do not want."[43] The 23 did not consider themselves defectors. They said they hoped to return to their homeland one day and make it a better place but were dismayed by militarism, discrimination, and McCarthyism. One of the men, Morris R. Wills, said he was not a defector, pointing out that the United States signed an armistice agreement "that gave me the right to go to China if I wanted to."[44] While the men felt they were forsaking imperialist elites, not the whole country, they did part ways with the United States government and its policies. In this sense they were defectors, and they were certainly seen as leaving one side for the other. Interestingly, many were not notorious Progressives in the camps. Several years later, federal attorneys tasked with deciding whom to prosecute wrote that they were mainly "relative non-entities" who became notable "chiefly by virtue of their decision to refuse repatriation."[45]

The announcement by the 23 was followed by months of suspense to see if they stuck it out while held by the NNRC. The American repatriation drama was thus extended into January 1954. While Indian troops protected a prisoner's right to meet privately with an explainer, there was no guarantee a POW would accept. When official American explainers tried to approach, the 23 showered them with catcalls. To be heard, American officials used loudspeakers to blast a recorded message into the compound. Family members were not received any better when they sent a series of letters and recordings to the boys. Portia Howe, the mother of Private Richard Tenneson, pleaded with her son to come home and asked to visit him in Korea. She was brushed off with a harsh note that all the guys helped compose. The 23 treated family entreaties as group events and letters were read aloud, turning the persuasive power of the group against private misgivings.[46]

The defectors touched a nerve in American life. They were seen as throwing away all that was of value—family, religion, freedom, and wealth—and substituting all that was ugly. The 23 became not just communist, but part of the alien Oriental way of life. Their ex-communist counterparts headed for Taiwan were not entering an entirely new culture, bereft of language skills. Just the thought of anyone rejecting freedom and plenty seemed to reveal an emptiness in America, setting off soul-searching and recriminations. Defection joined brainwashing as a totem of Korean captivity. The public's first impulse was to try and get them back. In Vandergrift, Pennsylvania, townspeople wrote James Veneris, asking him to return.[47] The governor of Maryland joined the mother of one stay-behind on a recorded plea. "Come home, John, come home to the freedom and the human dignity of America," intoned the governor. Played first on a local radio station, the recording was sent overseas where the GI would hopefully hear it. Taking the fatherly tone used on wayward youths, the governor explained, "We all make mistakes, particularly when we're young.... Regardless of what you may have been told, the United States has no imperialist ambitions." "Jack, please hurry," added the mother, her voice breaking.[48]

The 23 were certainly not without their critics. Many Americans needed no prompting to call them traitors. *The Knoxville Journal* said of a local man that it would "rather see him dead."[49] Writing them off, however, would have been a passive act at a moment when action was needed, and coaxing them home was the available outlet. The patient and sympathetic were rewarded on October 20, 1953 when one of the GIs changed his mind. Telling bunkmates he was ill, Cpl. Edward Dickenson headed to the infirmary in the middle of the night, then slipped away to the Indian guards. Dickenson was quickly flown to a Tokyo military hospital, where he stayed for thirty days of "rest"—and interrogation. The month he was out of sight provided plenty of time for conjecture to build about the response of the authorities. Would he be welcomed, or punished? Dickenson's legal fate may have been up in the air, but not public feeling. While the Dickenson family waited anxiously in Big Stone Gap, Virginia, they were showered with 30 letters a day from well-wishers around the country. Only two writers were said to be critical of his previous travel plans.[50] Despite the foreboding 30-day sequestration, the Pentagon also gave hints of magnanimity. Instead of arresting him when he arrived stateside, he was granted a 30-day leave. Dickenson married during that time and tried to start life anew. His change of mind fortified the inclination to treat the defectors with generosity. The chances of persuading them that life at home would be better than in China seemed excellent. Schoolchildren joined in letter writing campaigns to the remaining 22, assisted by Dickenson himself.[51]

Convincing the 22 became a national test. After letters, the next logical step was to send people—mothers especially—to appeal to the youths directly. The

California American Legion joined several locals in arranging flights to East
Asia. The Legion dubbed their project Operation Mom and issued a sympathetic press release. Legionnaires knew "the hazards of psychological warfare,"
and believed that the boys were caught in circumstances beyond their control.[52]
Sending the people closest to the refuseniks seemed humane and the best way
to get them back. However, parents needed cooperation from the Army to gain
access to a military zone. A Statement from the Pentagon's Office of Public
Information was curiously unenthusiastic about family visits. It expressed "deep-
est sympathy," but kept repeating the theme that the defectors had made a choice.
Rather than finding ways to make it happen, Defense looked for reasons why it
was "neither practicable nor advisable" to allow family meetings. For one thing,
the defectors would be released in civilian clothes in just a few months, and the
military felt they could arrange their own reunions then. For another, the terms
of the armistice seemed to stand in the way; it allowed only seven explainers per
1,000 nonrepatriate prisoners, and they could not be "coerced or intimidated
in any way."[53] The implication that mothers could coerce and intimidate was an
obstructionist interpretation of the armistice accords. Decades later, internal
documents revealed no fundamental reason why family members could not simply have been used as explainers. A cable to Washington from the Commander
in Chief of the UN forces argued against letting them visit, but acknowledged
that "nothing in the terms of reference" (the armistice) prohibited using relatives as explainers and asked for sufficient notice to arrange lodging if it came to
that.[54] The Army offered to relay letters and recordings, but seemed to be writing
the men off.

Pentagon discouragement stimulated more insistent calls for family visits.
*U.S. News and World Report* reported that Cpl. Edward Dickenson thought such
meetings would be helpful, while others began appealing to the president.[55]
"Fly the parents," demanded a Georgia Gold Star Mothers chapter, made up
of women who had lost a son in war. The Dallas Disabled American Veterans
argued that "mothers' love" could overcome any indoctrination.[56] The White
House staff kept a tally of messages, which were overwhelmingly sympathetic
to stay-behinds and their families.[57] There were groups of communiques from
the same towns (like Macon, Georgia), indicating that local people were taking
the initiative to mobilize friends and associates. Minnesota mother Portia Howe
was especially persistent, obliging officials to make embarrassing rejections of
her travel requests. Howe wrote to the Far East Command for permission to
visit in November 1953. When this was not granted, she applied for credentials
as a journalist for a newspaper in Ashland, Wisconsin. The editor telegrammed
the White House, requesting that mothers attend those "mentally wounded by
the most evil propaganda ever devised."[58] When that did not work, Howe simply
went overseas on her own, but the State Department stamped a restriction on

her passport to keep her out of Korea. Undaunted, Howe flew to Tokyo, where she got a half-hour audience with General John E. Hull, head of United Nations forces.[59] Hull denied her a pass to Korea, exposing the official face that stood between a mother and her son.

Despite pleas from across the country, the travel ban prevailed because of a political calculation. Decision-makers reasoned that if American mothers were sent to talk sense to their sons, then the other side might do the same. The 22 Americans were dwarfed by the thousands of Chinese and North Korean defections. If US relatives were allowed to visit, then communist mothers might show up too, even offering "their own lives as hostages for their sons."[60] An encampment of relatives in the repatriation zone pressuring their sons to return to communism might capture world attention for weeks. The UNC had gone to lengths to make sure enemy prisoners did not change their minds about refusing repatriation, and was not about to let American mothers open a window. Family ties had run up against reasons of state. The Pentagon cabled the Far East Command forbidding visits, especially by Portia Howe, which the Operations Coordinating Board (the PSB's replacement) concurred in.[61] Unlike Ike, mothers would not "go to Korea." Forbidding families to visit the 22 defectors was part of the contention between family love and government policy that ran through POW affairs.

The recordings sent overseas and attempts to visit had assumed that defections were not deeply considered. Actually, the nonrepatriates were a carefully selected and trained group, so persuading more to come home would be difficult. A little more than a month before the armistice, Chinese political cadres began selecting an exclusive group of westerners to stay behind, initially including 26 Americans. These men were known to the Chinese through detailed autobiographies and voluntary participation in political study classes. There were no officers, only enlisted men. All were captured early in the war and had spent two to three years behind the wire. Morris R. Wills wrote in his memoir that he felt his government had "abandoned" him in a prison camp for two years: "You have long ago given up hope of being rescued and the war being won. You give in to those realities. Then you search for something else, something to stand on."[62] For Morris, this meant taking an interest in Chinese civilization and Maoism. He was attracted to the lack of racism and the rational organization of society that socialism aspired to. By the time he was invited in early summer 1953 to live in China, he was ready. A variety of incentives were reportedly offered to the men, including secure jobs, education, travel, and family life, and the distinction of being significant persons. The Army said that another motivation was to avoid reprisals, alleging that twelve of the group were snitches.[63] The stay-behinds were aware that Progressives released earlier at Little Switch were put in a mental hospital, and they expected the same.

The initial choice to live in China was one thing; sticking to it was another. They would be away from their political handlers for months. The nonrepatriates faced not just the onus of joining the enemy, but also the culture shock sure to come. Several left behind wives. The Chinese would have to rely on the commitment of the stay-behinds, so the single most important criteria for selection was political reliability. They had to be believers. To weave a tight tether, the 26 were taken out of the prison compounds and domiciled as a collective. They ate, slept, played, and studied together for two months before entering custody of the Neutral Nations Repatriation Commission. Every day included group criticism sessions where members examined each other for deviations from proper political line. "Every member of every group must confess his sins and every member must criticize every other member," Morris Wills recalled. To fill this demanding regimen of criticism, there were endless discussions of little things, which soon became big things, keeping all on edge. Besides the public surveillance of each other, there was reportedly also an inner group who reported to the Chinese in private.[64] One of the strongest holds on the expatriates was the fear of being ostracized by the rest of the group, which was illustrated when three of their number were accused of smoking marijuana. The political chaperones orchestrated a meeting that put the suspects through a grueling, verbal dissection. They were then cast back among the rest of the POW population. For the 23 who remained, training continued with mock sessions with American explainers. They practiced their responses and appraised each other's performances. The strategy was not to argue with Pentagon representatives, rather to sing, ridicule, dance, and chant. When the time came to enter the neutral zone, they were prepared to keep a tight huddle. American explainers were never able to get one of the 23 by himself to talk. Between group criticism sessions and letters from families read aloud, they hardly had a moment alone with their own thoughts.[65] In the final month, one more soldier changed his mind. On New Years Day 1954, Cpl. Claude Batchelor had Indian guards turn him over to American authorities. As a leader who was supposed to keep the others strong, Batchelor's return bolstered hope that the rest might waver. None followed, and on January 22, 1954, the remaining 21 began their odyssey in China.

When the ex-POWs' severance from America could no longer be denied, attention turned from how to get them back to why they had been lost. Although the 21 were a tiny proportion of prisoners, they were considered a telling statement on the morale and character of American GIs and the society they came from. Journalists went to work. A *Time* magazine reporter searched their backgrounds and discovered that one GI was "raised in a city slum," had an unemployed father, a promiscuous mother, and a sister blinded by syphilis and locked in a girls' home.[66] Such stories suggested that the communists had found a weakness in America. The poor and maligned who were usually relegated to the shadows were emerging as an embarrassment and security vulnerability. Long Island *Newsday* reporter Virginia Pasley was so affected that she journeyed to all 21 hometowns, interviewing family, friends, teachers and priests. Pasley rushed into print a book with the self-explanatory title, *21 Stayed: The Story of the American GIs Who Chose Communist China—Who They Were and Why They Stayed.* Poet Carl Sandburg wrote in a prefatory note that it was Pulitzer material, and *U.S. News* ran a 16-page excerpt.[67] Pasley represented the social reformer's response to the 21. She began by defining the problem that horrified her: "Never before" had American soldiers chosen to stay and live with the enemy, she (mistakenly) wrote. Pasley had a social worker's tone, revealing that Lowell D. Skinner, "the boy who never smiled," was like millions who "grow up hurt and undereducated." A chapter was devoted to each man and at the beginning of each, Pasley defined them with vital statistics: IQ, religion, ethnic origins, social adjustment, and education. Pasley provided an appendix of statistics on the men, showing the incidence of divorce, social ostracism, and low IQ scores—a preoccupation of the day which she referred to constantly. The author regularly cited "slow learners" as a problem, but her own data demonstrated considerable variation in verbal skills. Race was noted for the African Americans only.[68] Like broken homes and skipping church, blackness was a risk factor for political delinquency. Pasley's analysis also reflected the pop psychology of the day, wherein dramatic moments of childhood were thought to determine personality in straightforward fashion. Hence, the very first thing to know about Otho Bell was his belief that his birth killed his mother.[69] Although not without compassion for the expatriates, Pasley dwelt on the pathology of the individuals involved and had nothing to say about the larger times in which they grew up. The inclination to understand oppositional political beliefs as mental illness led one noted psychiatrist to testify in court that Batchelor was a clear case of "induced political psychosis."[70] The social science attention to deviance pushed aside ideological issues, and did not consider that to young men born in poverty, the wrong color, and the wrong side of the tracks, the concept of social class might make sense and class struggle seem appropriate.

Without doubt, the 21 acted for reasons both personal and situational, but Pasley's effort to explain political deviance with the terminology of social science had an important implication for public debate. If the factors in defection could be isolated and measured, they might be fixed. Pasley may have begun with the psychology of the individual, but the effect was to shift attention outward, toward society. Pasley used the following logic to demonstrate the danger of poverty: The 21 switched sides because of deficiencies in their backgrounds, millions of youths had similar disadvantages, and therefore a whole underclass was a security risk. By choosing hometowns to research, Pasley quickly compiled evidence that society had failed the men as much as the other way around.

A parish priest said of one, "If we had had the staff then, and psychiatric advice, he could have been helped," and a former teacher was broken-hearted over "how utterly we have failed in that boy." A child guidance director in Santa Barbara, California lamented that their new Mental Hygiene Clinic was not established in time to help LaRance Sullivan. Pasley repeatedly found that the expatriates were socially isolated in childhood. An oil worker familiar with one of the youths told Pasley, "If anybody over there treated that boy decently, I don't blame him for staying. He sure never got a bit of good treatment here."[71] The search for sadness in youths' background was paralleled in some regional newspapers, both about the 21 and locals accused of collaboration.[72] While Pasley's analysis did point toward social problems, the therapeutic approach kept remedies politically safe. It pointed toward a new response to defection: social reform instead of punishment. This was one measure of how deeply the defections were felt: They raised the urgency for social betterment, both for its own sake, and for homeland security.

The social problems explanation of collaboration shared an important conclusion with those of brainwashing, youthful immaturity, and torture. All held that the subject was not entirely responsible for his actions. This was very different from the martial tradition that placed the blame squarely on the individual. Cowardice or treachery were traditionally answered with attacks on the body: flogging it, incarcerating it, displaying it. Reformers targeted the mind. The focus on measurement, analysis, and prophylaxis also made the experts who assembled the data into essential parts of a solution. Social reformers gave scientific credibility to responses besides the stockade. But in the effort to offer solutions, they also reinforced the scrutiny of prisoners. Although motivated by sympathy, the social reformers saw collaboration as a symptom of a national crisis, not a predictable occurrence of Cold War imprisonment. They helped turn the failure of the war into an interrogation of the younger generation, and shared assumptions with unsympathetic elements who wanted POW blood. The angriest critics favored hard labor over mental hygiene classes, but agreed that the nation's soul was corroding.

Repatriation sparked keen interest in what went on behind the wire, although debate continued over whether to blame POWs or a diabolical enemy. While collaboration might be the headline, the article underneath was likely to include voices downplaying the extent of collaboration or brainwashing. Some argued for a Spartan standard of conduct for POWs—that no sacrifice was too great—while others took the attitude that they were mistreated and the war was over, so they should be left alone. President Eisenhower himself had dueling inclinations. Answering press questions about what would happen to Dickenson and Batchelor, he recalled the Biblical story of the prodigal son who was welcomed home despite years of estrangement. While

Eisenhower encouraged "real sympathy" from the armed services, he also hinted that there was "something else" to be revealed about the men's conduct. Investigations would be made and justice done.[73] His tempered, even kind remarks were made at the same time that criminal charges were moving forward against Dickenson, Batchelor, and dozens of other returnees. A new debate was brewing over whether ex-prisoners should be imprisoned—and, by extension, whether the public was sacrificing enough for the Cold War. Although the ex-POWs returned as spectacle, the media frenzy might have died down. But the returnees would not retire from the public eye. Big agendas were at work, and the GIs' service life was not yet up.

# The Brainwashing Dilemma

## Atrocity Reports Undermine Punishment

> Civilian leaders talk about the state of morale in a given country as if it
> were some kind of uncontrollable event or phenomenon, like a thun-
> derstorm or a cold winter. The soldier leader looks on morale as one of
> the great factors (or greatest) in all his problems, but also as one about
> which he can and must do something.
>
> —Dwight D. Eisenhower

When prisoners returned, American sentiments were torn. Washington was
unsure whether to downplay collaboration or loudly denounce it, and the public
was divided between blaming prisoners for giving in or the enemy for coercing them. But worries about military readiness pushed officials toward a harsher
view of returned prisoners. One violent conflict was over, but the Cold War was
not. Washington was concerned that the end of the Korean emergency would
lower vigilance at home and abroad. To keep opposition to communism vigorous, security officials launched a variety of sometimes contradictory campaigns.
Fears that POWs were not tough enough led to prosecutions, training revisions,
and lectures about masculinity. At the same time, prisoners were featured in stories about torture, executions, and brainwashing. Reports of mistreatment complicated the focus on the weakness of soldiers. How could the boys be blamed
after going through death marches? Impugning prisoners soon provoked the
public and disrupted government management of public opinion.

Domestic morale for the Korean War was troubled from the beginning. It was
first called a police action, then became a full-fledged war that was perplexingly
distant. The conflict soon become an unpopular grind and was already called
"the forgotten war" in fall 1951.[1] This apathy stirred long-standing elite fears
about the competence of the public. The success of the fascists in the last war
was well remembered; their large following suggested that "the people" lacked
judgment. The inevitable name to come up regarding public opinion is that of
the commentator Walter Lippmann. Lippmann shared upper-class impulses,

but was open and incisive in explaining them. He considered the "volk" vulnerable to the "bribery and enchantment" of totalitarians. During deprivation and crisis, the masses might do as Russians did in 1917 and support Bolshevism, "the dinner the cooks happened to provide for hungry men."[2] The need for public consent put democratic governments at a dangerous disadvantage against dictatorial regimes, who could act without consultation. To make wise decisions, leaders had to be insulated from popular meddling. Once a course of action was chosen, however, the public would then be brought around through explanation. Democracy was distinct from totalitarianism because the masses were managed with education and persuasion rather than violence. This gave government a sacred duty to convince the people to agree with elite decisions.[3] For this, Lippmann coined the unvarnished phrase "manufacture of consent."[4] In his view, opinion management was not unsavory; it was a pillar of democracy. It was the only way to run society efficiently and keep it from falling into the abyss of disorder, where totalitarianism was sure to emerge. It was either manufacture consent, or succumb to dictatorship.

Lippmann's philosophy meshed with the growing interest in a science of propaganda. Although psychological warfare was usually used against an enemy, views like Lippmann's validated its domestic use as well. This was especially important in the confusing era of cold and limited wars. Civilian morale was more complicated when threats were not as clear as Pearl Harbor and fighting could drag on indefinitely. NSC-68 considered public support a foundation of the national security state. "The whole success of the proposed program" hung on the nation understanding the depth of the Soviet threat. "A large measure of sacrifice and discipline will be demanded of the American people," it continued. "Nothing could be more important than that they fully understand the reasons for this." This meant propagandizing the nation, making sure things were "clearer than truth," as Secretary of State Dean Acheson famously put it.[5] As the Cold War dragged on, American officials felt urgency to get the consent they needed for wider engagement and larger defense budgets. Under this pressure, the line between what was and was not permissible in domestic propaganda was fluid. Many of the same officials enthused about using psychological warfare against the enemy were also active in domestic public relations.

Psychological operations received more emphasis when Eisenhower took over the presidency in early 1953. Seeing civilian morale through a general's eyes, he resolved to "do something" to improve it rather than just observe it like the weather. One of his first appointments was a special assistant on psychological affairs, C. D. Jackson of *Fortune* magazine. Eisenhower also set up the William H. Jackson Committee to review how well the American image was being projected abroad.[6] The Jackson Committee advocated more active and coordinated information overseas, but also devoted Chapter 8 to "The Participation of the

American People," concluding that "a strong foreign policy begins at home." Unfortunately, according to the authors, the obligations "of our world position" have "not been grasped by many Americans." The Committee recommended presenting events "dramatically" in "clear and simple fashion."[7] In their more discreet moments, cold warriors spoke in terms of education, disclosure, and reasoned explanations to the public. But the publicity methods were indistinguishable from what in other contexts is called psychological warfare, propaganda, or advertising. It can be said that the nation itself became the target of psychological warfare. Prisoners of war were a case in point, for they were used during the Korean War and then at home for lessons in discipline, manhood, and the barbarity of the enemy. But these lessons sometimes undermined each other.

Changing international attitudes was just as crucial. The National Security Council staff sought ways to maintain western readiness even after the smell of cordite left the air. Of great concern was something termed the Soviet "peace offensive." After the death of Stalin, Kremlin leaders turned a softer face to the international community, trying to distinguish themselves from recklessly aggressive imperialists. Even before the last shot was fired in Korea, staffers in the State Department and NSC began planning a postwar diplomatic offensive. They set their sights on the upcoming general assembly of the United Nations. Much of the activity was in the Operations Coordinating Board, a new NSC office that replaced the Psychological Strategy Board. In May 1953 the OCB/PSB produced a document whose title told the story, "Exploitation of Soviet, Satellite, and Chinese Communist Psychological Vulnerabilities before and During the Eighth U.N. General Assembly." The document complained that "appeasement-mindedness" was spreading among American allies who might go so far as to let China into the UN. The document warned that US views could be "deprived" of a solid platform in the UN, "unless new events and revelations occur."[8] The Americans wanted issues. They needed debate materials for the floor of the General Assembly that would expose their enemies as aggressors just as clearly as the tanks that rolled across the 38th Parallel. In April 1953, staffer Horace S. Craig compiled 36 possible issues for a memo, "Subjects for Possible UN Exploitation." Soviet misdeeds ranged widely from absorption of the Baltics and cultural genocide in Eurasia to wiretapping embassies. Down at the bottom of the list was "brainwashing and forced confessions."[9] This seeming afterthought was chosen as the central theme of the UN campaign. Some of the planning for the OCB was done by NSC analyst Edward P. Lilly, who argued that "peace-mindedness" among the allies would be difficult to overcome because "the U.S. has been losing credibility as a Cassandra....We have cried 'Wolf!' about military aggression in Europe" too many times, leading some to worry more about a "trigger-happy America!" "What needs to be said," according to

Lilly, "is that there is a communist threat, and an enduring one, of a far deeper and subtler kind." This "total menace" threatened not just countries but "the soul of man." Even without Soviet invasion, societies were endangered from the inside. Returned prisoners fit right into the idea of a total menace, for their minds had been captured and tormented by the enemy. Communism now endangered the individual as much as national borders, and nothing demonstrated this more vividly than brainwashing. Publicizing mental aggression against prisoners would both show a generalized Soviet danger and discredit the pernicious germ warfare tales at the same time. Lilly suggested linking Korea POWs to Soviet rule elsewhere, with its purges, show trials, and public confessions. The "confession" was said to be a key way that communists controlled an individual; it was "designed to destroy his soul."[10] With the shooting war stopped, ex-prisoners would help keep the tocsin ringing.

In early fall of 1953, plans crystallized for domestic and UN campaigns. Primary participants were the Army and State Department, with staffers of the OCB providing research and coordination. They formed the ad hoc Prisoner of War Working Group (PWG), chaired by the OCB, which met almost every other day. State and USIA handled the group's international work while the Army carried out domestic publicity.[11] The "Basic Plan for U.S. Action to Discredit the Soviet Bacteriological Warfare Campaign" was authorized October 14, 1953 and was sometimes referred to as the Lodge Project, after UN Ambassador Henry Cabot Lodge. Also approved was the "National Operations Plan for Exploiting Communist Mistreatment of UN Prisoners of War," or simply the National Plan. It would "focus national and world-wide attention" on mistreatment of POWs. The National Plan organized TV specials, talks to civic groups, speeches by selected repatriates, and "domestic magazine and newspaper articles by-lined by prisoner of war returnees."[12] The first headlines were achieved with an address to the United Nations by Dr. Charles Mayo, of medical clinic fame. Dr. Mayo's talk before the Political and Security Committee of the United Nations focused on the Air Force fliers who were forced to make germ warfare claims. Mayo told the UN members that the confessions were the result of cruel attacks on the brain; the communist method was "calculated to disintegrate the mind of an intelligent victim." They used the "conditioned reflex," according to Mayo,

> essentially the same technique which the famous Soviet biologist Pavlov used in his experiments on dogs and rats.... When a rat goes through the wrong door, he gets an electric shock. When he goes through the right door, he gets a bit of cheese. Before long ... the rat has been conditioned to enter the door you want him to enter. The Soviet regime has used this same technique against its own people.[13]

Mayo did not use the word "brainwashing," but he might as well have. Accompanying handouts included recantations from the pilots and point-by-point accounts of what had been done to them. According to Mayo, mistreatment of fliers revealed the fundamental difference between the West and its enemies: "The ancient belief that man has the God-given ability to distinguish rationally between fact and fiction has no place in Communist thought." Truth was determined by the party, not man as a free agent. The lack of a scientific foundation for the occurrence of brainwashing in Korea was made up for by the high visibility and gripping content of the government propaganda campaign. With Mayo's speech on the record, the State Department's publicity machine went into action, sending reprints to 82 countries. It was the first major project of a new federal office, the United States Information Agency, which ran the Voice of America transmitters. Mayo's voice filled the shortwave frequencies, along with charges that 6,000 American POWs died in enemy hands. USIA used the words of former prisoners "to expose the Communist machinery, and its complete absence of moral standards." The PWG's Mayo talk became a standard authority on mind control and POWs for years.[14] Mayo's committee speech was the prelude to Ambassador Henry Cabot Lodge's address to the General Assembly on November 30, 1953. Lodge told delegates that 81 POW death marches were documented, 50 overseen by the Chinese. According to Lodge, about 38,000 prisoners from all UN nations had died. The General Assembly agreed to condemn the mistreatment of prisoners in North Korea. After surveying the results for a week, the OCB Working Group complimented itself on the impact of Lodge's speech. It broke "the wall of indifference" and was headlined around the globe.[15] Communist abuse of POWs became a regular feature of American UN statements and was cited for years as a reason to deny membership to China.[16]

PWG publicity made a splash domestically as well. The nationwide Sunday newspaper supplement *America* quoted from Mayo's talk, as did a *New York Times Magazine* article by military reporter Hansen Baldwin.[17] Unlike in the USIA broadcasts overseas, the government hand in domestic propaganda was covert. "Every effort will be made" to use "non-official channels" at home, wrote OCB staffer Charles Norberg. PWG officials made repatriates available for commercial media interviews individually rather than use a "government-sponsored speaking tour." A State Department participant suggested creating "an association of Korean prison camp alumni" because it "could do and say many things which would be embarrassing" if done officially.[18] Publicizing mistreatment of prisoners would make Americans "far more aroused" than previous communist misdeeds, officials calculated. The Pentagon sent public relations guidelines to generals telling them to stress atrocities in local media outreach, including the claim of 6,000 UN troops murdered after capture. The information sheets provided a stream of examples, such as 80 US prisoners executed in November

1950, and three wounded buried alive in February 1951.[19] A *Saturday Evening Post* story closely paralleling the PWG line was "Red Murder of 6000 GI's Finally Angers Us!" Repatriates then fanned out to speak on radio, TV, "civic organizations, clubs and similar groups," and to write stories for newspapers and magazines.[20]

Domestically, discrediting the germ war accusations was less important, since few Americans believed them. The participation of American servicemen in those charges, however, was another matter, and the domestic National Plan tried to massage public thinking about collaboration. The seemingly large number of collaborators necessitated a response, both to deter future misconduct and reassure concerned citizens that something was being done. The Secretary of the Army instructed base commanders that "any illusions about any justification for … collaboration with their captors … must be destroyed." Another goal of public announcements was "to minimize the attention given to UN personnel refusing repatriation or returning as Communist sympathizers."[21] Both these objectives would be well served by shifting attention over to heroes who refused to assist the enemy. Researchers scoured through Big Switch shipboard investigations to find candidates for medals and media appearances. Army Adjutant General William E. Bergin asked each continental command to forward 25 names of prospective spokesmen. Eventually, 57 were decorated for heroism in captivity.[22] The National Plan instructed base commanders to "exploit to the maximum" those who stood up to their captors. The PWG's minutes said it arranged for a magazine story by returnee Maj. David F. MacGee, which showed up in *Colliers*, entitled "Some of Us Didn't Crack." An Army memo reported working with big circulation magazines including *The Saturday Evening Post,* which ran a six-part series by General William F. Dean about his captivity. PWG publicists also placed Dean on the TV show of journalist Edward R. Murrow. Dean was joined by General Clark for another conversation moderated by Bill Downs, and he spoke on radio for 30 minutes on the 500-station Mutual Network.[23] Dean's series in the *Post* stressed several themes important to the PWG: the GI's inadequate understanding of communism, the cruelty and doggedness of communist torture and "brainwashing," and Dean's remarkable resistance. In the conclusion of the series, Dean wrote that his captivity taught him the need for "each of us" to understand "exactly why we are fighting, in Korea or anywhere else."[24] This echoed Edward Lilly's call for an individual response to a total menace.

Another article reflecting PWG views was by William A. Ulman in the *Saturday Evening Post.* This story made no mention of its high-level patronage, but it can be linked to the PWG through a memo from administrator Charles R. Norberg, which listed the Ulman article as a completed task.[25] The piece was titled "The GI's Who Fell for the Reds" and warned that some returnees belonged to communist cells. Alternating between alarm and reassurance, it reported that the "Reds" had made "powerful propaganda use of our disaffected soldiers," but their actual recruits were "largely foggy-minded half-jelled young converts" who posed no serious threat. They did, however, demonstrate the lack of ideological preparation at home. Ulman suggested that the fuss over the 21 was an overreaction, but quoted an unnamed defense official saying it might "wake the public up." He continued: "We weren't really ready for this new ideological warfare when the Korean scrap started, but we better be damn well ready for the next one." The source added that just as the Nazis tried out new weapons in the Spanish Civil War, communists used Korea to perfect "ideological warfare." Since there was a void in public knowledge of communism and democracy, it could easily be filled with Pavlovian indoctrination of "conditioned reflexes."[26] In other activity, the PWG "cleared for public release" an editorial in the weekly *America*. The Working Group briefly considered instigating a libel suit against the Communist Party USA newspaper *The Daily Worker* for alleging germ warfare attacks.[27] A diorama about POWs kicked off a national tour at the Waldorf Astoria hotel and was reportedly seen by 30 million people. The Army also drafted a special magazine on "Communist Inspired Atrocities in Korea" for distribution to 35 million American homes, but it appears they were deterred by the expense and hoped *Life* magazine would take over the topic. *Life* did run a two-page atrocity spread a short time later. It cited an interim Army finding of 57,559 murders, including a Chinese officer gouging out the eyes of POW stragglers.[28] OCB staffers deliberated sponsoring a stage production entitled *The Breaking Point*. Written by a Colonel Holst, it was performed by an amateur Pentagon theater group and there was talk of it becoming a movie. It is unclear if this specific project went further, but a soldier's breaking point provided the plot for two Hollywood films assisted by the Pentagon, *Time Limit* and *The Rack*.[29]

Another source of headlines was a Senate committee investigation headed by Charles E. Potter (R-Mich.). His committee wanted "maximum psychological guidance" from the PWG, which channeled reports and witnesses to its hearings. General Mathew B. Ridgway's talk to the committee was written by the PWG, and it was noted intriguingly in the minutes that "all media, both overt and covert" had been contacted about the hearings.[30] The Committee concluded that nearly 6,000 captives died in war crimes. Potter's report argued that these were not the acts of cold individuals, but "a calculated part of Communist psychological warfare." The PWG congratulated itself for the "widespread domestic impact" of the hearings. A Detroit paper's headline read, "Potter Report Shocks Senate With Details of War Atrocities." Senator Potter continued making waves by pushing for investigations of live prisoners thought to have been left behind.[31]

The atrocity stories publicized by the National Plan had their day, but what entranced people for decades to come was brainwashing. Since the air rushed so quickly out of the Little Switch brainwashing story, it might follow that its credibility would suffer, yet the legend grew larger. The images of brainwashing were too potent and resonant for Cold War publicists to ignore, in no small part because of the authoritative pseudo-science surrounding it.[32] The brainwashing of Little Switchers was disputed, but the phenomenon itself was taken seriously. It rapidly entered Americana as an explanation for involvement in charismatic cults, objectionable politics, or shopping. Government officials talked up brainwashing to discredit germ warfare accusations, damage Soviet prestige, and maintain citizen vigilance. But the public was so tantalized by the idea of mind control that it quickly escaped official guidance. The brainwashing story became too successful in that it damaged a parallel effort to hold soldiers responsible for collaborating. This was the brainwashing dilemma: The more people heard about coercion of POWs, the less tolerant they became of prosecutions and jibes about unmanliness.

The birth of the word "brainwashing" can be pinpointed. It was fabricated in 1950 by a CIA agent working undercover as a journalist. Edward Hunter introduced the term in a *Miami Sunday News* article about China, which he considered one big brainwashing camp.[33] He was identified as CIA in a Congressional hearing in 1972 and acknowledged it in interviews in 1978.[34] Hunter claimed the term came from a Chinese phrase, *hsi-nao*, literally "wash brain." He defined it as putting a "man's mind into a fog so that he will mistake what is true for what is untrue, what is right from what is wrong, and come to believe what did not happen actually had happened, until he ultimately becomes a robot for the Communist manipulator."[35] The word caught on so quickly and stayed current for so many decades that it clearly spoke to individuals' fears of losing autonomy to powerful institutions whether public or private. The idea of externally controlled minds is an old one. It is similar to the demonic possession in the Salem witch trials or the Jewish *golem*, a being created to robotically obey its master.[36] While cultural resonance explains its fast spread, brainwashing was still defined and introduced by US government propaganda. Hunter himself wrote several books on it and was widely cited. He claimed that "the plain people of China" coined the term as a resentful colloquialism for Maoist indoctrination.[37] But as researcher John Marks and others noted, *hsi-nao* was not a catchphrase in China and had no political meaning or usage. It does not appear in the standard reference work *Comprehensive Glossary of Chinese Communist Terminology*.[38] The paucity of evidence explains why Hunter stopped making the claim. Although *hsi-nao* was in the *Miami News* article, his first book said only that "brainwashing" was a translation of a popular, unspecified Chinese term. In his subsequent *Brainwashing, From Pavlov to Powers*, he stopped attributing it to peasant slang, claiming instead that it was used by an "intimate circle" of unnamed Chinese expatriates, derived vaguely from an unrevealed Buddhist term for "heart washing."[39] The truth is, he made it up.

Edward Hunter, the CIA agent who concocted the legend of brainwashing. While working undercover as a journalist inside the United States, Hunter introduced the term through articles, books, and Congressional testimony. Associated Press.

Hunter described a precise, scientific method for controlling behavior. The Chinese refugees he claimed to have studied were supposedly subjected to psychiatric treatments common to American mental institutions, except that doctors "had stopped treating the insane" and now cured "only the sane" of political deviance. Hunter had a clear purpose for his fairy tale. Despite the intensity of the Red Scare, officials constantly worried about public complacency. The undercover writer wanted to make a communist threat seem tangible in Kansas. In a revealing passage, Hunter claimed he had met a Chinese brainwashing victim and used him for a parable about civic responsibility in the Cold War. He determined that helping the man was

> a test of me and my whole civilization.... The ultimate success or failure of our way of life will depend on how we individually deal with the multitudinous cases, such as his, of people who want to be on our side. The way we act as individuals is much more important than what the government says.[40]

To protect against mind control, credulous scientists researched the brain. News reports hailed experiments with isolation tanks at Bethesda Naval Hospital as a new frontier in psychology, comparable to "basic theoretical research in physical science." Elsewhere, a researcher predicted it might become "a grisly necessity" to issue cyanide to soldiers. Supposedly the perfection of drug and environmental manipulation could change "the probabilities of verbal inputs from 98 percent pro-American to 101 percent pro-Communist."[41] Behaviorist theories of the day explained the mind as arising mechanically through the conditioning of reflexes with rewards and punishments. Emphasizing environmental stimuli over genetics, brainwashing was considered an extreme form of behavior modification. Dr. Joost Meerloo, author of a mass-market paperback, *The Rape of the Mind*, was one of the academics who gave scientific credibility to brainwashing. Meerloo believed human thought was as deterministic as "Pavlovian conditioning" of dogs. Punishment and reward determined thought as well as behavior, making totalitarian mind control possible. "Instead of conditioning man to reality," a dictator could condition him to follow "catchwords [and] slogans." Mere words from the brainwasher were potent, "the tone and the sound have a conditioning quality." He introduced the neologism *menticide* or "mind murder," which meant the replacement of a personality with a more politically compliant one. Meerloo published in academic and popular venues and was regularly cited. He testified as an expert at a hearing for one of the Air Force pilots. Interestingly, an important source for Meerloo was none other than Edward Hunter. Hunter, in turn, used Meerloo's work to back up one of his later books, congratulating him for providing "the fine laboratory word *menticide*."[42] The circle of invention was complete.

The flexibility of the word "brainwashing" helped it penetrate the language. To many, brainwashing was a near-magical process that turned victims into robots, while to the more discerning, it simply meant the systematic use of traditional methods of coercion, like sleep deprivation, isolation, and physical torture.[43] The term was rarely defined precisely; readers were free to understand it as something new and diabolical, or as old as bondage. Since the same word was used for distinct concepts, extreme notions gained credibility from more careful usage.

The most influential and extreme version of brainwashing was in the 1962 movie *The Manchurian Candidate*, in which an ex-Korea POW automaton kills on cue, then forgets. When shown the queen of diamonds, he would go into a trance and follow any instruction, even an accidentally overheard "go jump in a lake." Although clearly fiction, all the basic elements of a Manchurian killer were first established by Edward Hunter. He had claimed a brainwashed consular employee in Hong Kong was unable to recognize his wife, and another was certain he had committed a rape, despite being miles away at the time. Hunter suggested the neural mechanism was similar to hypnotism, citing a showman who convinced volunteers they were selling fish to the audience.[44] Entire hallucinogenic worlds could be evoked in people, who then acted accordingly, just like in the movie.

Brainwashing resonated partly because people in modern societies felt their independence under siege. A complex, interconnected society brings benefits, but also dependence on unseen authorities in government bureaus, banks, and insurance offices. Prospering in the consumption society required ever more elaborate conformity, right down to the uniform of the modern office, the "gray flannel suit."[45] Overweening, inscrutable bureaucracy grew not just in the corporate skyscrapers, but in a rapidly expanding government, as well as. As historian Abbott Gleason noted, brainwashing illustrated the state's "holistic reshaping of the individual" to conform to a new order. Gleason suggested brainwashing tales resonated loudly in the "organization man" who feared being overwhelmed by the administrated society. The brainwashing issue helped shift the concept of totalitarianism from the simple coercion of the police state to "the enslavement of the helpless individual psyche."[46] The encounter with communism became an unusually personal and intimate battle with demons of thought, encouraging scrutiny of repatriates from Korea.

There was a fuzzy line between the official hand and the more extreme visions of brainwashing. For example, the *Saturday Evening Post* assisted the government's public diplomacy, but it also had to turn a profit by exciting readers. Its 1955 story "The Brainwashed Pilot" by Sidney Herschel Small, showed how a government idea could morph into fantastic fiction. Anne, the main character, is a pretty young nurse whose husband had been shot down over Korea and captured. She moves to Hong Kong to work in a clinic and try to find him. She gets news of a furtive Caucasian living in the hills—it is her husband Johnny, who had escaped from the Chinese only to wander disoriented, living off the land. At the key moment when she finds him, he draws back from her embrace: "She saw the shell of her husband watching her with wide, unblinking eyes." The dull, flat, robot affect was already established as the face of the brainwashed. Johnny fails to recognize her and can speak only Chinese at first, but he is still drawn to her, eventually managing to ask her to "walk with me and we can gather wild grasses." This, Anne happily understands, was "an invitation to be courted," and soon Johnny is saying things like, "Can we put mouths together again?" An examination back at the clinic determines that he has been brainwashed and may need shock treatment. The medical cure is not necessary, however, after Anne and Johnny are set upon by Chinese soldiers sent to recapture him. At first, Johnny obeys their Pavlovian verbal cues, but the sight of Anne being fondled by the soldiers shatters the conditioning. He attacks them, shouting in Chinese, "but he was not fighting like a Chinese at all." He throws American punches, "short and sharp, snapping the man's head back with a crackling sound." His former self reasserts itself through punches. After chasing off the reds, "his eyes were no longer blank," and "he kept looking at her. 'A'n,' he muttered, and then, clearly, 'Anne.'"[47] Small's story fit romance and a Korean adventure into an established formula with oversized illustrations. By combining current affairs with standard themes, the story carried agitprop to the average readers that cold warriors considered apathetic. "The Brainwashed Pilot" was the classic Indian captivity narrative described by Richard Slotkin.[48] A pilot-warrior has gone native, living in the hills and speaking the savage tongue. He is drawn back to civilization by the virtuous, devoted, female. Through violence, he conquers the enemy and can throw off the savage skin, allowing his civilized self to reemerge. Updated for the Cold War, this captivity narrative served as both warning and hope. Brainwashing was diabolical, but it could be beaten, provided the home front stayed supportive, particularly women.

A project of the PWG's National Plan was publicizing reports of American POWs withheld by the enemy. Originally designed to buttress public support for the Cold War, it boomeranged when many people, families especially, concluded that the government had left behind live POWs to achieve an armistice. This was an early version of the Vietnam POW/MIA episode, where people believed there was government conspiracy to conceal abandoned POWs. This MIA story, however, clearly began in official statements. The PWG worked with the Army Signal Corps to produce a television episode of *The Big Picture*. When "Atrocities in Korea" aired on 261 stations in February 1954, viewers saw the recently retired General Mark Clark saying there was "no question in my mind" that the enemy retained live prisoners. Clark and government officials said there were 944 soldiers known to have been alive in POW camps who should have showed up at Big Switch. (The claim was controversial in the Pentagon, and excised from one version of *The Big Picture*.) The 944 figure regularly came up in PWG discussions, and Clark repeated it in his memoir *From the Danube to the Yalu*.[49] It was all the more plausible because it seemed to be just what communists did—the Soviets still had not finished returning German POWs. Fleshed out by reports of prisoners secretly moved to China (in Mayo's UN speech, for one) the number 944 entered the permanent record.[50] Prisoners held behind the "bamboo curtain" were the subject of heated letters pouring into Washington. Ambassador Henry Cabot Lodge had to dodge a delegation of MIA mothers trying to have a word with him.[51] Editorials picked it up; "A National Disgrace" in the *Chicago Tribune* moved a reader to write Washington complaining that it was "impossible to instill patriotism" in his draft-age son when the nation abandoned prisoners. Analyst Paul Cole found that in actuality, the 944 list was a hasty hodgepodge of missing soldiers of whom the communists "might have some knowledge." Some were actually presumed dead, others classified as prisoners based only on a witness seeing a parachute open.[52] The 944 figure's real use was for denouncing the communists. The number inevitably declined as more information emerged. Many people encounter a live prisoner, but only a few witness his death and it took time for that information to come out. The 944 were soon reduced to 768, then to 500 within two years, and below 389 in 1992.[53] It is possible a limited number of American POWs were kept after the war, but the 944 figure was premature.[54] It was first released during Big Switch, before the shipboard debriefings of ex-POWs could be parsed. Officials were so eager to amplify blame that for a time General John E. Hull blocked reducing the public number, according to PWG minutes.[55]

At the millennium, the Pentagon was still being bitterly accused of leaving behind Korea POWs.[56] Fascinatingly, a State Department analyst warned of this during Big Switch. Robinson McIlvaine wrote presciently that the 944 figure might "create a Frankenstein" by inciting the public to demand back prisoners who could not be verified or produced.[57] True or not, the MIA story was one of many that kept returned prisoners visible and politically topical. It also showed how opinion management was an endless task, as blowback from one story required corrective damage control, which might require its own adjustment.

The National Plan succeeded in its immediate goal of demonstrating prisoners' horrible experiences, but caused other problems for officials trying to prosecute collaborators. Plans to punish collaborators predated the National Plan and were now fortified by the shipboard interrogations. Soon after Big Switch the military began hearings, trial preparations, and noisy dishonorable discharges, all of which confused a public reading about forced marches and mind murder. Not only did atrocity reports contradict disciplinary measures, but the reverse was true as well. Punishing pilots for weakness undercut the story that germ warfare confessions were forced. The government was trying to push together the north ends of two magnets. One OCB staffer, frustrated by the news headline "POWs to Face Ouster if they Collaborated," complained that "our entire UN presentation" was based on forced confessions, and then "we oust or discharge them for collaboration."[58] Brainwashing was even more problematic than physical torture because resistance was wiped out. A tortured person still capitulated, but when minds were erased and replaced, the previous personality could not be responsible for aiding the enemy. In mid-November 1953, the PWG majority tried to persuade army representatives to keep disciplinary action quiet for the duration of the UN campaign. When punishment was imperative, publicity "should be kept to the minimum required under law." In addition, the Army was to try and make a clear difference between opportunists and those pressured into collaborating. The other branches were urged to go easy on the fliers who spread germ war stories.[59] Discharged soldiers had to be prosecuted by the Department of Justice. A DOJ memo complained that even "the most aggravated" cases were stalled by the UN problem and Navy and Air Force reluctance.[60]

The military itself was divided on whether to blame enemy mistreatment or soldiers' weakness. While the Army prosecuted and discharged, the Air Force and Navy tread softly, starting with the first and best-known case, that of Marine pilot Col. Frank H. Schwable. Already known from Mayo's UN talk, Schwable was the highest-ranking Marine taken captive. Schwable's court of inquiry (not a court-martial) began in February 1954 and went on for weeks. Front-page stories repeatedly brought up brainwashing and duress. Witnesses testified that after he returned to the general population, Schwable's arms twitched involuntarily and he seemed to hallucinate, crying out, "I'm surrounded by oil. What's all the oil doing here?"[61] Joost Meerloo appeared at the hearing, claiming that "communist mental torture techniques are so highly developed" that they could "inject" thoughts into a victim's mind who would "mechanically imitate" them. The highest-ranking repatriate of all, General William Dean, appeared and said he "had it easier" than Schwable, but still did not have the "strength or intelligence" to stick to name, rank, and serial number. Defense attorneys made sure everyone noted that Schwable held out months longer than the heroic Dean before signing propaganda statements. The court of inquiry eventually decided not to court-martial Schwable because, although he made propaganda statements, he did not disclose military secrets.[62] The panel found that his germ confession was "excusable on the ground that it was the result of mental torture," and he was demoted to a desk job on air safety. This set a balance between sympathy and refusing to condone those who gave in. It became a counterpoint to castigation, as in the U.S. News article "Is It a Crime to Crack Up?" President Eisenhower himself struck an empathetic tone, telling a press conference that in light of "incessant 'brain washing,'" condemnation of collaborators should not be severe.[63] How to receive repatriates became a nationwide dilemma. As one headline put it, "For the Brainwashed: Pity or Punishment?" Edward Hunter weighed in with the article "Frame-Up, Communist Style" in the U.S. Army Combat Forces Journal. "Chalk up another big success for international Communism's propaganda apparatus," Hunter wrote. The communists were behind the collaboration stories as a way to sow divisions. The camps were "huge brainwashing centers" that no one could resist for long.[64]

Supported by official statements, scientists, and urban legend, brainwashing became a defense for collaboration. To justify punishment, Army publicists had to draw a distinction between victims of mind-murder and opportunistic traitors. But this was difficult to maintain, since brainwashing overwhelmed the discussion. The Secretary of Defense's Advisory Committee on Prisoners of War concluded that reports of brainwashing were having the wrong effect. It complained of "the misconception that so-called 'brain-washing' was a hellish technique which forced the American POWs to collaborate." It distracted attention from the real nature of collaborators, "opportunists, cowards, and traitors."[65] It was too late, however; generals, preachers, and pundits were already weighing in on the issue. The Vatican expressed "understanding" and "forgiveness" for Cardinal Joseph Mindszenty, a Czech who served as a prototype brainwashing victim. A *Washington Post* editorial cited Edward Hunter to back up its argument that "no one who has not been subjected to comparable experiences has any right to pass moral judgments."[66]

The brainwashing issue offered an opportunity to demonize the enemy, but it also relieved the individual of responsibility for his actions. At a time when cold warriors sought commitment from each and every citizen, the "brainwashing" excuse threatened to erode the standard of duty. The irony is that the brainwashing fable began as official propaganda before it broke the leash. Army prosecutors preparing to make examples of collaborators were going to be seen as the bad guys. One effort to manufacture consent was disrupting another.

# 10

# Prosecutions Rile the Nation

Why not send some of these tallow bags we have in government that wants these boys punished sent over to Korea, let them go through the same punishment these boys took, two and three years of torture, then ask these fuse boxers what they think we should do with these boys.
—A. M. Evans to *Army Times*, December 1953

Air Force pilot Sam Johnson was shot down over North Vietnam in 1966. In a memoir, he wrote there was a serious problem with collaboration, particularly in the Hoa Lo prison where he was held late in the war. But when the Vietnam POWs were repatriated, the issue was handled entirely differently than it had been in Korea. Johnson was the ranking officer on his flight home from Hanoi and when it touched down, he took a call from General Chappie James at the Pentagon. The general ordered Johnson to pass the word not to discuss collaboration in public. Johnson disliked the "military and State Department edicts," but followed them and did not name names even twenty years later in his book. When the ex-prisoners were debriefed, their questioners were instructed not to ask about misconduct and to steer away if it came up.[1] The silence extended to the military justice system as well. To the consternation of some repatriates, none of the Vietnam POWs who came home in 1973 were prosecuted.[2] In contrast, Korea returnees were grilled, surveiled, discharged, demoted, denied pay, sentenced to hard labor, and paraded in a nationwide perp walk.

The POW stir has no parallel before or since Korea. Part of the reason was novelty. For all the things captors have compelled prisoners to do, none had ever demanded that so many sing in tune all at once. Another reason for so many repercussions was Americans' widespread innocence of the pressure and complexity of captivity. World War II set the bar for heroism. "There was not a man in uniform" who did not know that a good soldier provided only name, rank, and service number, one analyst noted. In 1942, *Life* magazine reprinted cartoons used to train troops to keep quiet.[3] This standard of honor was rarely violated, it was thought, including in encounters with the Japanese. There were several trials after World War II, but turncoats like Tokyo Rose or Axis Sally were caricatured villains quite unlike ordinary POWs. Although there were reports of misconduct under the Japanese, they were not dwelt on. Resisting captors to the end remained a cardinal legend. In an official Pentagon hearing on Korea, an Army officer called for the ultimate sacrifice from POWs, claiming history was "filled with the tradition of absolute resistance" to Indians, Nazis, Moros, and the like.[4] When veterans of Korea were repatriated, they returned to a country still on Pacific time. So when scores of troops seemed to have gone along with the Chinese, it was seen as a full-scale breakdown of discipline. The Army was the most worried, since controlling so many enlisted troops in battle was a bigger challenge. It sounded too much like an officer's worst nightmare: his own troops turning on him. When Korean War POWs came home, they were going to have to pay for their crimes in court.

On the ships home, much of the interrogating was done by criminal investigators. Michael Cornwell remembered questioning could go eight hours: "Those debriefing us wanted us to inform on other prisoners—to say this guy did this and this guy did that." Cornwell faced another investigation at home when he proposed to the daughter of an officer. His father-in-law, a West Point colonel, made "damn sure his daughter wasn't marrying a pinko." The Army reported to the president that it was conducting "intensive screening" for "undesirable individuals" among the repatriates.[5] All personnel files were administratively flagged with the phrase "RECAP-K," which stood for Returned and Exchanged Captured American Personnel in Korea. Paperwork with that designation followed soldiers from base to base as late as 1958.[6] It was an enormous monitoring program. According to FBI director J. Edgar Hoover, all the shipboard interrogation summaries were forwarded to local FBI offices as to who needed further watching. Some RECAP-Ks were visited over and over. Bill Smith said the FBI periodically came to his house and "run my wife and daughter off and sat up in my living room with their typewriters, and sometimes they'd stay three days." They wanted to know about everything, starting with the 21 who stayed. This went on for years, until his wife kicked them out for good.[7] Sgt. Donald L. Slagle said that he finally got tired of the visits and refused to answer any more questions: "I was trying to forget the past and get on with a new life." By 1957, Justice Department attorneys complained that the RECAP-Ks were "becoming uncooperative and even hostile." Some even felt the Progressives "performed a useful function" by satisfying the Chinese and taking the heat off everyone else.[8]

Also working against the repatriates was the pervasive fear of domestic subversion. Columnist Victor Riesel claimed in 1954 that there was a three-person Negro cell active in the South. For the Chinese they had broadcast "weird tales of alleged torture and persecution in the U.S.," and now were recruiting. Riesel reassured his readers that "even the cotton picker's unpainted

shack is a mansion along side the torture huts of that third of the world which
has its brains washed daily." Edward Dickenson claimed at his court-martial
that "most" repatriated Progressives had missions. The William Ulman story
planted in the *Saturday Evening Post* reported there was an "organized group
of Communists" among the returnees.[9] Brainwashing added credibility, since
creating an army of subversive robots would be the perfect use of the technique. Sometimes there was a specific number of secret agents reported—
namely 75. That number reemerged for years even though in 1959, the Under
Secretary of the Army's office did an "exhaustive" search of multiple agencies
and concluded there was no such list. There were a total of 67 names accused
here and there of having secret missions, but never compiled in one place. The
Assistant Chief of Staff for Intelligence concluded that none of the accusations were ever "adequately substantiated." The FBI concurred that "nothing
of a substantive nature" came up in surveillance of discharged soldiers.[10] This
was especially notable considering that the authorities thoroughly expected
agents and searched fervently for them. Attorney General Herbert Brownell
recalled that FBI surveillance was vast.[11] The spies just were not there. Some
of the Progressives accepted Chinese exhortations to organize at home. "Fight
for peace," reported Joe B. Vara. "That's all they told me." Henry Clark Corner
confessed his mission to investigators: "Improve his writing ability, become a
novelist and write in support of communism."[12] If Vara and Corner's missions
constituted being agents, then there were some. But if an agent is someone
communicating secretly with a foreign power about unlawful conspiracies
within the United States, then not one was discovered, much less prosecuted.
Nonetheless, in 2000 it was still claimed that recruitment of agents by the
Chinese was "frighteningly successful," with 20 percent of Progressives on
missions "inspired and controlled" by Beijing.[13]

Although nothing came of the espionage investigations, officials could not
know that then. They believed they were dealing with spies, subversives, and an
epidemic of collaboration, which all needed to be addressed. A punitive approach
was signaled early on. While Big Switch was only half finished, Attorney General
Herbert Brownell warned that collaborators might face treason charges and the
Army announced that all the POWs would be scrutinized. On January 23, 1954,
right after the NNRC explanation period ended, the Secretary of the Army, by
fiat, dishonorably discharged the 21 going to live in China. The *Columbia Law
Journal* noted that this "violated basic military law," which required a courtmar-
tial for a dishonorable discharge.[14] The Army regretted this later when the men
began returning and it had no jurisdiction to prosecute. There was concern that
discharges without hearings might be unpopular. The PWG decided to find
derogatory information on the 21 and release it to the media, "relating these
facts to the dishonorable discharge." Three days later, the Associated Press ran

an article quoting Army sources saying that 12 of the 21 were "squealers." *Time* magazine referred to the defectors as pot smokers and homosexuals.[15]

As collaboration stories swirled about, powerful voices called for retribution—such as Senator Richard Russell, who was incensed by petition-signing and propaganda statements. The best soldiers "were ready to die rather than to falsely stigmatize their country," according to Russell, in contrast to those "unable to withstand threats, tortures, or the promise of better food." The Pentagon assured Congress that collaborators would at a minimum be kicked out of the military, even if they had been tortured.[16]

The contest over punishing or forgiving POWs was encapsulated in the fight over pay bonuses. Under the War Claims Act, repatriates were eligible for $2.50 per day hardship pay—enough for most to buy a new car with a V-8 engine. But after Korea, the law was amended to deny benefits to anyone who collaborated willingly. An appointed body, the Foreign Claims Settlement Commission, examined Army records and in fall 1955, rejected 252 RECAP-K claims. All were army, because only that branch tried to block bonuses. The decisions of the Commission were based on secret information and applicants could not face their accusers. It quickly became a kerfuffle as spurned POWs called it a "kangaroo court" and congressmen and pundits went to bat for them. Decorated veterans were "being given the McCarthy treatment," columnist Drew Pearson charged.[17] The outcry prompted a senate subcommittee to investigate why the men were receiving "a badge of infamy" without a trial. The repatriates could appeal—to the same commission that rejected them in the first place. Nonetheless, several made good use of the opportunity and denounced the Commission at a heavily covered hearing in Chicago in early 1956. The Commission began backing down. It not only granted 110 appeals of its own rulings, it went back and reversed 58 cases that applicants had not even bothered to challenge.[18] The bonus pay issue was a microcosm of the POW affair. The impulse to discipline the repatriates was obstructed by public protest, primed by the government's own brainwashing and atrocity publicity at the UN.

Reining in prosecutions was another matter. The legal mobilization had inertia and took on the complexity of a battle campaign. After shipboard interviews of 3,600 returnees came compilation and follow-up. The data was used for prosecutions and administrative sanctions, such as discharge or loss of rank. A military prosecutor said that some cases required reviewing 2,000 separate POW statements, then tracking down witnesses around the country.[19] Derogatory reports led to detailed investigations of 565 of the RECAP-Ks. Others who had already been discharged were referred to the FBI and Justice Department.

Two early arrests were of Claude Batchelor and Edward Dickenson, the men who had thrilled the country by deciding not to live in China. The Army insisted that they were not charged for the temporary defections, only for previous offenses in the camps, but hardly anyone believed that. Author Virginia Pasley noted that scores of POWs who "committed similar offenses" were not tried. Many believed the Army tricked the men into coming home by promising not to arrest them. The Army insisted that no one in a "position of authority" had ever offered anyone immunity.[20] Politicians took note of public sympathy and protested the Army's decisions. Congresswoman Frances E. Bolton (R-Ohio) told the House she was "deeply disturbed" by charges against Dickenson: "Let's be human beings in these things." The Associated Press circulated a quote from a fellow prisoner saying Dickenson "didn't do anything more than I did myself, except to decide to stay."[21] A retired brigadier general offered to defend Dickenson, because a fair trial was impossible in "the present climate of emotionalism and vindictiveness." One of Dickenson's lawyers was confident enough of public opinion that he requested an open hearing. When Dickenson was convicted of collaboration in May 1954, a draft board member in Mississippi resigned and his protest was picked up by the national wires. The Hattiesburg man believed the Army had "lied" to get Dickenson to return, then gave him ten years breaking rocks.[22]

More resentment arose because the Navy and Air Force did not court-martial anyone. There were some administrative punishments, but no prosecutions, despite the fact that the airmen's germ war confessions were infamous. An Air Force board of inquiry took five weeks to consider 83 servicemen accused of collaboration. Ten were separated from the service with honorable discharges; the rest were exonerated. The *Christian Century* editorialized, "it is hard to escape the conclusion that somebody has suffered an injustice." There were discrepancies between services and also between enlisted men and officers.[23] The *Century's* audience was primarily ministers, and its arguments frequently turned up in pulpits across the country. A Gallup poll found that 61 percent believed the germ warfare confessors should not be punished; only 10 percent favored harsh prison sentences.[24] The resolution of the Air Force cases seemed to signal a precedent of going easy on former prisoners, so it was galling when other repatriates got hard labor.

The more the character of prisoners was challenged, the more exercised their defenders became. One letter writer suggested putting government bureaucrats through "two and three years of torture," then asking if they still wanted to punish GIs for misconduct. A Michigan veterans group telegrammed Washington complaining that the Army was "throwing the book" at POWs—part of a "great number" of similar comments sent to officials and members of Congress.[25] Presidential aide Sherman Adams prepared summaries of the mail for his boss. One day had 14 letters opposing the court-martial of Edward S. Dickenson, none in favor. Over several years, the flow of letters would resume each time a returning defector was put in cuffs. An August 1955 sample of letters included one from Macon, Georgia, asking that repatriates in custody be freed for Christmas.[26]

The sensitivity of the collaboration trials led the Pentagon to package them as carefully as possible. Starting in February 1954, the Secretary of Defense required all prosecutions to get special permission from a Board on Prisoner of War Collaboration.[27] The Judge Advocate General (JAG), the Army office that pursued collaborators, looked for the most egregious cases. "Usually," according to military justice personnel, there were no criminal charges if there was "substantial evidence of force or duress."[28] Although some GIs were charged only with participating in propaganda, JAG tried to portray defendants as the worst of the worst, such as Sgt. James C. Gallagher. He was a Progressive and informer convicted of murdering two dysentery victims by throwing them outside to freeze because they were too sick to clean themselves. Gallagher became a commonly cited example of POWs' lack of character. He was paroled in 1966.[29] Despite its efforts, JAG was never able to shake the impression that good soldiers were being victimized a second time. Ironically, this was partly due to reemphasis on name, rank, and serial number. Since that was so firmly entrenched as the standard of duty, many people assumed that this was what prosecutions were about. The POWs were used as a general criticism, and that is how the prosecutions were understood, not as highly select cases. In fact, not all charges were actually for heinous acts. Some convictions were purely for participating in propaganda, something many citizens were less exercised about.[30] William H. Olson received two years in prison for giving speeches and writing articles in the camp newspaper that were deemed disloyal. A letter Cpl. Harold Dunn sent to his parents while in captivity got him convicted for aiding the enemy under Article 104 of the Uniform Code of Military Justice. The letter spoke well of the Chinese and asked his parents to work for an end to the war. Propaganda was the only thing Dunn was charged with.[31] There may have been more behind the Dunn and Olson cases, but the narrowness of the charges fed the impression that soldiers were punished strictly for expression. Other cases seemed more clear-cut. Besides the infamous Gallagher murders, there were Pvt. Rothwell B. Floyd's convictions for assault and stealing food from other prisoners. Claude Batchelor's counts included one for telling the Chinese of a prisoner who had a camera.[32] Ronald Alley, the only officer convicted, was known in Camp 2 as a member of the "faithful five," a group of officers named for their earnest service to the Chinese. Alley served three-and-a-half years at Leavenworth Penitentiary.[33]

The public outcry over the prosecutions was strong enough to have two clear results: Prosecutions halted, and many sentences were reversed. In the end, only 14 soldiers ever went to trial and 11 were convicted, but the attention still fed the perception of vindictiveness. In summer 1955, a Pentagon committee found that the disparity between the service branches incited much of the resentment. It considered the perception misguided, but wanted to address "public misconceptions." In a section revealingly titled "Measures to Satisfy Public Concern for

Justice and Equitable Treatment," the committee suggested revisiting prison sentences.[34] In March 1956, the Ad Hoc Board for Review of Sentences in RECAP-K Cases began examining sentences that might appear to be unfair. A board member reminded his colleagues that their actions would "receive widespread attention" and would determine if the public believed the Army had "brought credit upon itself."[35] In other words, the sentences may have been appropriate, but they were causing negative publicity. The board decided to reduce the sentences of three out of four ex-POWs who were still incarcerated when it acted. Two sentence reductions were particularly large: Claude Batchelor's life at hard labor was reduced to seven years, and Rothwell Floyd's sentence dropped from forty years to ten.[36]

The unpopularity of prosecuting ex-prisoners led to a revealing spat between Army prosecutors and the Department of Justice. Most of the soldiers JAG wanted prosecuted were discharged normally before indictments could be prepared. The Army wanted the DOJ to go after these newly minted civilians, and began shipping over massive files. However, the vast majority of cases were for misconduct as a prisoner of war—something illegal only under military law, which the Justice Department could not touch. Under UCMJ Article 3a, the military was supposed to handle prosecutions of offenses that were not crimes under civilian law, even if the suspect had been discharged. Justice lawyers said that JAG should "reassert jurisdiction" of those cases rather than unload them on the DOJ, but that was not happening. Army press releases continued to say that Justice was taking over the prosecutions. This prompted a scathing analysis in a late 1954 Justice memo:

> These press releases were designed to shift responsibility for these cases to the Department of Justice and to divert public attention from the Department of the Army so that this Department will have to bear the brunt of any further unfavorable criticism and irate protests of the public against the prosecution of prisoners of war.

Some cases were so weak they probably could not be won even under military law. The memo wondered how the Army could have referred them "in good faith."[37]

The memo demonstrated the intensity of public hostility to prosecutions, but the Justice Department was not able evade the brickbats. In November 1955 in *United States ex rel. Toth v. Quarles*, the US Supreme Court ended military jurisdiction over discharged soldiers once and for all. That made the Justice Department the last resort, but it could still only enforce civilian laws. The potentially applicable civilian laws were for grave crimes: treason, sedition, and the Logan Act, which restricts citizen interactions with foreign governments. With the FBI doing follow-up investigations, Justice staffers continued poring over the 310 cases referred by the Army. Finally, in 1957 they decided that around 50 egregious cases were prosecutable. However, even the worst of the worst had legal hurdles. Treason charges applied only to wartime, but the Korea "police action" had never been clearly declared by Congress, and some offenses occurred after the July 27 armistice. Federal attorneys also worried how juries would feel about defendants' "extreme youthfulness" and "limited educational backgrounds." Many witnesses would be other collaborators who were given immunity—never favorites to put on the stand. Another issue was the high standard of proof for treason, especially when defense attorneys would be sure to provide evidence of pervasive duress. But federal prosecutors believed that assistance to the enemy was widespread, and were confident they had found flagrant examples of nonduress.[38] They had, after all, spent several years preparing. The cases were tough, but lead attorneys Victor C. Woerheide and John C. Keeney anticipated they could get convictions roughly two-fifths of the time. They may have low-balled the estimate, since they felt prosecutions "should not be undertaken" at all.[39] Besides the high crimes of treason and sedition, there was an entirely different option that would be easier to prove and had many more suspects. To get hardship pay from the Foreign Claims Settlement Commission, repatriates had to certify that they had not collaborated except under duress. If ex-POWs could be shown to have misrepresented themselves to the Commission, they could be charged under 18 U.S.C. 1001, a catch-all law against lying to federal institutions with a five year penalty. Assistant Attorney General William F. Tompkins actually preferred this over the more demanding charges.[40]

In the end, the Department of Justice did not make one indictment. The Army got the official word in October 1957 from Tompkins, who expressed "deep appreciation" for all the help, but there would be no trials. The stated reasons were the weaknesses in evidence and the issue of duress, especially after the federal declarations about brainwashing.[41] Although the cases were daunting, it strains credulity to think that not one person could have been successfully prosecuted by the Justice Department, especially with the bonus pay opportunities. Internal documents make it clear that the prosecutions were really dropped over public relations. In June 1957, two DOJ attorneys wrote an analysis of the prosecution environment. The big problem was that the public, and the juries drawn from it, would hang up on the issue of fairness: Only Army personnel were being indicted, while Marines and Air Force got off. Indictments could not be expanded to the other services, because Air and Navy refused cooperation. That still left the possibility of less serious indictments for misleading the Foreign Claims Settlement Commission. The authors thought this a better alternative, especially considering the public attitude against felony charges. In the end, though, public concern was trump. The attorneys eventually recommended closing out all the cases, since "it would be impossible to attain even a semblance of uniform 'justice' for all former Korean War POWs."[42] In a special issue devoted to POW legalities that included DOJ participants, the *Columbia Law Review* noted public opposition and said that prosecutions were halted because they were "too controversial."[43]

Dropped cases and reduced sentences showed the strength of the public backlash. The Justice Department did not want to take the heat, and neither did the Army. Similarly, when RECAP-Ks fought for bonus pay, they were aided by several years of government-encouraged stories of brainwashing and torture. The bulk of the public had dutifully absorbed these lessons and then rejected policies of retribution. This created something of a public relations emergency. Sympathy for ex-POWs needed to be corrected, it complicated support for global interventions.

Although the government eventually let up on punishment, prosecutions still helped tar all the returnees as suspicious and gutless. Ex-POW James Thompson wrote in a memoir that lice, cold, and dysentery were easier to get over than "the humiliation some of us suffered at the hands of our own government." Thompson believed African Americans were portrayed as the most craven and devoted his book *True Colors* partly to "correcting that perception." But for all the returnees, "the longest lasting agony may well have been the psychological impact, especially for those of us who came back to face later charges of collaborating with the enemy."[44]

# Target Mom

## Disciplining "Misplaced Sympathy"

Thus the massive squall of women interfered with warfare.
—Philip Wylie

In February 1953, an Air Force magazine ran an article entitled "Target: Mom, How the Reds' War of Words Is Aimed at the Next of Kin of Captured Fliers." The story warned that "Middletown" America contained "an age-old military target—the will to resist." The piece recirculated widely in *Readers Digest*, reporting that scores of letters containing antiwar messages were reaching families of POWs. It warned people not to be taken in because the reds were using family sentiment to promote propaganda. In this scenario, "The overjoyed parents read the letter to their relatives and friends. The local paper ran it in a front-page story. The mother dashed off a note to her Congressman, asking that he do what he could to end 'this senseless slaughter.'" Mothers and wives were weak links, desperate to "buy peace." According to the article, the reds considered female sentiment a vulnerability and skillfully exploited it to undermine support for the war.[1] Moms thus became a double target for their weakness first from the enemy, then from the cold warriors who had to restrain their sentimentality and baleful influence on men.

Geopolitical power was routinely thought of in terms of male strength, not as metaphor, but causally. Conversely, weaknesses in defense indicated a female hand. After Korea, masculine standards seemed to erode when the public halted prosecutions and cut prison sentences. This was an affront to officials and commentators who believed that the Cold War necessitated a military creed as demanding as ancient Sparta. Not only were the soldiers weak in captivity, their families were now making excuses for them. This perception impelled a sustained criticism of the repatriates and the nation said to coddle them. It was a jeremiad—all the anxiety about weakness and dishonor were channeled into a call for renewed strength. The word "jeremiad" derives from the Book of Lamentations in the Old Testament, where the Prophet Jeremiah gave a litany of man's failings and how to right them. The POW affair spawned a whole group of Jeremiahs, some coached by the Army, some freelance. Their central theme was effeminacy. The undue influence of mothers and easy living of an abundant society was weakening young men and crippling defense. The failure to win the war was the jeremiad's first proof. More evidence came from sources like Sgt. Lloyd Pate, who was quoted in a *Saturday Evening Post* article arranged by Prisoner of War Working Group (PWG) staffers. Pate complained that "this Army of ours just isn't tough enough to fight this new kind of war, on account of women are always softening it up." According to Pate, the POW death rate was high because the men were "spoiled and pampered" as kids, "too much mamma."[2] His attitudes tapped into resentments brewing among officers since reforms in treatment of enlisted men instituted after World War II. Pate later published a memoir, first serialized in the *Washington Daily News*, which a POW task force cited as evidence it was getting Defense Department views into print.[3] Interviewed years later, Pate expressed no knowledge of an official hand promoting his views—a regular reporter approached him about doing the memoir—and he was also considerably more forgiving of POW behavior.[4]

The 1950s crisis of masculinity is easy to overemphasize, since historians find a gender panic in every age, but it is unavoidable in Korea discussions because it comes up incessantly. The POW jeremiad took place at a time when men were freshly worried that women were displacing them. World War II had brought more females into male professions, companionate marriage was encroaching on the male-dominated variety, and the economy was replacing rugged individualists with office cooperators. As historian James Gilbert put it, "the effects of conformity, suburban life, and mass culture were depicted as feminizing and debasing." The editors of *Look* magazine reflected the times in a book called *The Decline of the American Male,* which claimed scientific research showed that conniving women were weakening men. Firm discipline was being displaced by mothers' technique of withdrawing affection. This set sons up to be controlled by girlfriends who were "imposing monogamy earlier" by using sex as a lever, made possible by permissiveness. Once married, wives concentrated on their own pleasure, causing an alleged rash of impotence in husbands, scientists said.[5]

There were endless permutations of female dominance; it was no wonder the boys failed in Korea. Senator John Stennis was so disturbed by POW performance he demanded that collaborators not receive honorable discharges even if tortured. "My views may be extreme," he said, "but we must have a lot of austerity in our military."[6] One of the most thorough and influential contributions to the jeremiad was Eugene Kinkead's book *In Every War But One.* Kinkead first published a 40,000-word piece in the *New Yorker,* then a mass-market version in *McCall's,* claiming that POWs did their duty in every war until Korea.[7] Kinkead's work was an authoritative statement of the thinking of the Army brass at that

time, at least the dominant part. The Army General Staff (G3) gave Kinkead special access to classified information and reserved the right to veto content. An
internal progress report said the *New Yorker* article was "edited and cleared for
publication" by staff and that it reflected "the Army position on POW problems."
Kinkead acknowledged that it was not "an independent journalistic survey."[8] His
book concluded that prisoners collaborated "casually" and in "large numbers."
To prove that male debility was the cause, he claimed (among many things) that
POWs were afraid to try and escape, but the accusation was worded in a tricky
manner: "During the entire Korean conflict not one of our men escaped from a
permanent enemy prison camp and successfully made his way back to our lines."
The qualifiers masked another reality: 647 men got away from makeshift corrals or
while in transit. The first "permanent" camps were not in operation until January
1951, after the bulk of captures and escapes. Several hundred did flee established
camps.[9] Debriefings of returned prisoners were peppered with escape reports,
such as that from Cpl. Theodore Jackson, who fled with three companions from
Camp 5 but did not get far: "It was very cold. The ice got too thin and we turned
around and came back."[10] True, no prisoners successfully traversed hundreds of
miles of Korean countryside back to UN lines, but that said more about the difficulty than the toughness of American men. Nonetheless, the no-escapes tale
spread through the literature, sometimes with Kinkead's lame qualifiers, other
times as a flat claim that "not a single American attempted to escape from captivity."[11] A detailed rebuttal to Kinkead called *March to Calumny* was written by Air
Force researcher Albert Biderman. *Calumny* systematically tore apart Kinkead's
claims and also challenged the idea that he spoke for the military. The Air Force
in particular rejected the legend of warriors that never cry. Revered military historian S.L.A. Marshall was another dissenter who stated that soldiers in the 1950s
were as strong as those "at the Alamo." Certain writers were "waxing fat" ped-
dling a "holy cause," according to Marshall, who ridiculed the idea of "national
repentance and wholesale moral reform."[12] Forceful as they were, Marshall and
Biderman's comments came in the early 1960s, after years of jeremiad.

Kinkead and others believed in the superior manliness of Turkish prisoners
who supposedly put Americans to shame. This was based in part on the lower
death rate of the Turks. The Pentagon's Burgess committee investigated Korean
imprisonment and believed that "the Turks lived while the Americans died"
because of better discipline and stronger men. They looked out for each other,
made no propaganda statements, and none defected at the end of the war. A general announced that "the average Turkish soldier isn't accustomed to the corner
drug store type of life."[13] A comparison with the Turks was not valid for several
reasons. For one, most of the Turkish troops had the good fortune of being captured after the deadly winter of 1950–1951. Officers were allowed to stay with
their men and maintain discipline. The biggest difference may have been that the

Chinese lacked translators and could not indoctrinate or exploit them for propaganda anyway.[14] Despite barely being asked to collaborate, the story of the Turks' primitive vigor outshining effete Americans grew with the telling.[15]

American prisoners' 40 percent death rate was used to suggest that they died too easily. Army psychiatrist Col. William E. Mayer gave speeches on the chicken dinner circuit for years where he claimed that "about half" of the deaths were the result of "passivity among the soldiers." A callow young soldier would supposedly,

> walk into his hut in North Korea, look despairingly about and decide there was no use trying to participate in his survival. He would go off into a corner by himself, pull his blanket over his head, and in 48 hours was dead. You could stop these deaths by picking up these fellows, hitting them, spitting on them, slapping them. If you could just get them angry, they'd survive. If you couldn't, they didn't.[16]

Attributing half the deaths to passivity was unclinical, but Dr. Mayer had a diagnosis: "morassmis" he called it, and claimed that "we had never before seen it among adults." Captured American physicians seemed to substantiate this, reporting soldiers who stopped eating or cleaning themselves and faded away. They gave it a name, "give-up-itis," which caught on. A novel that picked up the theme, *Valley of Fire*, said GIs "died as quietly and unobtrusively as they had lived." The article placed by the Psychological Strategy Board in the *Saturday Evening Post* claimed that "literally hundreds of men died because they simply would not try to adjust to camp life and camp food."[17] These conclusions derived not from research but an assumption of fragility. A spirited constitution can help an individual survive, but humans do sometimes curl up and refuse food and water in order to hasten the end. But this is ancient behavior common to all starving times. One study demonstrated that the give-up-itis in Korea was the same phenomenon accompanying starvation in the Holocaust, or Jamestown, Virginia in 1609, where a "most strange Condition" afflicted the "distracted and forlorn" colonists. The POWs' nutritional deficiencies in the first year produced the same symptoms as the alleged character deficiency of give-up-itis. Their thin grain diets lacked niacin and thiamine, causing pellagra and beriberi, conditions that affect the nervous system and produce classic symptoms of depression, resignation, and ataxia.[18] Ataxia (weakness or stiffness in the limbs) in particular discouraged victims from getting up and hustling for survival. To postwar critics, the stillness of prisoners was a sign not of malnutrition but of retreating to an infantile state. They died "in a foetal position," read one account, "like a baby safe in its mother's womb."[19] According to the jeremiad, even dying was a failure of duty.

A common charge was that too many GIs told the enemy more than name, rank, and serial number. The Chinese actually wanted political agreement from prisoners far more than military information, but the claim that one-third of POWs collaborated was assumed to include a great deal of talking. A Pentagon committee looked into it, but kept this part of its findings secret. Although talking to the enemy was a taboo, the more discerning military planners understood that name, rank, and serial number was less a commandment than a fiction created for team spirit. Even without physical torture, the compulsion to say *something*, even a subterfuge, is great. Not even General William F. Dean, the highest-ranking officer captured in Korea, stuck to name, rank, and serial number. When seized, Dean knew the juiciest intelligence imaginable: the surprise invasion planned for Inchon. Dean reported that he was never assaulted, but was repeatedly interrogated for 72 hours at a stretch. He talked, and talked some more, about the most inconsequential things he could muster, but he never gave up the prize. Dean privately told the Burgess Committee that his babbling was "to divert them from really starting those oriental tortures." Eventually, Dean sensed he would break and was narrowly prevented from committing suicide. He was not questioned intensively after that, perhaps because the North Koreans did not want to lose their prize catch.[20] The Burgess committee knew that few humans could resist as well as General Dean, let alone remain silent. A rear admiral told the committee that his interrogation experts could "extract information from anybody, and they say they can do it even without using actual torture." A study of Air Force POWs in Korea reported that only 6 percent (12 men) recommended a policy of silence, but none claimed to have stuck to it.[21] A Joint Chiefs of Staff study of World War II had suggested trying to satisfy interrogators with vague, ignorant-sounding answers. But this doctrine of the indefinite answer was not implemented and when prisoners returned from Korea, their country still expected them to have stuck to name, rank, and serial number. The jeremiad blamed the nation for POWs' not following a policy that the Pentagon knew was an ideal. Nonetheless, in public one Army general called for resistance to the death rather than give more than name, rank, and serial number: "The tree of liberty…thrives only when it is watered by the blood of patriots." Lloyd Pate noted that this would require a prisoner to get "the hell" beaten out of him for refusing to reveal his unit when the patch was right there on his uniform.[22]

The hypersensitivity to collaboration and masculine failure can be seen with a quick comparison to the 2008 presidential campaign of Vietnam POW John McCain. By the harsh standards of Korea, Senator John McCain would never have had a political career. The son of an active duty admiral and a prize catch, McCain's captors at the Hoa Lo prison in Hanoi forced him to record a confession. Prisoners listened to loudspeakers play an endless loop of McCain saying "I am a black criminal and…an air pirate." But once he recovered from a

round of torture, he resumed impressing other POWs with his steadfastness and
contempt for his captors.[23] There was enough forgiveness for Vietnam POWs
that the recording could not be used against him politically and McCain almost
became president.

Army psychiatrist Mayer connected prisoner weakness to a wide range of
social ills. He said he personally interviewed 1,000 ex-POWs during Big Switch
and that "one third of prisoners lacked faith in America," a dauntless use of statistics.[24] Mayer believed that docility was an inherently female trait while asser-
tiveness was male; therefore, the appearance of passivity anywhere reflected the
influence of women. Military training had been softened to "please mama's boys
and boys' mamas," and welfare and government grew because men had "abdi-
cated their own positions of responsibility." Mayer linked the erosion of male
influence to the emancipation of women. While it was fine for women to have
gotten the vote, they were spreading passivity by taking on male roles. Docility
could "easily destroy us" before nuclear fallout had a chance; "this is what we
learned from prisoners of war."[25] Mayer closed his speeches by saying prisoners of war needed to have courage and personal responsibility which military
training could not provide, "they are issued in your house." Mayer gave talks at
least into the early 1960s and reported selling 100,000 recordings and 500,000
transcripts. He rose to Assistant Secretary of Defense for Health.[26]

The most caustic critic of women during the Cold War must have been
Philip Wylie, inventor of the term "momism" and author of the notorious screed
*Generation of Vipers*. Wylie delighted in playing around with gender tension—
the more offensive, the better. Behold Mom, "whose very urine will etch glass."
Wylie defined momism as interfering women creating "sickly dependencies" or
a "psychic umbilicus" in sons and husbands. Although the rhetoric was play-
fully overheated, beneath it all he meant every word of it. First published in
1942, Wylie updated *Generation of Vipers* for Korea, after "the moms and the
mom-pinioned pops tore the government apart to get a truce." He added, "thus
the massive squall of women interfered with warfare."[27] Fans applied his invective
to POWs. Patricia Highsmith of Fort Worth, Texas wrote to Wiley in December
1953: "I thought of you at once when I saw this photo in my local paper. I should
imagine there are many things in Korea a young man would rather face than
this."[28] The photo was of a family waiting to greet a returning POW as he got off
a plane. An emotional mother was being held back as she tried to sprint across
the tarmac. Overeagerness to hug was vulgar, even dangerous. Wylie expanded
on Korea in a 1960 essay written for *True* magazine:

> Marines, MacArthur, and a lot of masculine joes halted and eventually
> turned the flood of Marxist marksmen . . . when mom started screaming.
> Screaming what? "Come back, son, with your shield—or on it!"—the

Lt. Col. Dr. William E. Mayer used psychiatric jargon to argue that Korean War POWs were effeminate and unresisting. Associated Press.

war cry of Sparta's mothers in ancient days? No, pals. America's moms screamed, "Come back, tootsy-wootsy, safe and sound to mom. You might get hurt in that Korean thing!"[29]

The fear that women would weaken men reached a comic peak in a report that atomic spy Klaus Fuchs had given Moscow the secret to a hormone ray that would feminize troops.[30]

The Freudian preoccupation with mother-son incest gave seeming scientific explanation for maternal damage to male independence. The 1990s was the decade of father–daughter incest in TV and novels, but in the 1950s, it was the mothers. Freudians believed that incest or its subconscious desire could enfeeble the male psyche. An ex-prisoner reported that on the ship back, the psychiatrist really did ask if he had sex with his mother.[31] Several novels and a TV episode traced collaboration to mother–son incest, as did the film *Manchurian Candidate*, with its lip-lock between Angela Lansbury and Laurence Harvey. Although the subject was more often treated fictionally, it came up enough to suggest a common association. Incest was the dark secret that allowed the enemy to control a captive. In the 1960 novel *Night*, an American POW resisted physical coercion, but a shrewd cross-examination zeroed in on his secret shame—intimate fantasies about mother. "Bed!" shouted the interrogator. "Did you sleep in her bed?" "How big were they?" Mentally shattered by this exposure, the POW gave up the name of a resistance leader, whose head got chopped off. After the war, he committed suicide.[32] The incestuous link to Korea POWs was still strong in the 1976 novel *Turncoat*, whose antihero lacked "drive," stammered, and defected to China. His disorder began as a child. After his father called him a "goddamn queer," he received solace from mother, whose lips "were moist and full." He finally breaks his life of effete treason by raping a maternal figure and committing suicide.[33] *The Manchurian Candidate* also ended with a suicide, apparently the only way to resolve incest plots. Men not devitalized by incest were still weakened by the clamor of woman. Scholar Michael Rogin noted this pattern in Cold War movies like *My Son John*, where an apron-bound son became a communist, while his athletic brothers were the patriots. In red matriarch stories, young men dominated by women escape by enlisting and becoming warriors. In this way, cultural resentment of female strength was relieved by joining the Cold War—a fortuitous circumstance for a military trying to fill boots.[34]

A theme beneath the surface of the jeremiad was same-sex attraction. Few sources explicitly blamed collaboration on homosexuality, but it was there. The newsweeklies did make the connection outright in short blurbs about the 21 who went to China "bound together more by homosexualism than Communism."[35] Pundits were usually more circumspect, but doubts about POW masculinity reinforced suspicion that lavender was the color of treason. Communism and homosexuality had already been linked during the Red Scare, especially when the Truman administration pushed hundreds of alleged security risks out of government. Most of them—400—were suspected of being gay. A "nexus between political and sexual subversion" developed in 1950s thought, according to one historian.[36] Male homosexuality was often blamed on domineering or incestuous mothers, giving sexual deviance the same roots as collaboration. In a time when the fem-ray story could see print, commentators did not have to allege outright that the Progressives were gay.

The nation's faint-heartedness prompted government action. Writers and cultural workers could chastize the nation, but concrete steps were also needed. Perhaps the signature initiative of the Pentagon was to create a formal code of conduct for prisoners to follow and get the nation behind it. In spring 1955 Secretary of Defense Charles Wilson organized the Advisory Committee on Prisoners of War, known informally as the Burgess Committee after its chair, Carter L. Burgess, the Assistant Secretary of Defense. Members from the three branches of the military began an intense pace of expert briefings and study sessions and delivered a final report six inches thick in little more than two months. The main goals of the Burgess Committee were to win public support for stricter standards in captivity, and to toughen POWs with a new creed. For the soldier, the Committee set out to design "a simple, easily understood code to govern his conduct while a prisoner of war." This Code of Conduct would then be explained to the public with a booklet and publicity blitz. The domestic opinion problem was the more sweeping one, the Committee believed, noting that nuclear war could make combatants out of civilians:

> The Committee's approach to the prisoner of war problem is to arouse national conscience as to equal public responsibility. When the American enters the brutal contest of war, his strength lies not alone in the armament and training provided by the military. The foundation of his strength is derived in large part from his early environment and education.[37]

In the view of the Burgess Committee, the nation's survival rested on "the collective effort of its people," and the Korean POW affair had revealed shortcomings, like indulgence of misconduct. The conclusion of the Committee report clearly showed how the Code of Conduct was, in significant part, opinion management:

> Wide distribution of the Narrative Report will indicate to the public what conduct is expected from prisoners and why this standard of conduct is essential. Further, it will inform the public there was no injustice in service actions concerning misbehavior cases.... If necessary, where such action does not jeopardize fairness of the trial, publicity concerning specific offenses committed will do much to offset misguided public sympathy.[38]

The Committee was handicapped by a dispute over just how much prisoners could be expected to endure. The Army demanded that soldiers stick as closely as possible to name, rank, and serial number, and never participate in propaganda. The Air Force considered this unrealistic, pointing out that they could not document "any Army ex-prisoner" who fulfilled this to the letter in Korea.[39] Since no one stuck to name, rank, and serial number, the Air Force suggested an alternative concept: the indefinite answer. Prisoners could give vague, empty answers rather than attempting to remain mute. Only by giving interrogators "harmless information with which to 'bargain' will the soldier be able to withhold vital data." "A determined interrogator is never actually 'resisted'; he can only be 'satisfied.' "[40] Acting dumb and jousting with interrogators fit the Air Force's situation. Pilots were captured alone or in small groups, and as knowledgeable officers, they received greater pressure. They could get training in playing word games. The Army, on the other hand, worried about the discipline of masses of enlisted men and doubted their capacity for repartee. General John E. Hull told the Committee that if they allowed troops to go one step beyond name, rank, and serial number, "we may open the floodgates."[41] The Burgess Committee had to fashion a code that addressed the public, while also reconciling the hard and soft lines. The final result was purposefully ambiguous so that the different branches could interpret it as needed. The pertinent section read: "Should I become a prisoner of war, I am bound to give only name, rank, service number, and date of birth. I will evade answering further questions to the utmost of my ability. I will make no oral or written statements disloyal to my country and its allies or harmful to their cause."[42] Contrary to common belief, the Code is flexible; it is not necessarily unforgivable to go beyond personal identification. When the code is read carefully, "bound to give only name, rank, and service number" is a minimum, not an absolute limit. This key phrase accommodated a provision of the Geneva Conventions, which directs prisoners to identify themselves. The Code directed a prisoner to resist further interrogation "to the utmost of my ability"—a less-noticed, more realistic standard. Giving more is up to the individual's stamina and the tradition of his branch. A lawyer from the Judge Advocate General's office recognized that the Code was more of a slogan and did not carry the weight of law. "It is obviously a training device," wrote George Prugh, a standard of what servicemen "should strive" for. It was partly for morale and "increasing unit fighting strength" before capture. Attorney Prugh insisted that the goal was set very high, but decisions to prosecute would take duress into account and be based on the Uniform Code of Military Justice, not the Code of Conduct.[43]

In August 1955, President Eisenhower signed an Executive Order making the Code of Conduct canon. He announced that "every member of the Armed Forces" had to live by it.[44] Despite the element of forgiveness built into the Code, its public description was narrow. The Burgess Committee circulated a booklet *POW: The Fight Continues After the Battle*, it explained that interrogators might push through the first lines of a soldier's resistance, but he must "stand on the final line to the end—no disclosure of vital military information and above all no disloyalty in word or deed." This went against recent experience, where Chinese indoctrination was not *mano a mano* between interrogator and captive. The setting was in classrooms where even obstreperous prisoners recited political lessons, yet still disrupted them later on. POWs included antiwar rhetoric in letters home so they would be delivered, but did not take it seriously. The ideological statements forbidden by the Code were some of the most difficult to prevent and caused the most indistinct damage. The penultimate sentence of the booklet *POW* read: "The Korean story must never be permitted to happen again."[45] This faulted soldiers and the nation, with no allowance for the circumstances of limited war in East Asia.

Officials fanned out across the country explaining the Code to civic groups. At a national education convention the Assistant Secretary of the Army spoke on POWs, "A Challenge to U.S. Educators." Army psychiatrist William Mayer went to Tokyo to instruct troops.[46] Signed and framed copies of the Code went to VIPs including the president of CBS and Dr. Charles Mayo. The Secretary of Defense required bimonthly reports on progress in popularizing the Code. He held a luncheon to rope in big names to talk up the Code, including Herbert Hoover Jr. and Nelson Rockefeller.[47] The biggest push was in the broadcast media. The Pentagon featured the Code in its own quasi-news program *The Big Picture*, but also got it into dramas like *The Avengers*. CBS did an hour-long radio documentary. By December 1955, 46,000 copies of the booklet were distributed, mainly to public schools.[48] The sympathy for POWs apparent during prosecutions was answered with a reemphasis on toughing it out.

The "every war but one" proposition was never logically complete. Structurally, it was a comparison, but there was no systematic contrast with data from other wars. Research from Korea was judged against the mythology of Indian fighters. Similarly, the explanation of prisoner weakness did not go beyond homilies. Since Samson was captured by the Philistines, women and comfort have been blamed for weakening men; the Spanish-American War of 1898 is particularly notable.[49] The 1950s jeremiad did not identify an event so dramatic that it could turn warriors into sissies right after World War II.

The Code succeeded in reestablishing intransigence as the standard for captivity, but did not undo the perception that ex-POWs were unfairly treated. Outcry still halted prosecutions and restored bonus pay. Newspapers still ran stories about an Air Force "torture school" that trained potential POWs with "an orgy of sadism."[50] The touchy issue of prisoners of war seemed to require a more sensitive medium. Hollywood was going to try and persuade the nation to raise its sons' right, usually with the assistance of the Pentagon's motion picture office.

# 12

# Missing Action

## *Hollywood Films Try and Fail to Fix Captivity*

The sufferings of the war prisoners in North Korea are reenacted so
realistically and the cruelties inflicted are shown in such horrid detail
that it will serve to sicken people rather than entertain them.
—review of the Army-assisted Ronald Reagan movie *POW*

The POW affair needed a new storyline.[1] Korea seemed to show that prisoners were weak and the nation weary of the Cold War, but arousing the public
with communist atrocities undermined punishment of collaborators. The war
was unpopular and its conclusion too awkward to be readily recast as a stirring
triumph. Military readiness required a revival of national morale, but POWs—a
strong association of the war—were difficult propaganda vehicles. Pentagon
officials were too clumsy and formulaic to refashion the Korea POW story. But
there was a professional group of artists who might be better able to engage public emotion. As citizens, filmmakers are exposed to the same events as everyone
else, but they are not just barometers; they often display social consciousness
and pursue agendas. Film producers and the military often collaborated. The
Pentagon helped make movies visually engaging by lending ships and tanks,
in return for a say in the scripts.[2] Screenwriters needed to have a sense of the
current concerns of the military in order to ensure access to all the wonderful
equipment. After Korea made prisoners current among audiences and problematic for the Pentagon, it was inevitable that Hollywood would take it up. But
the cinematic versions of Korean POW camps largely failed, and for many of
the same reasons that the real story proved unmanageable. Several films rejected
official military concerns; they engaged instead with popular resentment of how
ex-POWs were treated. Cinema mirrored politics.

Putting Korea POWs on the big screen presented immediate challenges.
Prisoners stay in one place and are controlled by others, constraining plots. To
sell tickets, movies have to stay sufficiently within genre for audiences to follow

them. The result was that films about captivity were firmly established as adventure fables about escape. The 1963 film *The Great Escape* is a strong representative of the genre. In a climactic scene, actor Steve McQueen is fleeing from a World War II German prison camp on a motorcycle. As soldiers close in from all sides, he uses an earthen embankment as a jump and his motorcycle sails over a ten-foot barbed wire fence. The scene is emblazoned in the memories of several generations of young males, along with an elaborate tunnel. Prisoner of war camps are built in a heroic landscape where natural motorcycle ramps abut barbed wire fences and no one gets dysentery. The daring breakout is a defining element in *Man at Large, Stalag 17, Von Ryan's Express*, and *The McKenzie Break*, to name a few. The genre took on a new life in Vietnam POW/MIA films such as *Missing in Action*, where commandos went back to free cinematic prisoners left behind at the end of the war.[3] If it is a movie set, the purpose of bars and wire is not to confine, but to provide something to escape through. This adventure formula dominates every group of POW films except those set in Korea.

Almost invisible in prison camp adventures is the subject of collaboration. Informing and betrayal are fixtures of real incarceration, but not in war movies. POW films set in World War II and Vietnam focus on the brave but rare event of escape, and skip the complications. *Stalag 17* came close to addressing aid to the enemy, but its informer turned out to be a German spy educated in America, not a real turncoat. The adversary in POW films remained simple: the enemy without, not weakness within. With few exceptions, Hollywood concentration camps are places to celebrate masculinity, not question it.[4] POW films set in Korea depart from convention in every case. Some form of collaboration with the enemy is a central issue in all six feature films about American soldiers imprisoned in Korea. Prompted by the misperception of whole-scale collaboration in Korean prison camps, these dramas were forced to depart from convention and acknowledge frailty, weakness, and unfaithfulness. They followed swings in public opinion and often tried to counter them, guided by Army advisers. They often addressed public sympathy for collaboration, but then tried to redirect it. There was a clear progression in movie formulas as Hollywood patriots searched for a way to approach Korea. Judgmental stories that blamed POWs for capitulating would be callous and unentertaining. The first films were heroic adventures, but they lacked verisimilitude for an audience aware of the record of collaboration. Scenes that focused on the torture and tribulations of incarceration were too depressing and implicitly questioned whether war was worth it. The subgenre finally settled on the courtroom drama as the best way to present the complexities of captivity.

The 1954 films *Prisoner of War* and *The Bamboo Prison* both featured stock heroes who snuck into prison camps and pretended to be collaborators so they could spy. *Prisoner of War*, starring Ronald Reagan, was released just a few months after the real prisoners, reportedly making it MGM's quickest production to date. The military initially assisted production by providing former prisoners for interviews and a repatriated officer as a consultant. The Army also requested and got four pages of script revisions.[5] In the film, Ronald Reagan plays Web Sloane, who crept into a prison camp to collect proof of violations of the Geneva Conventions. He pretends to be a Progressive, but the secret agent angle is drowned out by the film's main theme: communist torture, whose depiction is unsettling even by today's standards. In one scene, a prisoner refuses to confess to germ warfare. Guards put his pet puppy in a burlap bag and smash it with rifle butts. He still doesn't talk, but other prisoners are shown breaking under horrible torture. In one frigid scene, guards dump buckets of water on a man and a grotesque mantle of ice forms around his head. In another, a haggard face is repeating name, rank, and serial number, the camera pulls back to reveal his arms twisted around a bar and stretched with boulders. Prisoners are also shown boiling in the sun, hung up in trees, and capitulating before mock firing squads. The film's focus on atrocity themes paralleled Washington's initial approach. Officials tried to downplay collaboration and used the United Nations to talk about brainwashing and massacres.

*Prisoner of War* flopped. The torture served to "sicken people rather than entertain them." The industry press pronounced "War Atrocities Pic Limited in Appeal." The producers had tried for realism by depicting reported incidents of torture, only to have it called "a brutal, sadistic, and thoroughly cheap attempt to exploit public interest."[6] Although the movie was almost universally hated by critics, the portrayals of torture were accepted as accurate. The reviewer for the Parent-Teachers Association (PTA) warned parents it should have been "presented in documentary form to a prepared audience" rather than as entertainment. At least four reviewers used forms of the word "documentary" in their treatments.[7] A telling explanation for why a seemingly realistic movie was a "botch" came from Moira Walsh in *America* magazine, who called it an "endless succession of physical brutalities" without balance from a "counteracting moral and spiritual force."[8] Portraying men breaking under torture was too pessimistic. It was necessary to believe that faith and masculinity provided honorable ways out of all situations. If captivity was examined too closely, a film undermined the morale it was supposed to improve. This was true of *Prisoner of War* despite the fact that hero Reagan prevailed in the end. Critics also faulted the secret agent subplot, because the real record was considered shameful. The film "shockingly suggests," wrote *Saturday Review*, that collaborators "were really secret agents."[9] Treason, then a foremost association with captivity, had been dealt with by denying it. The movie claimed collaboration was a ruse or the result of extreme torture, not personal inadequacy. Perceptions of rampant assistance to the enemy were strong enough that suggestions to the contrary were immediately attacked.

After assisting production from the beginning, the Defense Department repudiated the film on the eve of general release. Army commands were ordered not to aid publicity or allow military bands to play at openings. Although there was no detailed official explanation, the circumstances and statements from the filmmakers suggest the ways in which the movie transgressed sound management of public opinion. A movie about torture of prisoners came out just as the Army was preparing to indict repatriates. Director Andrew Marton said the Pentagon did not want to be in the position of "investigating soldiers who were treated understandably in the picture." A *New York Times* report suggested that the brass objected to the film's portrayal of collaborators as secret agents. A short statement released by the Defense Department did refer to the plot as "too fictional."[10] The film *Bamboo Prison* provoked a similar criticism from a Pentagon official who considered "representing progressives as American Agents" to be a problem.[11] Supposed traitors were portrayed as having been tortured, or they were turned into secret agents at a time when the military was prosecuting POWs and citing them as proof of the need for patriotic renewal. No prosecutor wanted to face a public who had been persuaded the GIs were forced to comply.

The turncoats-as-agents plot was repeated later in 1954, but with an entirely different tone. *The Bamboo Prison* was a lighthearted B-movie. Unlike the Reagan film, this one was denied assistance by the Army from the beginning.[12] In *The Bamboo Prison*, a Sergeant Rand infiltrates a prison compound to gather proof of unreported prisoners so that negotiators at Panmunjom can demand them back. This reflected contemporary headlines about prisoners remaining behind. As in the earlier movie, Rand works undercover as a Progressive. The sergeant spends most of the movie in heat. His strategy is to seduce Tanya, a Russian ballerina married to a top communist (an effete American from *The Daily Worker*) whose office might contain revealing documents. When queried by a confederate about how he is going to get to the files, Rand explains, "I'm in the process, let's say, of climbing under the covers with the proletariat." Tanya is responsive and joins the scheme, believing that the communists "have ceased to be men." The movie ends with Tanya escaping to the West, while Rand stays behind as an ersatz defector.

*The Bamboo Prison* did not follow the sober approach of similar films, but it was still very much a response to Korea's prisoner of war trauma. It was not just that in those unsure times, American males would be pleased to be found more sexually desirable than Marxist intellectuals. The real-life defections of soldiers to China added to the concern that communist ideology might have a real appeal to the downtrodden, to which the film replied with cutting ridicule. In one scene, the high income of Americans is celebrated by a POW who had been a car salesman. He vroomed around the camp making car sounds like an eight-year-old and managed to enrapture the camp commander with a vision of cruising in his very own American convertible, radio blasting. Unfortunately, his salary is only 100,000 Chinese yen. "What's that in American money?" asks the salesman. "Four dolla twelve cents," is the reply. The auto guy makes a face and loudly vrooms off, speed-shifting into high gear. During an interminable political education class for POWs, the camera pauses on a student's eyes, which appear fishy. He blinks, and the audience realizes he has been asleep with eyeballs painted on his eyelids. During a Marxist recitation exercise the Chinese instructor calls on "Arkansas," a gangly, endearingly mischievous youth. Arkansas recites class-struggle dogma in a mocking manner, which the pupils get but the Chinese do not. The instructor is tipped off by a collaborator, and he begins shouting wooden rhetoric at Arkansas: "You have insulted the politburo. You have answered proletarian hospitality with bourgeois ingratitude." Arkansas feigns stupidity with his hillbilly accent: "Did Ah do ahll thaat?" This black and white film has the raucous high-energy of *Stalag 17* and the gritty texture of a working-class conscript army. The film portrayed the sly, earthiness of street-wise proletarians, who despite coarse manners and little education, see right through Asiatic communism. The film affirmed the soundness of American institutions, despite the real-life defectors.

Although *The Bamboo Prison* is infectious as a period piece, it was barely noticed at the time. One of the few reviews complained that its light tone was "incompatible" with the reality of the prison camps. Another critic, Mrs. Louis Bucklin of the Parent-Teachers Association, was disturbed that the film's most devious collaborator posed as a Catholic priest. The Memphis Board of Censors sought to ban the film, citing the priest as an affront to the memory of Emil J. Kapaun, an Army chaplain who died in captivity.[13] The script did not tap into the seriousness of concern in 1954. Similarly, Bob Hope scratched plans for a farce after the Army refused to assist it. A letter to Hope's agent explained that the Army valued its previous work with Hope, but the POW issue was too grave to be "treated in the farcical manner indicated by the outline." The plot involved a USO tour of Korea, theft of a helicopter, and "Jane, Jimmy, and Bob" somehow ending up in North Korea.[14]

Neither realism, satire, nor heroic adventure were sufficient to address the POW predicament, so a new plot device was employed: the courtroom drama. Three out of the four remaining movies were court-martial films. This paralleled real life, where the court-martial became strongly associated with POWs. Although more sophisticated than adventure flicks, courtroom films faced other problems: They were visually stagnant and had to convincingly answer public resentment of the collaboration trials. Screenwriters responded by incorporating public sympathy into the stories, then trying to finesse it into patriotic renewal.

The first Korean POW feature film that satisfied the Defense Department enough to give full assistance was released in 1956.[15] MGM, the studio responsible for *Prisoner of War*, got it right with *The Rack*, starring Paul Newman as an

Army officer returning from captivity. A moving, brooding, talky film, it was the most thoughtful of the bunch and favored by critics, but it offered nothing to the action market. *The Rack* explored treason, but with surprising empathy for its antihero. It suggested that honest men might collaborate, and pondered what should be done about it. Captain Hall (Newman) returns from prison camp a psychiatric casualty. Although decorated for bravery before being captured, he is about to be tried for collaboration. He is greeted by his father, a tough officer of the old school. And if that were not enough, Captain Hall's brother was killed heroically in battle. "Why didn't you die like your brother did?" the father demands.

Captain Hall wants only to plead guilty and get the trial over with, but his kind attorney, puzzled by the early record of bravery, insists on a defense. During cross-examination the script reveals Hall's background and the circumstances surrounding his aid to the enemy. He grew up lonely in a family bereft of warmth. His mother died when he was ten and his father was cold and distant, never kissing or touching his sons. The Chinese jailers exploited his emotional vulnerability by putting him in solitary confinement. There are no prison flashbacks. Hall's anguish is communicated with just courtroom dialogue and Paul Newman's acting. Solitary confinement crushed Hall with hunger, cold, and worst of all, loneliness. After months of pressure, Captain Hall's jailers sensed a vulnerable moment and revealed the death of his brother in combat. They threaten to leave him alone forever, and Captain Hall finally began signing propaganda statements. After setting up an empathetic premise mirroring public sympathy, the Rod Serling script changes course and begins undermining Captain Hall's account. In a key sequence on the stand, Hall reveals the loneliest day of his life: It was not in prison camp, but the day his mother died. The prosecutor points out that even after this, the worst day of his life, he still bounced back and became an officer, but in what was only the second worst experience, prison camp, he cracked. The prosecutor argues that the defendant was not at the limit of his endurance; rather, his character failed, rendering him culpable. In a nod to a debate of the day, the prosecutor adds in his peroration that even if society were remiss in preparing youths for the rigor of duty, it must not compound its error by failing to punish the guilty: "If you find Captain Hall innocent of collaboration, you find all those other Americans who refused to collaborate guilty of stupidity."

*The Rack* subtly tried to redirect sympathy for collaborators. In a scene near the end of the film, the father breaks down and acknowledges his emotional neglect of his family. The son forgives him in an embrace, and the movie suggests that if they had achieved such closeness earlier, the Captain, who was never physically tortured, would have had the spiritual strength to resist. By admitting that even well meaning men can falter, *The Rack* added sophistication to the call for an unyielding Spartan code. The movie's understanding tone showed respect for the backlash of sympathy for supposed collaborators, but civic-mindedly tried to correct it. *The Rack* made compassion part of the rationale for unyielding discipline in captivity. Newman's spiritual pain did not come from the discomfort of a cell, but from his own failure to act heroically. The film called on society to steel its young soldiers for anything, or face the shattered spirits who come home. *The Rack* optimistically concludes that valor is possible even during extreme isolation and deprivation. Capitulation is still portrayed as a choice; character is the key variable, not the conditions of confinement. Captain Hall belatedly recognizes this and uses the court-martial for atonement and to provide a lesson for others. In a clear, strong voice just before sentencing, he says, "I wish that everybody could feel the way that I feel now. Because if they did, they'd know what it's like to be a man who sold himself short." He accepted the prosecutor's argument that he had given up faith in himself just when he needed it most.

*The Rack* informed a humiliated nation that a solution to the POW disgrace was already at hand: rededication to traditional values and paternal involvement, as belatedly done by the Hall family. The message was well taken by critics. *Saturday Review* said *The Rack* showed "the emotional and ideological unpreparedness of our own armed forces." *Catholic World* called for "better psychological background" for soldiers and approvingly noted the film's contrast between Newman and fellow-POW Lee Marvin, who did possess "the inner resources" to maintain his honor. *The New Yorker* added that the problem was society's inadequate nurture of children.[16] The only caveats came from reviewers who seemed to feel that empathy for alleged cowards strayed from a manly ideal. Collaborators were certainly "more to be pitied than scorned," according to a *Nation* reviewer, but the scriptwriter committed "ethical mugwumpery" by not condemning them unambiguously. *Newsweek* made a similar point and compared it to a Broadway play called *Time Limit*.[17] The response to the prisoners of limited war remained divided between a sympathy that seemed to excuse weakness and a Spartan code that was unrealistic and heartless.

One year after *The Rack*, the play *Time Limit* was made into a movie. Shot in black and white, it opens on a grim, windswept scene. A POW collaborator is giving a propaganda talk to his fellow prisoners about cooperation. "Communism is peace," intones the senior officer, played by Richard Basehart. As the fellow prisoners contemptuously wander off, Basehart's character breaks down and desperately pleads with them to pay attention: "Listen to me, don't be such heroes." *Time Limit* was a variation of the court-martial plot. A brave, selfless officer had collaborated with the enemy in order to save his men from mass execution. The film is a meditation on whether Basehart should be prosecuted for violating the military code, even though it was to save lives. In weighing common decency

against the exigencies of war, *Time Limit* specifically addressed the lively public debate over the military's new Code of Conduct. The film may have been
inspired by the court-martial of Maj. Ambrose H. Nugent, who was acquitted of
propaganda and other collaboration after claiming that the Chinese threatened
to execute his subordinates.[18]

Like *The Rack, Time Limit* built sympathy for a man accused of failing his
duty, yet still received an imprimatur from the Army's Motion Picture branch.
Basehart had a high motive: The lives of his men were more important than
maintaining his honor and reputation as an officer. The climactic clash between
duty and sentiment is played out by a gruff general and Richard Basehart. In a
somewhat involved element of the plot, it is revealed that the general's son had
been murdered by other POWs for collaborating (despite enduring protracted
torture). The general is appalled to learn his son died ignominiously, saying "he
was raised to know better." Basehart pleads for understanding of prisoners' situation: "Your son was a hero for hundreds of days.... And on only one day did he
break. In the name of God, aren't all those other days worth something?" He suggests putting a "time limit" on heroism. Just when the script seems to favor the
explanations of collaborators, the general is given his soliloquy: "You talked to
me of sixteen men. Multiply that by thousands. Try carrying that weight on your
shoulders. Try sleeping with the cries of those wives and children in your ears.
I've done that, Major, every war commander has, because until a better world is
built, it's got to be done. That is why we have the Code, Major. The Code is our
Bible and thank God for it." On that note, the charges are not dropped and the
court-martial proceeds. Like *The Rack*, a nod was given to the defenders of the
POWs. The movie then explained that because the enemy would use American's
basic decency against them, harsh decisions were unavoidable. In order to minimize suffering in war, heroism had no upper limit.

Some critics did not comprehend the military's rationale for assisting a production like *Time Limit*. Reviews reveal a debate locked into a simple-mindedly
heroic conception of captivity. *Films in Review* called the story "tendentious." "A
time limit on heroism?" it asked, "what an insidious implication!" *Newsweek* was
just as unforgiving of the Basehart character, "The Code of Conduct condones
no collaboration of any sort under any circumstances. It is always the sad duty of
an officer to sacrifice the lives of a few rather than risk the loss of many—in this
particular case, the minds of many through false propaganda."[19] *Newsweek's* com-
ment showed how the flexibility of the Code was little in evidence in its public
presentation, as well as the tizzy over POWs making propaganda statements that
few of them believed. One reviewer had such a shallow appreciation of captivity
that he denied that there were dilemmas to consider. Robert Hatch wrote in *The
Nation* that *Time Limit* conjured "brain-teasing" choices for entertainment, even
though disloyalty in Korea resulted not from "honorable dilemmas" but from

"confusion, ignorance and bad conscience."[20] The negative reaction to a film approved by the military illustrates the trickiness of using POWs to stimulate patriotic verve. Respecting popular sympathy for the POWs seemed to violate the propaganda imperatives of the hardliners. But in order to be effective, a film had to address the public horror at enemy treatment of prisoners. But the revelation that strong, honest people can collapse, even without physical torture, threatened the heroic narrative on which morale seemed to rest.

Interestingly, neither main character in *the Rack* or *Time Limit* would have been court-martialed in real life. In actual disciplinary policy, collaboration in Korea was mitigated by duress. Internal Pentagon documents were explicit in saying that "no disciplinary action" was taken if POWs colluded under duress.[21] However, common currency gave a dogged impression that name, rank, and serial number was the test used for legal action. The very movies favored by the Pentagon reinforced the perception that shattered young men were being tormented a second time. The ceaselessly violent portrayal of Chinese captivity was also overblown. Physical attacks on POWs were usually distant from the indoctrination programs, and collaboration came more from toadying than atrocity.

The next feature, John Frankenheimer's *Manchurian Candidate* (1962), does not fit easily with the other films, but it does connect with the sentiment that POWs were blameless because free will had been washed from their brains. In this inventive fantasy, a young POW is brainwashed to the point that he can enter a memory-less state of suggestion and commit murder on cue. He returns to America programmed to murder a presidential candidate as part of an elaborate communist coup. The completeness of brainwashing is displayed in a surreal scene early in the movie. A group of young men, American prisoners of war, are sitting in a hotel meeting room. There is a lecturer, a middle-aged woman in a colorful hat droning on about hydrangeas to a ladies' flower club. The camera does a slow, 360-degree pan showing the POWs sitting listlessly while the flower club members fan themselves. But when the camera rotates back to the lecturer, she is no longer the flower lady, but a sinister-looking Chinese communist named Yen Lo. Lo is a stereotypical Asiatic villain played by Khigh Dhiegh (who was also the camp commandant in *Time Limit* and a recurring master criminal on television's *Hawaii Five-0*). Yen Lo explains to his real audience of malevolent, communist officials that he has brainwashed the men in three days to think they are at a flower talk. The camera view keeps cutting between middle-aged dears with big hats and menacing men with scars and jackboots. Yen Lo reveals to his official audience the plan for the repatriated POW to assassinate an American presidential candidate, clearing the way for an agent to reach the White House. The effectiveness of brainwashing is proven by having a prisoner strangle a friend on stage, which is done with all the pleasant decorum of a flower lady making cuttings.

*Manchurian Candidate* was the only one of the Korean War POW films to receive Academy Award nominations or to sell many tickets. Its success demonstrates how deeply the fear of capture and absorption by an enemy organism resonated with the audience, and how far the imagination might go to explain collaboration. One critic, Bosley Crowther, worried that although "as wild a piece of fiction as any," the film might agitate the more "anxious minds" of the day. Another reviewer considered the film's robot assassin plot just plausible enough to need a corrective: "I do not believe," wrote Moira Walsh, "that brainwashing…is as precise or efficient a process as the film makes it out to be."[22] Brainwashed prisoners could hardly be held responsible for their actions, putting into sharp relief the callousness of POW critics. The success of this film shows how completely the Army publicists had lost the battle of public opinion. With the legend of brainwashing so well established in the audience, there was sure to be reflexive sympathy for captured soldiers who went beyond name, rank, and serial number. Although the main plot tended to exonerate prisoners, the film also offered a cultural critique of the corrosive influence of mothers. When the brainwashed POW returns home from Manchuria, his control agent is none other than his mother (Angela Lansbury). She held the queen of diamonds playing card that triggered his control state. She kisses him deeply on the lips as she sends him off on the mission to shoot a presidential candidate. Her son finally shatters the incestuous hold on him by turning the rifle on her at the last moment.

Chinese brainwashing was still topical enough to be taken up in 1963's *The Three Stooges Go Around the World in a Daze.* The Chinese capture the Stooges and brainwash them, then demand signed confessions, which they refuse. Moe explains, "sorry general, with these boys, no brainee to washee." The soldiers who were supposed to have brainwashed the three then enter the room. They are Chinese stooges, now under Moe's control, who immediately start smacking and poking. Moe shouts "62" and they deface a Mao portrait, "41" and they double eye-poke the general.[23] The scene's edge came from providing comical relief from disquieting legends.

The theme of unfair treatment of POWs is explicit in a 1963 episode of the science fiction TV show *The Outer Limits.* The episode "Nightmare" is a parable on the pernicious danger of suspicion. It warns soldiers to build group loyalty and avoid feminine weakness because the enemy will destroy solidarity by sowing suspicion. In the story, a group of warrior-astronauts from "United Earth" are taken prisoner by an alien race, the grotesque Ebonites. The plot revolves around determining which prisoner will collaborate first. A creepy voice warns the new prisoners "you will cooperate in all ways, resist in none." One by one the men are subjected to torture, trickery, and hallucinatory mind-control. The parallel to Korea is explicit: Human traitors assist the Ebonites in interrogation, and one prisoner pessimistically refers to the success of brainwashing in Korea, noting that the Chinese achieved it even without the Ebonites' telepathic mind control. In an interrogation booth, the Ebonites probe for personal weaknesses. They terrorize Private Dix (Martin Sheen) by taking his voice away. Dix continues to mouth name, rank, and serial number. He is then drugged and his mother comes to him in a hallucination. Dix's voice returns in the dream, but he hesitates to talk out loud because the Ebonites might hear. His mother's voice is comforting: "Whisper all about it in my ear." Another prisoner also has a maternal hallucination. Krug, the German, is distressed-to-death when his mother berates him for turning a relative into the Nazis when a boy. Another man is blinded. At one point, the camera cuts to two off-scene humans who are evaluating the affair. They are trying to guess which one will collaborate first. One suggests it will be Private Dix, because "there's too much mom in those eyes."

As individuals return from interrogation, apprehension grows that someone has talked. They all claim to have given only name, rank, and serial number, but each man has a reason to be mistrusted by the others. Deals are hinted at when the Ebonites restore the sight of the blind prisoner and the voice of Private Dix. Even more suspicious, one man was never touched at all, possibly because he cooperated. Suspicion fixes on Jong, the Asian member of the group. Mistreatment suddenly ceased after Jong's interrogation and food and living conditions improved. An Ebonite appears and confirms there was collaboration by reciting classified information that could only have come from a POW. The alien wants them to know there is a turncoat. The prisoners take the bait and decide to execute Jong. They draw straws, but the man with the short straw hesitates. He suspects the enemy is inducing mistrust: "We must not let them make us do this to ourselves." The pause allows attention to turn to Private Dix and what it was he whispered to his mother during the dream. Dix begins breaking down; his mother reappears in another hallucination and confirms that he gave classified information to her, which she relayed to the aliens. Dix falls to his knees, blubbering: "Tell me I didn't say anything to you, please Mommy." The Ebonites had used mutual suspicion to get men to turn on one another, just as America had blamed the Korean POWs. Above all, soldiers must retain their masculine camaraderie, because the diabolical enemy will use anything, even a prisoner's weakness for mother.

Although men were killed, injured, and nearly executed, it is revealed in the end that it was all an elaborate ruse to train the men for real captivity. The Ebonites turn out to be friendly aliens—they were helping the humans prepare for encounters with less amicable space beings. The Ebonites are incensed that the exercise became so heartless and deadly. An officer defends the harsh training regime, saying it was necessary in light of the "shameful record" of Korea. He recites Eugene Kinkead charges, including that no one escaped. At the conclusion, however, a voice-over seems to side with the more advanced and compassionate Ebonites. The narrator sadly intones that military strategists would study the Ebonite episode intently, and "perhaps they will learn something." The episode was careful to speak to both sides of the POW controversy.

The theme of Cold War America out of control is more explicit in the 1968 feature *Sergeant Ryker*. Lee Marvin is Sergeant Ryker, sentenced to death in the midst of the Korean War. (The name "Ryker" may have been chosen to echo John Wayne's heroic Sergeant Stryker in *Sands of Iwo Jima*, 1949.) Technically not a POW movie (he's in prison in the United States, not Korea), it nevertheless makes collaboration the central theme. The drama takes place concurrent with the second evacuation of Seoul, lending an air of hysteria that might trigger a rush to justice. The case against Ryker seems open and shut: The Sergeant never denies joining the Chinese army. But as another compassionate defense attorney investigates, doubts and sympathy rise. A general warns the lawyer not to risk his career defending a man like Ryker, especially when thousands of non-traitors in the capital are fighting for their lives. But this is disingenuous. Plot developments make it clear Ryker is being railroaded. The establishment general is putting the system ahead of justice. The betrayal theme is carried further by Ryker's wife, who would really rather be with the lawyer.

Eventually, cross-examination reveals that Ryker was a hero, not a turncoat. He had been on a secret mission when he crossed over. The truth was known only by his superior officer, who was unfortunately killed in action. The real security breach turns out to be, significantly enough, an officer whose Korean mistress is exposed in court as a spy. Ryker was not only falsely charged in court, but he had been serving his accusing compatriots in a mission of extraordinary danger. The Chinese had believed his defection; it was his own people who did not. A moment of justice comes on the witness stand when Lee Marvin erupts in a hissing, spitting tantrum: "Go ahead and hang me, I risked my life for you brass types....I only made one mistake, boys, I came back."

Originally a 1963 TV movie, a film distributor added outdoor shots to the courtroom dramatics and put *Sergeant Ryker* in theaters in early 1968. The rerelease took advantage of the developing Vietnam antiwar audience by resurrecting a previous injustice.[24]

The prisoner of war film genre was briefly transformed in the years after Korea. A failed war and images of collaboration contributed to a crisis of confidence. Patriotism and the beneficence of the Pentagon encouraged films that gave proper guidance to the wayward audience. But a touchy public made it a treacherous process. To be plausible, movies had to go beyond the escape formula and address collaboration, but this made it hard for screenwriters to make Korea saleable. The films were too grim, unbelievable, or missing visual action. Filmmakers tried different formulas and eventually found a way to acknowledge the pressure soldiers were subjected too, but still demand unending resistance. The films paralleled the contest in the real world, where the initial shock at collaboration prompted an examination of captivity, followed by greater sensitivity, then disillusionment with renewed military austerity.

Korea brought an unusually close examination of captivity that went beyond valor and considered torture and human limits. Extended attention to the obligations of captives, in film and elsewhere, gave high profile to a rarely filmed agony of war. A prisoner is a victim. Surrender is followed by dependence on the captor and often onerous conditions. This violates a maxim of public opinion management: War must never seem so horrible that it is not worth it.[25] A dead soldier is easier to heroicize; the story has an end and fulfills a desire that sacrifice be worthwhile. But former prisoners keep the cost of war conspicuous with their continuing presence, especially when they are criticized at home. The POW saga darkened the Cold War mentality culminating in *The Outer Limits* and *Sergeant Ryker* in which POWs were clearly treated shabbily.

The Korean War was an example of the difficulty of managing the image of POWs of limited wars. The Pentagon learned from Korea that prisoners did not make good subjects for parables about faint-heartedness and played Vietnam differently.[26] Vietnam prisoner movies also returned to simple heroics. During the second Gulf War, the Pentagon was sufficiently savvy that it essentially tried to turn a real capture into an action picture. In March 2003, Pfc. Jessica Lynch was badly injured and seized in an Iraqi ambush. The Pentagon made a drama of it, claiming she fought to the last bullet, made even more gripping by her gender. She was then dramatically saved by special forces in a seeming midnight shootout, all captured on camera, then released in a five-minute edited version. Later, Lynch said with simple honesty that she had never fired a shot. Iraqi medical personnel welcomed her rescuers with a key to hospital floors. Contrary to early reports, the special forces team was not fired on. The early tales of derring-do became one of the embarrassments of the war. "They used me as a way to symbolize all this stuff. It's wrong," Lynch said.[27] Heroicizing captivity keeps it from demoralizing the public. A hostage, especially a female, induces helplessness. The hasty effort to make an icon of Jessica Lynch stemmed from the same impulse that hides the disfigured and forbids photographs of caskets returning from war. The killed in action can have their pictures censured, but a soldier in captivity is a casualty that keeps repeating. POWs must be heroes so that people do not dwell on what they go through. The backlash against the Korean War jeremiad succeeded in ending the use of POWs as whipping boys, but not their use in propaganda. Pentagon morale builders learned from Korea to either heroicize POWs—or keep them in the background. But like the discourse about real captivity, Korean POW movies revealed the constant pitfalls of opinion management.

# 13

# The Hidden Reason for Forgetting Korea

For obscure reasons the case of the Chinese and Korean prisoners who chose freedom has not been given the type of exploitation which it deserves. In fact, the liberation of these people is about all that we have to show for our Korean effort.

—Charles H. Taquey, Operations Coordinating
Board analyst, August 20, 1954

On a Sunday night, the general who became president, Dwight D. Eisenhower, stepped before the TV cameras and announced the end of the Korean War. The day was July 26, 1953. The armistice was actually signed in Korea on the 27th, but it was still the 26th in the United States. Like the date, understanding of the war would always remain a step behind.[1] After announcing that the shooting had stopped, the President paid tribute to the soldiers, widows, and families who sacrificed "to keep freedom alive." He praised UN allies and complimented Syngman Rhee and wished a swift return to captives "wearied by many months of imprisonment."[2] At a moment for recognition, however, there was a curious omission: the central issue of half the war. He made no mention of the Chinese and North Korean prisoners whose nonrepatriation had been secured with great effort. Through blood, death, and fears, Washington had compelled the enemy to accept partial repatriation, yet Eisenhower never even hinted at its part in the conflict. It is understandable that the initial success of the war—defending South Korea—would be the lead, but that had not been in doubt since spring 1951. Eisenhower made no oratorical flourishes about humble peasants rejecting communism or about how American steadfastness helped them start new lives in Seoul and Taiwan. The president might have looked to the future, calling for the nonrepatriates to be reunited with their families one day in liberated homelands. Helping former soldiers escape communism was full of rhetorical possibilities, but he availed himself of none. In the valedictory speech about the war, voluntary repatriation was invisible.

The president's omission was part of a heretofore unrecognized reason why Korea faded from memory: POWs. The conflict is reflexively referred to as the "forgotten war" and the standard explanations for Korean amnesia are largely true, as far as they go. Fighting certainly ground on without clear purpose. If President Truman had stopped at the 38th Parallel, the war would have been victorious in four months and outshone the Berlin Airlift as an American Cold War triumph. The limited war that followed was shapeless, so it is not surprising that people's minds had trouble engaging it. In David Halberstam's words, Korea neither united like the Second World War, nor divided like Vietnam; "it was simply a puzzling, gray, very distant conflict" going on and on. The war was being forgotten even when it was still going on; the *Army Times* complained in January 1953 that GIs were "lonesome symbols of a nation too busy or too economy-minded" to pay attention.[3] Perhaps the strongest evidence of a longing to move on was the end of two men's political careers: Truman and MacArthur. President Truman's reelection bid fell apart because of the war, providing an opening for his nemesis, MacArthur, who ran as a Republican. However, the general's acclaim did not transfer into politics. He was too closely associated with the war no one wanted to think about, and his personality did not hold up well in a Senate hearing. He lost the nomination, but was allowed to give the keynote address to the Republican convention in 1952. It was calculated to be a great moment, but it became his swan song. The two old politicians did not fade away—they tumbled. When an armistice finally came in summer 1953 there were, as one author put it, "no victors, no vanquished."[4] With the fighting over, Americans could commence forgetting in full. Grave markers in Arlington Cemetery were initially not even going to say "Korean War." A compromise added the "Korea" but not the "war."[5] South Korea built memorials to allied soldiers before the United States or England did. The American memorial did not open until 1995. Except among a few scholars, military history buffs, veterans, and families of casualties, Korea drifted away.

This amnesia raises a question: Since governments have a talent for spin, why wasn't Korea retold after the fact in a more pleasing manner? The past is full of wars that were remembered differently than they were experienced. Americans won no important concessions in the War of 1812; the capital was sacked and the invasion of Canada trounced, but they still got the "Star Spangled Banner" out of it and an effervescence of patriotism. This example pales before the Myth of the Lost Cause that dominated writing in the American South about the War Between the States. A devastating defeat was turned into a source of inspiration and honor that still sustains sons and daughters of the Confederacy. Yet officials could not find the words to heroicize Korea. This is even more curious considering the longstanding anxiety about public morale and the effort to cultivate it. The Cold War demanded public forbearance of an expensive, permanent, global projection of power. The planning document NSC-68 called for educating the nation so that "intelligent popular opinion may be formed."[6] This was the specialty of the Department of State's Edward Barrett, who was enthused by NSC-68 but warned that "the US public would rapidly tire" of its crusade and candidly recommended "a psychological 'scare campaign.' " Declining morale worried President Eisenhower immediately after the ceasefire. "We may not now relax our guard nor cease our quest," the general intoned. "We have won an armistice on a single battleground, not peace in the world."[7] Public apathy was an enemy. If there were ways to repackage Korea, clever minds would have done so.

The armistice agreement actually contained a possibility: voluntary repatriation. The substitute for victory was just that—victorious. Communism's foot soldiers seemed to have voted with their feet. Enemy negotiators fulminated for 18 months, but in the end accepted an armistice that withheld thousands of POWs despite knowing that most were coerced. Seemingly, Washington finally had something to celebrate after the long interval since Inchon. But this was a victory that security officials could not revel in. There was a hitch in celebrating voluntary repatriation because few citizens registered on it. The White House had slow-played it. The Truman administration did promote it on the editorial pages after it was first proposed at Panmunjom in January 1952 and succeeded in framing it as a refusal to return certain prisoners to tyranny and execution.[8] But this outreach was more to editors and opinion leaders. The administration was securing support in order to head off possible opposition, not trying to motivate the general public with a new war aim. Pentagon briefers did not give it a more memorable moniker like "Operation Free Return." Voluntary repatriation was not used to rejuvenate morale or stir troops in battle. It was never "why we fight." That the armistice talks foundered over prisoners was not a state secret, but it was a public secret. Partial repatriation was purposely muted because it was politically dangerous. Washington feared that if the only thing standing between American families and their boys was a Korean prisoner, support for the war would collapse. Even the truncated effort to recruit columnists in early 1952 revealed this danger. "Isn't our first business," a radio commentator asked, "to return to their homes the American and other allied prisoners the Reds have reported to be alive?"[9] An NSC staffer who tracked the media reported:

> Articles now beginning to appear in the press raise the specter that the issue might be presented to the American public as an "exchange of Chinese lives for American lives." Should this develop, it is likely that the public outcry would obscure the basic moral issue and jeopardize the effectiveness of the US policy.[10]

It was still a "specter," but the State Department's Charles Stelle worried that if the nation concluded that communist prisoners were being put first, "U.S. domestic opinion would shift against support of general principle of 'voluntary repatriation.'"[11] State's public relations guru Edward Barrett feared being "accused of sacrificing the moral obligations of any government to rescue its own prisoners" in order to help Chinese and Koreans "who were once shooting at us and who surrendered to save their own skins." Possible citizen opposition was also a reason not to rescreen Koje-do in 1952, despite the unlikely results the first time. A second headcount would have kept Koje chaos in the headlines for several more days. State's Charles Bohlen feared that repatriation might come to be seen as "*the* outstanding issue" blocking an armistice (emphasis in the original). This could arouse the public to go "get our POWs back."[12]

Hovering over the situation was the issue of race. In all the memoirs and archival documents I examined, not one source acknowledged an obvious consequence of partial repatriation: broken families. It was easier to overlook because the prisoners were of a different race. The officials who saw faceless Orientals and the soldiers who called them Chinks came from the same society that was so impatient for the war to end. Much of the public would oppose prolonging the war over voluntary repatriation, not just because the prisoners were the enemy, but because they were Asian. No official wanted to be confronted by a father demanding to know why his son stayed captive over a gook.

Hints of disquiet were apparent in late 1952 when State public affairs analyst Joseph B. Phillips wrote that newspaper editorials were on board, but not all the readers:

> There has been a constant under-current of privately circulated petitions demanding the return of our prisoners as a first concern. One such petition, started some months ago by the parents of a prisoner and with no known Communist inspiration, is believed to have gathered about 250,000 signatures. At present the Department has received about 12,000 petitions or form messages calling for a cease-fire and a large proportion of them demanding the return of our prisoners.[13]

Gathered without media buzz or social media, this impressive number of signatures spoke to the potential of a backlash. POW issues could not be erased from the public record, so the administration was very careful not to fan them. Pollsters hewed to the Washington line by not bringing up prisoners. In a White House summary of polls taken from fall 1952 through spring 1953, POWs were never mentioned. The surveys asked about support for escalation and whether the current battle line was acceptable for a truce, but not the main issue.[14]

Lowering the profile of POWs was so important that Washington declined to dwell on mistreatment of prisoners. In early 1953, Secretary of Defense Charles E. Wilson was worried that the germ warfare accusations were succeeding. He decided it would be "effective counterpropaganda" to take the confessions forced from pilots and turn them against the Chinese. In a letter to the director of the CIA, Wilson suggested accusing China of a new type of war crime, "menticide." Brainwashing could explain not just germ warfare collaboration, but also the 29,000 letters sent home containing antiwar comments. But even as he suggested splashy denunciations of menticide, Wilson realized it would not be received well:

> To date, the ugly specter of American prisoners of war having been 'brain-washed' has received but sporadic attention. Because of feared public reaction against the UNC position on repatriation, U.S. public information and foreign information agencies have aped the ostrich and buried their collective heads.[15]

This aside clearly reveals a policy of misdirection. Officials said little about prisoner abuse so that the country would not get overeager for peace and question voluntary repatriation more forcefully. Washington waited until after the war to take brainwashing accusations to the United Nations. Even then, the substitute victory "was blurred," complained OCB analyst Charles Taquey, replaced by the "less profitable issue of brainwashing."[16]

The administration could leave repatriation out of conversations, but it still had to explain why peace negotiations languished. It was commonly said that for murky reasons of their own, the communists "insist on prolonging the war." One UNC commander suggested peace hinged purely on military pressure: "Reds to Quit if Korea Going Gets Tough," read the headline.[17] The reds were also said to use petty obstructions. With talks deadlocked, there was little to discuss at Panmunjom and meetings ran fifteen minutes one day, eleven the next. Peninsula commander General James Van Fleet said this was proof of the enemy "not wanting a cease-fire." Often tight-lipped about negotiations, officials were sure to let people know of the shrill haranguing that dominated meetings. Lead negotiator Admiral C. Turner Joy told a reporter that after each morning's "dose of verbal vitriol," he lost himself in an hour of horseshoes. "I never pitched a horseshoe till I came here," he said, and after the assignment "I'm never going to pitch a horseshoe again."[18] It was a challenge to bury something in plain sight since the communists regularly inveighed against it. To keep them from gaining traction, American officials invariably described their policy as opposing "forced" repatriation. A senior negotiator publicized a question he asked enemy negotiators: "Are you insisting that our side handcuff, chain, or otherwise bind these persons and ship them to you like cattle?" This was an outlandish demand, "deliberately intended to make settlement impossible," and of course involving no issues of compulsion.[19] Even with it framed as strictly a rejection of force, many people did not think voluntary repatriation was worth a war. To avoid outcry at home and abroad, a State Department public opinion manager recommended against allowing talks to "break down on the single issue of forcible return of POW's." Negotiators held the line as long as possible against three communist demands: improvement of northern airbases after an armistice, Soviet representation in a postwar committee on Korea, and full repatriation. There would be "a great uproar," Charles Bohlen told the JCS, unless "there were three good reasons why an armistice could not be concluded."[20]

Although alert citizens could not be kept in the dark, Washington succeeded in keeping the political class united. The Republican Party did not accuse the Democrat president of preventing peace over red captives.[21] Without major political figures dissenting on repatriation, there was no debate reputable enough for timorous journalists to report. Similarly, there were no personal interest stories about individual anticommunist prisoners, or national tours featuring brave young Chinese men choosing freedom, despite a powerful Taiwan lobby. The lid was kept on so well that when a few GIs did not voluntarily return, the Army could punish them without any pundit noting that the 21 were doing exactly what the second half of the war was fought over. Three days after the war ended, the State Department's Division of Public Studies devoted its "Weekly Summary of Opinion on Far East" to newspaper reactions to the armistice. Eleven pages of summaries were provided and POW repatriation never showed up, even in stories structured as balance ledgers of the war's successes and failures.[22] To this day, many twentieth-century Americanist historians have no idea why peace talks took so long. Nonforcible repatriation had been declared and carefully pitched to opinion editors in early 1952, but its absence at the end of the war in polls, news stories, and political announcements demonstrates successful bamboozlement of the nation.

Voluntary repatriation was not the nation's motivation for war, so President Eisenhower could not proclaim it as a victory in his July 1953 announcement. He could point to saving South Korea as a success, but that news was two years old. A few credited the war for creating a new human right for POWs to seek asylum, but the knowledge never became common wisdom.

Cold warriors who might try to redeem the "sour little war" lacked materials for creating a usable past. National security planners had run up against a basic conundrum of limited war. Korea was sold like WWII, as necessary for survival, but then the government settled for a tie. When a nation is moved to fight by existential threat, but the war is conducted according to realpolitik, the memory can become unmanageable, and maybe best forgotten. Prisoners provided no way to see Korea in a more positive light; they were central to both the war and its dissipated memory.

# Conclusion

## *Two Wars, the Visible and the Cloaked*

> He seldom read newspapers because working in intelligence had con-
> vinced him that most stories never reached the press.
> —description of World War II veteran and
> DNA biologist Francis Crick

In 2008, the Korean War Ex-POW Association held its annual reunion in
Denver, Colorado. Membership may have dwindled, but new faces were still
turning up, reconnecting for the first time since 1953. I attended and brought a
batch of archival photographs from inside the prisoner of war camps. The veterans poured over them, searching for familiar faces and finding quite a few. One
afternoon in an open area where the ex-POWs congregated, a hotel employee
dropped a large steel tray with an earsplitting crash. It triggered an event in Bill
Smith that the eye could not immediately take in. He began hopping up and
down shouting one-syllable vocalizations which seemed to be in time with the
jumps: "jyb, jyb, jyb." With a practiced motion, his wife Charlotte grabbed his
hands, got close, and began repeating "look at me, look at me." This went on for
easily five minutes until his mind began returning to the hotel; movement and
vocalizations slowed and eventually his eyes refocused on the woman in front of
him. Other veterans carried on with calm familiarity. The Smiths said in an interview that explosive sounds had been inducing seizures for 55 years.[1] Bill Smith
was captured by the Chinese in late 1950 after intense combat in extreme cold.
He was the man put in solitary discussed in Chapter 4, and one of the medical
cases released early at Little Switch. The fits that Smith suffered are part of the
numberless traumas of Korea, each a reason to reflect on the war. The origins
and nature of the war are debated, but one thing that should not be disputed is
that the survivors deserved a clear description of why the war lasted as long as
it did. They did not get it. Partial repatriation's significance remained murky to
veterans, just like everyone else.

Bill and Charlotte Smith, Denver, CO, 2008. C. S. Young.

Nations commonly fight two wars at once—one public, one shrouded. There is an official war described by government and cooperative media, and an undisclosed war as understood and conducted by decision-makers. The gap between open and secret wars is sometimes wide, which was why Francis Crick did not like to read the newspapers.[2] Not just tactics or incidents, but fundamental goals may be understood differently by civilians and leaders. In Korea, Washington was not candid about what underlay the impasse in armistice talks. The second half of the war was incomprehensible without knowing that peace waited on the enemy accepting forced nonrepatriation. The nation understood the general goal of containing communism, but the specifics of how that would be measured and accomplished in Korea were hidden in mist, spied only by determined skeptics. War challenges democracy, and a public that does not know why it fights is excluded from the processes of a republic. Korea inaugurated not just limited wars, but special difficulties in maintaining national consensus, and the temptation to replace it with secrecy.

In Korea, the public/private divergence began with calling it a "police action," although the nation soon knew it as war from the carnage. People tended to trust their government and assumed it was a war of necessity. But Washington had concluded that Korea was not a vital interest when it pulled out combat troops in 1949. After Kim Il-sung's invasion, President Truman believed it was a Soviet war and that Korea was a good place to draw a line. Protecting South Korea was a clear objective, but wise or not, it was a choice, predicated on staying within the peninsula and made possible by having an army in Japan. Entering Korea was a calculation; it sought deterrence and credibility from a limited investment. But these goals contraindicated military victory after China made costs and thermonuclear risks too great. Truman's calculations were a step removed from a fight for survival, which turned the war into an enigma on the home front. A war deemed not important enough to win made little sense. Adding to the confusion were the shifts in fundamental military goals as events progressed. South Korea was secured in fall 1950, soon after Inchon. Conquering North Korea and rolling back communism became the new goal but only for a few months until survival of the Eighth Army became the priority. By summer 1951, early objectives had either been completed or dropped. The most confusing period began with truce negotiations. If neither side intended to win, what of importance was left to fight over? In comparison to winning a war, the aims that followed were secondary and tactical: propaganda, attrition, frontline adjustments, readiness, credibility. Public frustration with Korea emerged from a fundamental difference in how defense planners and most citizens understood war. To civilians, war was Germany crushing France in 1941, a direct invasion and occupation, which communism seemed to be of the same variety. But Korea was part of an expansive struggle for geostrategic power that rarely looked like the Blitzkrieg. Before 1941, military bases were limited to the Caribbean and Philippines, but now the United States competed for world influence, a less tangible concept than safe borders. The breathtaking scope of postwar activity ensured that Washington would conduct its limited wars differently than the public understood them.

In Korea, the government and public wars pulled the furthest apart when officials decided to temporize on peace negotiations. Washington prolonged the fighting for wider Cold War advantages and in President Truman's case, a poorly informed sympathy for anticommunist prisoners. But the substitute victory became the central goal and the method for achieving the others. Protecting the rights of prisoners would show strength, integrity, and expand defense in the process. While attractive on the surface, these objectives were rather intangible compared to the triumphant rollback they replaced, and they faded from exposure to time and blood. The geopolitical calculations behind the new military goals were unlikely to be attractive, especially when putting enemy prisoners ahead of American. Voluntary repatriation was pitched so narrowly to the domestic audience that it hardly clarified the war. A war over enemy prisoners was not saleable; negotiators in Panumjom strived to keep a jumble of issues from simplifying into one. Unclear war aims were better than an objectionable one, so Washington allowed support for the war to erode rather than risk repudiation. The official story was that it was purely the communists who blocked peace. Armistice negotiation strategy was so closely held that most of government and the military were as unaware as the public. Citizens could not judge the desirability of war goals they did not know about. POWs on Koje-do were well aware that the hands of Seoul and Taiwan reached into the yards. It was the American and other UN nations that did not know they fought for partial repatriation.

Voluntary repatriation, the mechanism of delay, began as a psychological operation so secret that commanding generals were blindsided by riots on Koje-do. It was not common knowledge that the 704th Counter Intelligence Corps supervised indoctrination and defections on Koje-do. Even more secret were the agents infiltrated from Taiwan and Seoul who ran the terror campaign and took control of the interior away from the UNC. Military stalemate transformed the psyops program. What started as a sideshow became the war, but it retained the secrecy of its origins. "I think we are God damn lucky there hasn't been more interest in our press," Chief of Naval Operations William Fechteler said of Koje violence in spring 1952. The strife on Koje-do was so poorly understood that *U.S. News* attributed it to a "standing general policy of treating prisoners tenderly."[3]

Possibly the most damning secret of the shadow war was that the Army would never have had to force prisoners home, anyway. Early parole was a humane solution for militants and could have been done at any time. Unilateral release was actually anticipated; preliminary plans were made in February 1952 and used later that year for 38,000 South Koreans. But Washington preferred to force a capitulation. Admiral Joy wrote after the war, "fifteen months were required to impose our principle of voluntary repatriation on the Communists.... It must have been a painful year for Americans in Communist dungeons."[4] It was also a lonely life for the Asian men withheld from families and infuriating to Americans if they had known. In the decades since the end of the war, a few ex-prisoners in Taiwan have made it back to the mainland for visits. Some North Koreans undoubtedly feel fortunate to have ended up in the South, while for others, separation from family was not worth it. Even if they would not want to go back now, they had no say then. It is commendable that South Korea formed a Truth and Reconciliation Commission to investigate its massacres of political prisoners during the peninsula's conflicts.[5] The withholding of POWs is another story needing acknowledgment by South Korea, America, Taiwan, and the United Nations in whose name the war was fought. An accounting could accompany pressure on North Korea over the 83,000 South Koreans it kept. Family reunions will be possible for another decade or so.

The failure to rescreen prisoners on Koje-do in 1952 was pivotal in opening the door for a cloaked war outside public understanding. The Far East Command was rather aghast when the low repatriation count put an armistice in doubt, and for a moment the Command noticed terror and compulsion on the prison island. But defectors were an enthusiasm of the Cold War and an honest recount would have meant expelling the secret agents and dismantling a successful political operation. Rescreening was undesirable, and they calculated they could get an armistice without one. Without a corrective, the low repatriation results were the only figures available and became received wisdom. Few knew better. It was accepted that nearly 40 percent of POWs wanted to stay with the United Nations even though their experience of the allies was behind the wire of a deadly police state. Men with inside knowledge, like Admiral Joy, released their doubts and soldiered on. The refuseniks were treated as an uncontrived problem thrust upon the United States, creating a choice between brutally returning them or continuing the war. This orthodoxy crippled opposition to prolonging the war in government and out, even though early parole was always practical. Forgetting about the duress led the UNC to protect prisoners from the wrong threat during the NNRC period. Barracks bosses, not communist explainers, endangered the new human right. The phrase "voluntary repatriation" really should be used more sparingly; "partial" is more accurate.

Not knowing that the communists fought on over prisoners confused many issues besides the length and purpose of the war. The Chinese germ warfare charade required extravagant fakery and frenetic publicity. The sheer scale was curious and grasshopper pandemics comical, but it made sense as a reply to voluntary repatriation. Mass defections were a serious political threat and the war crime accusations kept vilification from being one-sided. The mothers of the 21 American stay-behinds never got a satisfying explanation why they could not coax their sons home. It appeared to be just stupefying bureaucratic rigidity, when really the problem was that mothers from the other side might do the same. Lack of information from Koje-do allowed administrations to spin events that could not be covered up entirely, like the mutinies portrayed as fanatical convulsions. Riots were ordered by callous leaders who perversely kept prisoners "in combatant status," according to UN commander Mark Clark.[6] This was true, but it was in reaction to the UNC already turning the compounds into battlefields. If the public had understood that the rebellions were responses to a forced defection program, it might have been even less patient with the war. Such knowledge would also throw different light on the bombing of the north. Air attacks of unprecedented scale were in service to an apocryphal position on repatriation.

Although the objective of the war was not announced, many civilians figured out that peace hinged on communist prisoners and 250,000 signatures called on the president to drop the issue. The petition was gathered old-school, on paper, door-to-door, and despite the canard that forced repatriation was at issue. But this public participation in politics was still stunted by the lack of candor about the repatriation issue. The president did not explain the purpose of the war, opposition politicians did not call him on it, and the press deferred to defense officials. The petition signers figured it out themselves by parsing the news. Openness would have prompted wider participation in public affairs. The fact that a basic military objective was not explained is an example of how the Korean War was toxic to self-governance. Much of the war news was handled by military men who were used to owning the minds of recruits. Lives depended on how well they controlled information, and they guarded it closely. Traditions of discipline and secrecy stopped any whistle blower from announcing that unilateral release was being sat on. Clandestine habits spilled into the democratic process, sped by the fundamentally objectionable nature of the repatriation strategy.

The public had difficulty discerning the importance of voluntary repatriation, and it was also unaware of being a psyops target at home. The initial audience for the brainwashing hoax was the American people, since they were the readers of Edward Hunter's books and articles. The CIA's intent was to frighten citizens with an occult threat to their minds, since shooting wars were judged too distant and intermittent. Officials were as taken in by brainwashing as civilians, but the OCB's fall 1953 National Plan took rumor and legend and presented it as scientific research. This plan to expose atrocities against prisoners began with Dr. Charles Mayo's address to the United Nations. Mayo alleged that "the science of Pavlov" was used to extract germ warfare confessions, but there is no reason to believe the Chinese operatives had heard of conditioned reflexes, much less acted out the fiction of a CIA novelest.[7] The flyers who confessed described beatings and isolation in cold and filthy cells. Mayo's ghostwriters took traditional torture and called it Pavlovian conditioning. The Chinese indoctrination classes used methods out of their own long experience; POWs sang communist songs when closely supervised, not as a conditioned reflex. Possibly no covert action has reached so far into a culture as the fabrication of brainwashing. One of the great successes of psyops was carried out against the perpetrators' own community.

The records of the Operations Coordination Board, which coordinated the National Plan, provide a behind-the-scenes look at opinion management in process. The sponsorship of articles, books, and speeches by the OCB were classified. The National Plan directed that "private channels" be used to inform the American people of the abuse of prisoners. This was to "avoid the tag of government propaganda."[8] The timing was calculated. Major publicity waited until after the war so the nation would not get too antsy for POWs to come home. Citizens were first shielded from facts so they would remain inactive, then bombarded by information because inaction no longer served federal policy. OCB staffers saw the public as a problem, an object to be manipulated. It could hardly be otherwise since the aims of the war were not transparent. Media outlets welcomed the OCB as a silent partner. William Lindsay White, an editor at *Readers Digest*, got access to confidential material and was willing to publish his compilation "in any form that the government desired." His book, *The Captives of Korea,* included the disinformation that personnel from Taiwan were not used on Koje-do.[9] The *New Yorker's* Eugene Kinkead acknowledged that he presented the Army's view of things, but he did not reveal that he actually handed editing over to the OCB, making him a publicist, not a journalist.

Desire to stir the public encouraged putting out information that was not just misleading but false, as in the list of 944 prisoners supposedly unrepatriated by the Chinese. These were the GIs that a variety of officials said were known to have been captured but not returned. But a researcher who checked the raw intelligence found problems with hundreds of names. The paper casualty forms always listed the last known status of GIs, and for many of the 944, it was MIA, not POW. They had never even been reported as captured; they were soldiers or flyers who *might* have become captive. The names were misrepresented "from the very first day," according to analyst Paul Cole.[10] Mischaracterization of MIAs as prisoners gave families false hope. The 944 list still reverberates in the twenty-first century, when families use it to accuse the Pentagon of knowingly abandoning POWs. Defense Department employees assailed at conferences can thank their counterparts from the 1950s who wanted a single, vivid number with which to accuse the communists. Blowback occurs when wars are limited and opaque and the populace is a problem to be finessed, rather than reported to.

One propaganda success was the portrayal of captivity in North Korea as unbroken terror and suffering. Security officials waited until after the armistice to launch the National Plan, but once begun, it established mistreatment as the norm. There was plenty of evidence to draw on—mass executions, icy death marches, hunger, disease, and poor medical treatment. But in two out of three years, the basic needs of most prisoners were met. The impression of nonstop anguish colored the indoctrination program as worse than it was. Classes were tedious and harassment could be nasty, but instruction itself was not deadly, as seen in the pranks and backtalk directed at the Chinese. Since captivity was portrayed as continuous danger, the Army could not credibly claim that only willing collaborators were prosecuted.

When POWs returned to the United States, their behavior was questioned from many quarters, which was predictable. But what was not apparent was that an organized group of administrators was at work behind the scenes. The new Code of Conduct was not simply an internal military reform, but a choreographed national event. The Burgess Committee on prisoners of war announced it was fixing behavior in captivity, but it was also fixing the public, which needed to provide recruits with better character. The Code restated the position that prisoners needed to be unyielding. Not released from the secret report was the Committee's conclusion that captors get what they want from captives, or that the Code was flexible and accommodated the branches' different standards of resistance. The Burgess Committee wanted POWs to be tougher, but the Code's further significance was in setting an example of sacrifice for the public to follow.

The media jeremiad about GI toughness was only partly the work of the Department of the Army, but it provided much of the raw data that supported it. Eugene Kinkead and William Mayer were conduits for Army views and data; claims like no escapes, one-out-of-three collaborated, and give-up-itis became staples of editorials and polemics. The effectiveness of the jeremiad came not from a military cabal but from mutual reinforcement of social doctrines. The supposed primitive manliness of Turkish soldiers resonated with a nation raised on cowboy and Indian stories, while the arriviste psychoanalytic trade rushed to show the relevance of mother–son incest. Give-up-itis seemed related to the women who were walking over men and the husbands who let them. The jeremiad was not purely manipulative since proponents worried passionately about manhood. After all, they mistook pellagra for creeping effeminacy. Fixating on masculinity and character evaded the morale problems created by limited war. The Jeremiahs did not think the problem was shifting military goals, unarticulated national interests, or a startling reach for global influence, it was cloying mother. Families were blamed for weak POWs, but it was the authorities who limited the war, prolonged it, misread China, made prisoners a measure of success, and then judged them on performance in an anomalous situation.

The organized nature of the jeremiad was no less true because the military bureaucracy was divided over it. OCB staffers railed against the Army for going after collaborators just when Charles Mayo said that the biology of free will was under attack, and prosecutors complained that brainwashing was contaminating juries. Management of the public mind was contradictory, but still pursued assiduously. When critics pointed out what everyone knew—that the 21 were dishonorably discharged without court hearings because they went to China—OCB staffers started leaking information accusing them of other misconduct. Fellow prisoners were often angered by those who repeated Chinese views beyond necessity, but political collaboration was notable for being temporary. Except for the 21, it occurred in the unusual circumstances of the camps and did not carry over to America, to speak of. The FBI dug for years, but could not find effort to circulate Chinese ideology in the United States. No Friends of China alumnae group tried to soften the image of captivity. Germ warfare would be a likely issue for continuing collaborators to bring up, but there is little sign of it.

The criminal justice system is expected to be insulated from outside concerns, but the prosecution of collaborators was heavily politicized. Many indictment counts were for acts of expression. Decisions to go to court were guided as much by institutional interests as POW actions, as seen by the Air Force and Navy refusal to indict men who did the same things as Army personnel. The Army retracted sentences and stopped prosecuting collaborators because of the hostile public reaction, and the Justice Department never started for the same reason. But the cause of this reversal was not announced, prosecutions petered out over years. Citizens could not appreciate how successful they had been.

Hollywood war movies commonly thanked the Defense Department in credits and rolled cameras with patriotic lenses. What is less apparent until digging into the archives was the amount of coordination of ideas. The credits thank the Army for providing tanks, but not editing scripts. Movie fiction may have been the only chance for fixing the brainwashing dilemma. People convinced of torture and mind murder in Korea could not understand courts-martial and were impatient with philippics about servicemen becoming dainty. The Paul Newman movie *The Rack* was shrewd at trying to correct them. The film invited empathy for collaborators, then insisted that real compassion required an unyielding code of conduct. Films are expected to manipulate emotions to entertain, but the official hand tries to avoid notice. The Pentagon's interest in films is primarily ideological and for recruiting—not the technical accuracy of reel fighting. Bob Hope's Korea film never went forward because it was insensitive to Pentagon concerns, and political vetting was rigorous enough that the Ronald Reagan film *POW* was caste adrift at the last moment, even though the producers predictably raised a stink. Korea POW films fell into obscurity because they failed to move the audience, but it was not for lack of trying. The films languished because they tried to solve something intractable—morale under limited war.

Perhaps Korea should not be called the "forgotten" war, since many of its essentials were never well understood in the first place. The unknown Korea stretches beyond POWs to include the war's effect on the size of the military, its impact on the republic, and the conduct of the Cold War. Despite Korea's impact, few people on the street would answer "Korea" if asked "What was the most far-reaching episode of the Cold War?" Measured by the height of the event versus the shortness of its shadow, Korea is the most unknown war. Korea inaugurated permanent mobilization. Traditionally, troops demobilized after fighting; the 1870s military of 16,000 was not 3 percent of those killed in the Civil War. During Korea, the defense budget quadrupled in size, then never returned, nor did the habit of balanced federal budgets.[11] The institutions engaged in foreign affairs become leviathans, what is often called the "national security state." This was long in the works, but its blueprint, NSC-68, was rejected as a budget buster—until Kim Il-sung's invasion. Voluntary repatriation served as a cement catalyst, it sped the hardening of the foundation of the national security state. Although prisoners had minor parts, the great scope of this development multiplied their contribution. The security state was built to fight the Soviets but served many purposes, including the predilection of human organizations to grow and profit. The smoking gun is that when the USSR abruptly vanished in 1991, the military budget hardly dropped a canteen. Defense spending nearly equals that of the rest of the world combined.[12] In 2010 there were more than 750 military bases overseas, not including Afghanistan. "Base world" constitutes a parallel nation, with shopping malls, bus lines, and 234 golf courses.[13] The nation's turning away from an unmemorable war may have helped permanent mobilization slip into place smoothly.

As the Korean War dragged POWs along, it also militarized the "containment doctrine" which originated principally as economic and diplomatic. George Kennan, the diplomat who first formulated containment, spent the rest of his life lamenting that the Marshall Plan for rebuilding Europe after 1945 did not remain the preferred model of containment. After Korea, superpower rivalry was measured more by the number of tanks and nuclear bombs than economic advances. In a way, militarizing containment, necessary or not, played to the Soviets' strength, since they were always better at making tanks than blue jeans. They could not fill store shelves, but an arms race was one place they could compete. Through its part in sharpening the military rivalry (with POWs playing a small part, rearming Germany a big one), the west helped the Kremlin maintain a siege mentality, distracting citizens from their empty shelves and dreary media. This does not excuse the Kremlin's many crimes, but the arms race fertilized the Soviet system.

President Eisenhower's farewell address where he coined the phrase "military-industrial complex" is cited endlessly, but there was also a final press conference two days later. In it, the President looked beyond corporate profiteering and regretted how militarization captured the imagination. He said every other magazine had a picture of the Titan missile, "an insidious penetration of our own minds that the only thing this country is engaged in is weaponry and missiles." He might have called it the military-industrial-academic complex for the way scholars were getting on board. Universities, "the fountainhead of free ideas," were changing the questions they asked; "a government contract becomes virtually a substitute for intellectual curiosity."[14] When Eisenhower said this, the national security complex was still reaching its stride. It has now come to full fruition. Militarization's capture of the polity is such that major political figures who want to stay major never say "military industrial complex," and even the President said it only as he cleared out his desk.

Eisenhower believed the national security complex was necessitated by the Soviets, but that did not make its rise less worrisome to him. Similarly, the

Freed POW Jose Garcia, 29, leans from bus window to greet his younger brother. Travis Air Force Base, California, May 1953. Associated Press.

Korean War and voluntary repatriation helped militarize the nation, regardless of their wisdom. The military-industrial complex is a massive structure, every stone carried into place on the backs of common people. American POWs carried an extra load and when they got home, were told that was not good enough.

# ABBREVIATIONS

| | |
|---|---|
| AFP | Agence France Presse |
| AFPDF | Air Force Plans Decimal File, 1942-1945, RG 341, Archives II |
| AGO | Adjutant Generals Office, RG 407 |
| AGO CCAF | Adjutant Generals Office, Classified Central Administration Files |
| AP | Associated Press |
| ANZUS | Australia, New Zealand, United States Security Treaty |
| BRSRK | (Ad Hoc) Board for Review of Sentences in RECAP-K Cases, 1956–58; RG 153, JAG |
| CCF | Chinese Communist Forces |
| CDF | Classified Decimal Files of Adjutant Generals Office, RG 407 |
| CF | Confidential File, archival series at Eisenhower Library |
| CIC | Counterintelligence Corp, Army |
| CIE | Civil Information and Education |
| CINCUNC | Commander in Chief, United Nations Command |
| CINFO | Chief of Information |
| CR | Command Reports of AGO |
| DMZ | Demilitarized Zone |
| DOD | Department of Defense |
| DOJ | Department of Justice, RG 60 |
| DOJCSF | DOJ Classified Subject Files, part of RG 60 |
| DPRK | Democratic Peoples Republic of Korea (North) |
| FEC | Far East Command |
| *FRUS* | *Foreign Relations of the United States*, US State Department Document Series |
| G3 | Records of the Office of the Assistant Chief of Staff for Operations 1943-58, RG 319 |
| GHQ | General Headquarters |

| | |
|---|---|
| JAG | Judge Advocate General (Army), RG 153 |
| JCS | Joint Chiefs of Staff, US |
| KMT | Kuomintang, Chinese nationalist party |
| KPA | Korean Peoples Army (North) |
| K-POWs | Korean War Prisoners of War |
| LST | Landing Ship, Tank, a World War II vessel for delivering troops and vehicles |
| MIA | Missing in action |
| n. | A footnote or endnote |
| NA | National Archives |
| NARA | National Archives and Records Administration |
| NATO | North Atlantic Treaty Organization |
| NNRC | Neutral Nations Repatriation Commission |
| NSC | National Security Council Staff Papers, 1948-61, Eisenhower Library |
| *NYHT* | *New York Herald Tribune* |
| *NYT* | *New York Times* |
| OCB | Operations Coordinating Board Central Files, NSC Staff Papers, Eisenhower Library; the OCB replaced the PSB Sept. 2, 1953 |
| OCBS | Operations Coordinating Board Secretariat Series, NSC Staff Papers |
| OPI | Office of Public Information, Assistant Secretary of Defense |
| OSANSA | Office of the Special Assistant for National Security Affairs |
| OSD | Office of the Secretary of Defense |
| PCIIA | President's Commission on International Information Activities |
| PLA | People's Liberation Army, China |
| PPS | Policy Planning Staff, State Department |
| PSB | Psychological Strategy Board Central Files, NSC Staff Papers, Eisenhower Library; PSB replaced by OCB Sept. 2, 1953 |
| PSF | President's Secretary's Files, Truman Library |
| POW | Prisoner of war |
| Pro | Progressive, a POW receptive to Chinese indoctrination |
| PW | Prisoner of war |
| PWG | Prisoner of War Working Group, ad hoc body within the OCB |
| RECAP-K | Returned and Exchanged Captured American Personnel in Korea |
| REO | Records of the Executive Office, Office of the Secretary of Defense |
| RG | Record Group within the National Archives |
| ROK | Republic of Korea |

| | |
|---|---|
| SCAP | Supreme Commander of the Allied Powers, Tokyo |
| SMOF | Staff Member and Office Files, Truman Library |
| SMOF-PSB | Staff member and Office Files, Psychological Strategy Board, Truman Library |
| UN | United Nations |
| UNC | United Nations Command, which headed UN military forces in Korea |
| UP | United Press |
| UPI | United Press International |
| USIA | United States Information Agency |
| *USNWR* | *U.S. News and World Report* |
| USSR | Union of Soviet Socialist Republics |
| WF | (Ann) Whitman File, Eisenhower Library |
| WHCF | White House Central Files, Eisenhower Library |
| WHO | White House Office Files, Eisenhower Library |
| WHOF | White House Official Files, Eisenhower Library |
| WHTO | White House Telegraph Office, Eisenhower Library |

# NOTES

## Introduction

1. See also Carlson, *Remembered Prisoners of a Forgotten War*, 1.
2. Clark, "U.S. Army Welcomes Home United Nations Personnel."
3. "The Tough Prisoners." "Veterans Groups Divided."
4. "'Red Rumor' Chills POW's Welcome," 3.
5. "Ex-POW Assails 'Kangaroo' Trial," 20.
6. Ulman, "GI's Who Fell for the Reds," 64.
7. Kristol, "The Shadow of a War," 41.
8. Biderman, *March to Calumny*.
9. "Veterans Groups Divided."
10. "PW In 'Progressive' Group Says He's For Capitalism."
11. *Foreign Relations of the United States (FRUS), 1952–1954*, 15:1730.
12. Biderman, *March to Calumny*; Carlson, *Remembered Prisoners of a Forgotten War*; Lech, *Broken Soldiers*; Carson, *The Guilty of the Korean War*.

## Chapter 1:   Limited War

1. Zellers, "I Was a Prisoner in Korea," 713. Zellers, *In Enemy Hands*, 114.
2. Nitze, "NSC 68," in *American Cold War Strategy*, May, ed., 34.
3. Leffler, *A Preponderance of Power*, 518.
4. Hoopes, "Role of the Defense Department in the Cold War."
5. Laurie, *The Propaganda Warriors*.
6. Joint Chiefs to Johnson, "NSC 74 – A Plan for National Psychological Warfare."
7. Mitrovich, *Undermining the Kremlin*, 177. See also Lucas, *Freedom's War*; Rawnsley, ed., *Cold-War Propaganda in the 1950s*.
8. Peterson, "The Role of the Defense Department in the Cold War, Section II."
9. Simpson, *Science of Coercion*, 18. "Project TROY Report to the Secretary of State," found in Needell, "Truth is Our Weapon," 411.
10. *FRUS 1949*, 1:276. "Project TROY Report to the Secretary of State." The PSB was succeeded by the Operations Coordinating Board in late 1953.
11. Weathersby, "To Attack, or Not to Attack? Stalin, Kim Il Sung, and the Prelude to War."
12. Casey, *Selling the Korean War*, 31.
13. Norman, "'Lightning Joe' Talks," 50. Schaller, *The American Occupation of Japan*.
14. *FRUS 1951*, 6:53.
15. Norman, "'Lightning Joe' Talks," 50.
16. Goncharov, Lewis, and Xue, *Uncertain Partners*, 144.

17. Li, Millett, and Yu, eds., *Mao's Generals Remember Korea*, 4–5. Hermes, *Truce Tent and Fighting Front*, 503.
18. Hanley and Mendoza, "U.S. Policy Was to Shoot Korean Refugees." Hanley and Choe, *The Bridge at No Gun Ri.*
19. Cumings, *Korea's Place in the Sun*, 284.
20. Li, *Mao's Generals*, 69.
21. Halberstam, *The Coldest Winter*, 16.
22. Associated Press, "Curtain on War News."
23. "Where Yanks Suffered Disaster."
24. "Seoul Abandoned to Red Armies." "Reds Now Half Way to Pusan Beachhead."
25. Whitehead, "Withdrawal Inevitable."
26. Sandler, *The Korean War*, 140.
27. Kaufman, *The Korean Conflict*, 50.
28. Ibid., 54.
29. Li, *Mao's Generals*, 41.
30. Ibid., 46.
31. *FRUS 1951*, 6:36.
32. MacDonald, *Korea*, 220.
33. Hermes, *Truce Tent*, 179.
34. Gacek, *The Logic of Force*, 70.
35. Mansourov, "Stalin, Mao, Kim, and China's Decision to Enter the Korean War," 105.

## Chapter 2:   The Middle Passage

1. "Comparison of POW Deaths: World War II and Korea," *Committee Documentation of the Secretary of Defense's Advisory Committee on Prisoners of War* (July 1955) tab 12, AFPDF 1942-1954, 383.6, entry 336, box 441, RG 341.
2. Army Security Center, *U.S. Prisoners of War*, 46.
3. Toland, *In Mortal Combat*, 81–83. Army Security Center, *U.S. Prisoners of War*, 24. Carlson, *Remembered Prisoners*, 102.
4. Army Security Center, *U.S. Prisoners of War*, 24. Peters, "When the Army Debunks the Army," 78.
5. Snyder, *A Soldier's Disgrace*, 120.
6. Army Security Center, *U.S. Prisoners of War*, 20, 25. Anderson et al., "Medical Experiences in Communist POW Camps in Korea," 120.
7. "Death Skims Road in U.S. Jets' Dives." Allen, *My Old Box of Memories*, 35.
8. Carlson, *Remembered Prisoners*, 97–98.
9. Allen, *My Old Box of Memories*, 55. Berens, *Limbo on the Yalu and Beyond*, 68.
10. Young, *Oral Histories of Korean War POWs*; Funchess, *Korea POW*, 70.
11. Grant, *Operation Big Switch*, 13. Berens, *Limbo on the Yalu*, 73.
12. Young, *Oral Histories*. Knox, *Korean War*, 338.
13. Young, *Oral Histories*.
14. Anderson et al., "Medical Experiences in Communist POW Camps in Korea," 120. Peters and Li, *Voices from the Korean War*, 224.
15. "Interrogation Reports of Personnel Returned to Military Control in Operation Little Switch, 1953."
16. Young, *Oral Histories*.
17. Bassett, *And the Wind Blew Cold*, 54. Jones, *No Rice for Rebels*, 41.
18. Zellers, *In Enemy Hands*, 160.
19. Ibid., 161–62.
20. On the camp system, see Latham, *Cold Days in Hell*.
21. Army Security Center, *U.S. Prisoners of War*, 21–22.
22. Booth, *Operation Big Switch*, 13.
23. Rowley, *Korea POW*, 40. Allen, *My Old Box of Memories*, 33. Carlson, *Remembered Prisoners*, 108.

24. Allen, *My Old Box of Memories*, 50. Brown, "Archie Edwards, Korean War Educator Memoirs."

25. Cline, Wilbert Estabrook Interview," 227–8.

26. Peters, "When the Army Debunks the Army," 78. Sommers, *The Korea Story*, 10, 13.

27. Young, *Oral Histories*.

28. Gittings, *Role of the Chinese Army*, 133, found in Lee, *Korean War*, 83. Li, *Mao's Generals*, 63.

29. Young, *Oral Histories*. Hinkle and Wolff, "Communist Interrogation and Indoctrination of 'Enemies of the State,'" 168.

30. Army Security Center, *U.S. Prisoners of War*, 21–22. Davis, "Prisoner of Korean War Shares Story of Capture."

31. Segal, "Factors Related to the Collaboration and Resistance Behavior of U.S. Army PW's in Korea," 32.

32. Bassett, *And the Wind Blew Cold*, 58. Hinkle, "Communist Interrogation and Indoctrination," 129.

33. Brinkley, "Valley Forge GIs Tell of Their Brainwashing Ordeal," 116. Segal, "Factors Related to the Collaboration and Resistance," 97.

34. Schein, "Man Against Man: Brainwashing," quoted in Mitford, *Kind and Usual Punishment*, 121.

35. Spiller, *American POWs in Korea*, 108. Wills, *Turncoat*, 50.

## Chapter 3:  Andersonville East

1. Report of Boards of Officers-POW Division.

2. US 8th Army, *Logistics in the Korean Operations* (1955), v. 1:58, found in Lutz, "Epistemology of the Bunker," 265.

3. Vetter, *Mutiny on Koje Island*, 199. Hermes, *Truce Tent and Fighting Front*, 404.

4. Vetter, *Mutiny on Koje Island*, 106.

5. Bradbury, "The Political Behavior of Korean and Chinese Prisoners of War," in Meyers and Biderman, eds., *Mass Behavior in Battle and Captivity*, 223, 240. Vetter, *Mutiny on Koje Island*, 60; Hansen, *Heroes Behind Barbed Wire*, 95.

6. Hermes, *Truce Tent and Fighting Front*, 234. Boatner, "Mistakes Made with POW Under 2D Log Command."

7. Bradbury, "Political Behavior," 257. Vetter, *Mutiny on Koje Island*, 138. Bradbury, "Political Behavior," 220.

8. Ibid., 239–40, 245–46.

9. Oh, *Stalag 65*, 104, 106.

10. Oh, *Stalag 65*, 86–8, 117.

11. Lucas, *Freedom's War*, 140–41.

12. AP, "Red MIG-15 Jet Lands Near Seoul."

13. Bradbury, "Political Behavior," 225.

14. *FRUS 1951*, 6:549. Prugh, "Prisoners at War," 124.

15. *FRUS 1950*, 7:782. Peters and Li, *Voices from the Korean War*, 244.

16. CIC presence: Oh, *Stalag 65*, 169; Young Sik Kim, "Eyewitness: A North Korean Remembers," web; Burchett, *Koje Unscreened* (1953), 10; "The Communist War in POW Camps," 16 n.2.

17. Bradbury, "Political Behavior," 219.

18. Vetter, *Mutiny on Koje Island*, 99.

19. Benben, "Education of Prisoners of War on Koje Island," 161.

20. John Osborne, *Dispatch 44*, 27.

21. Bradbury, "Political Behavior," 259. Benben, "Education of Prisoners of War," 162.

22. Arzac, "Intelligence Briefing by Dr. Carleton Scofield."

23. Hansen, *Heroes Behind Barbed Wire*, 54. Norberg, "To Kenneth Hansen."

24. King, *Tail of the Paper Tiger*, 510. West and Li Zhihua, "Interior Stories of the Chinese POWs in the Korean War," 168.

25. Benben, "Education of Prisoners of War," 162–63. Godel, "Psychological Warfare Operations During the Korean Conflict."
26. Vetter, *Mutiny on Koje Island*, 100.
27. White, *Captives of Korea*, 115.
28. Hansen, *Heroes Behind Barbed Wire*, 67–68.
29. Bradbury, "Political Behavior," 220, 291–92, 259.
30. Ibid., 100.
31. Oh, *Stalag 65*, 169. Prasad, *History of the Custodian Force (India) in Korea*, 69.
32. Bradbury, "Political Behavior," 265.
33. Oh, *Stalag 65*, 172, 163.
34. Bradbury, "Political Behavior," 245. Also Hermes, *Truce Tent and Fighting Front*, 233.
35. *FRUS 1952–1954*, 15:369. Hess, "Oral History Interview with John J. Muccio."
36. Bradbury, "Political Behavior," 292.
37. Ibid., 298.
38. "Petitions," RG 319.
39. Burchett, *Koje Unscreened*, 15, 17, 10, 18.
40. Oh, *Stalag 65*, 175, 182, 177.
41. Millett, "War Behind the Wire." *FRUS 1952–1954*, 15:370. Vetter, *Mutiny on Koje Island*, 19, 76.
42. Hansen, *Heroes Behind Barbed Wire*, 19. Vetter, *Mutiny on Koje Island*, 77. John Osborne, *Dispatch 44*, 2.
43. Jin, *War Trash*, 351, 111, 241. Freeman, "Talking with: Ha Jin."
44. Further details and photos see Young, "Voluntary Repatriation and Involuntary Tattooing of Korean War POWs."
45. Georges Gallean, undated AFP clip attached to "Telegram 604 to Secretary of State."
46. West, "Interior Stories of the Chinese," 152, 172, 166.
47. John Osborne, "Personal and Confidential."
48. King, *Tail of the Paper Tiger*, 509.
49. West, "Interior Stories of the Chinese," 171.
50. Gallean, AFP clip, "Telegram 604 to Secretary of State."
51. Zhao Zuorui, "Organizing the Riots on Koje," in Peters and Li, *Voices from the Korean War*, 245.
52. *FRUS 1952–1954*, 15:98.
53. Stelle to Nitze, "The POW Issue in the Armistice Negotiations," found in Bernstein, "Struggle Over the Korean Armistice," 285.
54. Feather, "Life on Prison Island." Bradbury, "Political Behavior," 285, 314.
55. Clark, *From the Danube to the Yalu*, 36.

## Chapter 4:   Welcome, Fellow Peasant

1. Wang, *They Chose China*.
2. Rowley, *Korea POW*, 86–87.
3. Young, *Oral Histories of Korean War POWs*.
4. Army Security Center, *U.S. Prisoners of War*, 27, 15. Hinkle and Wolff, "Communist Interrogation and Indoctrination," 154, 167. Funchess, *Korea POW*, 20.
5. Rowley, *Korea POW*, 67. Army Security Center, *U.S. Prisoners of War*, 51.
6. Arzac, "Intelligence Briefing by Dr. Carleton Scofield." "GIs Freed by Reds Tell of Good Care," 2. Funchess, *Korea POW*, 36; Young, *Oral Histories of Korean War POWs*.
7. "P.W. Flyers Reveal Torture."
8. Atul Gawande, "Hellhole," 36–45.
9. Army Security Center, *U.S. Prisoner of War*, 59.
10. Hinkle and Wolff, "Communist Interrogation and Indoctrination," 134. Yoo "U.S. Dept. of Justice, Deputy Assistant Attorney General John Yoo To Alberto R. Gonzales;" also Haynes, "Counter Resistance Techniques."
11. "Too Late to Kill Germs," 187. Elie Abel, "6 Testify."

12. Army Pamphlet 30-101, *Communist Interrogation, Indoctrination, and Exploitation of Prisoners of War*. "Facts and Figures Used in Secretariat Briefings on Problems A & F," *Committee Documentation*, tab 12. Young, *Oral Histories*. Segal, "Factors Related to the Collaboration and Resistance Behavior," 84.
13. Edited for flow. Young, *Oral Histories*.
14. History Book Club, *Remembering the Forgotten War, Korea*, 7. Young, *Oral Histories*.
15. Brinkley, "Valley Forge GIs Tell of Their Brainwashing Ordeal," 121.
16. Young, *Oral Histories*.
17. Berens, *Limbo on the Yalu*, 69. Zellers, *In Enemy Hands*, 161. Army Security Center, *U.S. Prisoners of War*, 34; Young, *Oral Histories*.
18. Army Security Center, *U.S. Prisoners of War*, 30. Jones, *No Rice for Rebels*, 48. Lech, *Broken Soldiers*, 103.
19. Brinkley, "Valley Forge GIs," 110. Jones, *No Rice for Rebels*, 59. Brinkley, "Valley Forge GIs," 113.
20. Jones, *No Rice for Rebels*, 58.
21. Funchess, *Korea POW*, 74. Army Security Center, *U.S. Prisoners of War*, 77. Army Pamphlet 30–101, 51.
22. Hinkle and Wolff, "Communist Interrogation and Indoctrination," 157. Jones, *No Rice for Rebels*, 60.
23. Lech, *Broken Soldiers*, 158. Colegrove, "AF Freed Officer," 3.
24. Deane, *I Was a Captive in Korea*, 26. Wiltz, "The Korean War and American Society," 117. Kolb, "Korea's 'Invisible Veteran,'" 24.
25. Army Security Center, *U.S. Prisoners of War*, appendix XX.
26. POW Korea collaboration Literature.
27. Pate, *Reactionary, Revised 2000*, 82. Maffioli and Norton, *Grown Gray in War*, 157.
28. POW Korea Collaboration Literature; "A Complete Account," 45.
29. Segal, "Factors Related to the Collaboration and Resistance," 81.
30. Pate, *Reactionary!* 69, 136. Lifton, "Home by Ship," 734.
31. Hinkle and Wolff, "Communist Interrogation and Indoctrination," 163–64. Pate, *Reactionary!* 69. Segal, "Factors Related to the Collaboration and Resistance Behavior," 71. "Preliminary Findings on Army Prisoners by the Human Resources Research Office," *Committee Documentation*, tab 12.
32. Examples: AP, "P.W.s Say Pro-Red G.I.s Return to Propagandize," 3; Ulman, "The GIs Who Fell for the Reds," 17; Jones, *No Rice for Rebels*, 47.
33. Segal, "Factors Related to the Collaboration and Resistance," 75, 38.
34. Pasley, "21 American GIs Who Chose Communism," 43, 121. Crenson and Mendoza, "6 of 21 Who Defected After Korean War Now Live Quietly in U.S." Wang, *They Chose China*.
35. "Transcripts and Related Records Pertaining to Radio Peking Broadcasts."

## Chapter 5: Prisoners of Limited War

1. "Who Won the War?" 14.
2. *FRUS 1951*, 7:1296.
3. McClure to Army Chief of Staff, "Policy on Repatriation of Chinese and North Korean Prisoners."
4. Carroll, "To Gordon Gray, Repatriation of Prisoners of War."
5. Bradley, "To Secretary of Defense, Policy on Repatriation of Chinese and North Korean Prisoners."
6. Kaufman, *Korean Conflict*, 59–60.
7. International Committee of the Red Cross, "Third Geneva Convention."
8. "U.S. Policies, from the Psychological Strategy Standpoint, Governing the Exchange of Prisoners of War."
9. Stelle to Nitze, "The POW Issue in the Armistice Negotiations," (Jan. 24, 1952) PPS; found in Bernstein, "Struggle over the Korean Armistce," 280. Bernstein mistakenly cited "Frank" Stelle instead of Charles C.

10. Fechteler to the Secretary of Defense.
11. "PSB Staff Study on Repatriation of Prisoners of War in Korea."
12. "Russian Captives Riot at Fort Dix." Moore, "Between Expediency and Principle," 383, 396.
13. *FRUS 1951*, 7:1073.
14. JCS to CINCFE, (Jan. 21, 1952) JCS 92490, Matthews Files, found in Bernstein, "The Struggle Over the Korean Armistice," 279. J. A. C. Gutteridge, "The Repatriation of Prisoners of War," 207–16.
15. *FRUS 1952–1954*, 15:494.
16. *FRUS 1951*, 7:1339.
17. Joy, *Negotiating While Fighting*, 175–80. Hermes, *Truce Tent and Fighting Front*, 149.
18. Joy, *Negotiating While Fighting*, 259.
19. *FRUS 1951*, 7:993–94.
20. *FRUS 1951*, 6:53.
21. Fechteler, "State-Defense Conference on Korean Armistice Negotiation."
22. Stueck, *Korean War*, 211, n. 36. Lloyd C. Gardner, "Korean Borderlands: Imaginary Frontiers of the Cold War," in Stueck, ed. *The Korean War in World History*, 142.
23. Foot, *A Substitute for Victory*, 96. " 'Voice' Taunts Foe Over 'Volunteers.' "
24. Stueck, *Korean War*, 5.
25. Pierpaoli, *Truman and Korea*, 227.
26. Stueck, *Korean War*, 211. Li, *Mao's Generals Remember Korea*, 216, 222.
27. Mao to Stalin, (Nov. 14, 1951). "Stalin to Mao, Politburo Decision with Approved Message."
28. Joy, *Negotiating While Fighting*, 191. Foot, *A Substitute for Victory*, 97.
29. Li, *Mao's Generals Remember Korea*, 188. "War and Disease," 43.
30. "Germ Warfare: The Lie That Won," 92. "Big Lie," 24.
31. "U.S. the New Hitler: USSR," 25. Lindesay Parrott, "Allies Accuse Foe of Outright Lying," 2.
32. "Germ Warfare: Forged Evidence," 22. Henry R. Lieberman, "Freed American Tells of Drugging."
33. Endicott and Hagerman, *United States and Biological Warfare*.
34. Cumings, *The Origins of the Korean War Volume II*, 753.
35. Endicott and Hagerman, *United States and Biological Warfare*.
36. Beria, "To G.M. Malenkov and to the Presidium of the CC CPSU. Question Regarding Soviet Role in Falsifying Evidence of American Biological Weapons."
37. Chang and Halliday, *Mao: The Unknown Story*, 376. See also Furmanski and Wheelis, "Allegations of Biological Weapons Use."
38. Bradbury, *Mass Behavior in Battle and Captivity*, 225.
39. Joy, *Negotiating While Fighting*, 319, 330, 343.
40. *FRUS 1952–1954*, 160.
41. Joy, *Negotiation While Fighting*, 350, 347, 342.
42. Benben, "Education of Prisoners of War on Koje Island."
43. *FRUS 1952–1954*, 15:161.
44. Hansen, *Heroes Behind Barbed Wire*, 18.
45. Joy, *Negotiating While Fighting*, 355. Benben, "Education of Prisoners of War," 170–71; Joy, *Negotiating While Fighting*, 365.
46. Benben, "Education of Prisoners of War," 170–71.
47. *FRUS 1952–1954*, 360.
48. *FRUS 1952–1954*, 15:183–84.
49. Joy, *Negotiating While Fighting*, 355.
50. *FRUS 1952–1954*, 15:192–93. Stelle to Nitze, (Jan. 24, 1952) box 20, PPS, found in Stueck, *Korean War*, 259.
51. Bradbury, *Mass Behavior in Battle and Captivity*, 317, 312, 337.
52. Weintraub, *War in the Wards*, (1964).
53. Ibid., 31, 38, 28, 29, 34.
54. Ibid., 26–27, 41–42, 5, 32.
55. Joy, *Negotiating While Fighting*, 365.
56. Bradbury, *Mass Behavior in Battle and Captivity*, 278, 280, 337.
57. John Osborne, "Cable."

58. *FRUS 1952–1954*, 15:146, 183. Joy, *Negotiating While Fighting*, 355.
59. *FRUS 1952–1954*, 15:370. Joy, *Negotiating While Fighting*, 361, 365, 364.
60. *FRUS 1952–1954*, 15:155–56.
61. Joy, *Negotiating While Fighting*, 367–68.
62. *FRUS 1952–1954*, 15:396, 402.
63. *FRUS 1952–1954*, 15:447.
64. Hansen, *Heroes Behind Barbed Wire*, 19.
65. Clark, *From the Danube to the Yalu*, 330.
66. *FRUS 1952–1954*, v. 15.
67. Connelly, "Notes on Cabinet Meeting," (Sept. 12, 1952), Connelly Papers, found in Bernstein, "The Struggle Over the Korean Armistice," 296.
68. Futrell, *United States Air Force in Korea*, 449–51.
69. Allen, *My Old Box of Memories*, 41. Clark, *Journey Through Shadow*, 218.
70. Crane, *American Airpower Strategy in Korea*, 168.
71. Clark, *Journey Through Shadow*, 408. *FRUS 1952–1954*, 15:469.
72. Halliday and Cumings, *Korea: The Unknown War*, 195.
73. Hermes, *Truce Tent and Fighting Front*, 432, 500.
74. *FRUS 1952–1954*, 15:1506.

## Chapter 6:   The Failure of Chinese Indoctrination

1. Young, *Oral Histories*.
2. Segal, "Factors Related to the Collaboration," 62, 34–37.
3. Kinkead, *In Every War But One*, 16.
4. Young, *Oral Histories*.
5. Army Pamphlet 30–101, 51.
6. Biderman, "Effects of Communist Indoctrination Attempts," 310. DeRosa, *Political Indoctrination in the U.S. Army*.
7. Biderman, "Effects of Communist Indoctrination," 308.
8. Rowley, *Korea POW*, 77.
9. Strassman, "A Prisoner of War Syndrome: Apathy as a Reaction to Severe Stress," 998. "City P.W. 'Played Dumb,' Beat Red Propagandists," 3.
10. Tomedi, *No Bugles, No Drums*, 230–31.
11. Young, *Oral Histories*.
12. Dower, *War Without Mercy* (1986).
13. Segal, "Factors Related to the Collaboration and Resistance," 73. Pate, *Reactionary*, 91. Jones, *No Rice for Rebels*, 59. Rowley, *Korea POW*, 62.
14. Pasley, *21 Stayed*, 134. Adams, *An American Dream*, 54.
15. "Ordeal by Captivity," 38. Colegrove, "They Weren't All Pros," 3.
16. "Briefing by HUMRRO," *Committee Documentation*, tab 15A:6. "Preliminary Findings on Army Prisoners by the Human Resources Research Office," *Committee Documentation*, tab 12:2.
17. Rowley, *Korea POW*, 64–65, 102.
18. The 1954 movie *Bamboo Prison* had a similar character.
19. MacGhee and Kalischer, "Tortured in Pak's Palace," 75. Other versions of Rotorhead appear in Funchess, *Korea POW*, 116; Clark, *Journey Through Shadow*, 283; and Peters and Li, *Voices from the Korean War*, 231.
20. "Back from Death Camps, POWs Rediscover Freedom," 29. Carlson, *Remembered Prisoners*, 45. Spiller, *American POWs in Korea*, 10. Funchess, *Korea POW*, 115. Rowley, *Korea POW*, 80. Lois Mitchison, AP (Dec. 15, 1955) untitled article found in DOJ Classified Subject Files 146-28-2259, box 150, RG 60.
21. MacGhee and Kalischer, "Tortured in Pak's Palace," 75. Funchess, *Korea POW*, 116.
22. Cline, "Wilbert Estabrook Interviewed."
23. Pate, *Reactionary-Revised 2000*, 122.
24. Young, *Oral Histories*.
25. Wang, *They Chose China*.

26. Lech, *Broken Soldiers*, 150. Rowley in Young, *Oral Histories*.
27. Hinkle and Wolff, "Communist Interrogation and Indoctrination," 118. Army Pamphlet 30–101, 51. Biderman, "The Image of Brainwashing," 552.
28. Lifton, *Thought Reform and the Psychology of Totalism*, 150, quoted in Gleason, *Totalitarianism: The Inner History of the Cold War*, 247. Gleason has an excellent chapter and bibliography on brainwashing.
29. Hearst, *Every Secret Thing*.
30. Kinkead, "Study of Something New in History," 114–53.
31. Editors, "Coercion: A Defense to Misconduct While a Prisoner of War." Hogan, *The Irish Soldiers of Mexico*. Kirkpatrick, "In '74 Thesis, the Seeds of McCain's War Views."
32. Daws, *Prisoners of the Japanese*, 307, 310, 99, 282, 261.
33. Allied Translator and Interpreter Section, "Japanese Methods of Prisoner of War Interrogation."
34. Daws, *Prisoners of the Japanese*, 316.
35. Masaharu and Kushner, " 'Negro Propaganda Operations.' "
36. Board of Editors, "Misconduct in the Prison Camp," 753.
37. Snyder, *A Soldier's Disgrace*, 119.
38. Endicott, *United States and Biological Warfare*, 162.

## Chapter 7:   The UNC Withholds POWs

1. "Status Report on Korea." Vetter, *Mutiny on Koje Island*, 19–23.
2. Burchett and Winnington, *Koje Unscreened*, 70. By other accounts, they were carrying trash (Peters, *Voices from the Korean War*, 254) or scrap canvas (Hermes, *Truce Tent*, 245).
3. Vetter, *Mutiny on Koje Island*, 136, 130.
4. Ibid., 200.
5. Clark, *From the Danube to the Yalu*, 33.
6. Fey, "Greatest Victory in Korea," 655.
7. Vetter, *Mutiny on Koje Island*, 169, 171, 139.
8. Vetter, *Mutiny on Koje Island*, 176. Clark, *From the Danube to the Yalu*, 64.
9. Vetter, *Mutiny on Koje Island*, 174. Hansen, *Heroes Behind Barbed Wire*, 95.
10. Boatner, "Prisoners of War for Sale," 39. Boatner, *Saga*, quoted in Zweiback, "The 21 Turncoat GIs," 354.
11. Arzac, "Intelligence Briefing by Dr. Carleton Scofield," quoted in Bernstein, "Struggle Over the Korean Armistice," 287.
12. Radio Peiping, "Concerning Repatriation of Chinese and North Korean POWs."
13. Weintraub, *War in the Wards*, 3. Zhai, *The Dragon, the Lion, and the Eagle*, 120–21.
14. "Canada Has Koje Sequel," 7. *FRUS* 15:309, 311.
15. Stueck, *Korean War*, 287, 306.
16. Li, *Mao's Generals Remember Korea*, 46.
17. *FRUS 1952–1954*, 15:59; 436.
18. Zhai, *The Dragon, the Lion, and the Eagle*, 131, 124. Foot, *Substitute for Victory*, 19.
19. Pasley, *21 Stayed*, 12. Toland, *In Mortal Combat*, 566–71. Mark Clark (July 2, 1953), quoted in Foot, *Substitute for Victory*, 186. Also Fehrenbach, *This Kind of War*, 446.
20. Hansen, *Heroes Behind Barbed Wire*, 145.
21. Ibid, 121, 145, 127, 122.
22. "Chiang Kai-shek's Letter to Anti-Communist PW's."
23. *South China Morning Post* (Aug. 24, 28, 1953), found in Foot, *Substitute for Victory*, 193. Hansen, *Heroes Behind Barbed Wire*, 107.
24. "Contingencies for the War in Korea."
25. Godel, "Psychological Warfare Operations During the Korean Conflict."
26. Ibid. *Heroes Behind Barbed Wire*, 300, 200, 152 164, 162.
27. Dayal, *India's Role in the Korean Question*, 197.
28. Hansen, *Heroes Behind Barbed Wire*, 133.
29. Clark, *From the Danube to the Yalu*, 284; also in Prasad, *History of the Custodian Force*, 22.
30. Hansen, *Heroes Behind Barbed Wire*, 149.

31. Ibid., 149, 154.
32. "U.N. Captives Plot Charged by Indian."
33. Hansen, *Heroes Behind Barbed Wire*, 145, 134. Georges Gallean, AFP.
34. Prasad, *History of the Custodian Force*, 69–70, 36.
35. Ibid., 23–4.
36. Prasad, *History of the Custodian Force*, 22–23, 95–96.
37. Dayal, *India's Role*, 196.
38. *The Hindu* (Oct. 11, 1953): 7, found in Dayal, *India's Role*, 225. Prasad, *History of the Custodian Force*, 44. Alden, "Korea Foe Delays P.O.W.'s Sessions."
39. Dayal, *India's Role*, 228, 212.
40. Prasad, *History of the Custodian Force*, 76.
41. Toland, *In Mortal Combat*, 592.
42. Prasad, *History of the Custodian Force*, 38, 40, 42.
43. Ibid., 25–26.
44. White, *Captives of Korea*, 286, 303, 294.
45. Prasad, *History of the Custodian Force*, 56.
46. FO 371/105597, (Dec. 23, 1953), PRO, found in Foot, *Substitute for Victory*, 194. Dayal, *India's Role in the Korean Question*, 214.
47. AP, "Neutrals, 3-2, Bar Reds' P.O.W. Plan." Foot, *A Substitute for Victory*, 194.
48. White, *Captives of Korea*, 280. Dayal, *India's Role*, 217. MacGregor, "3 Neutrals Rebel at Red 'Explaining.'"
49. "India Ignores Red Protest, Gives Allies Prisoners." Prasad, *History of the Custodian Force*, 52–53.
50. Ibid., 62. Dayal, *India's Role*, 256–57.
51. AP, "Fellow Captives of Reds Armed, Corporal Reveals."
52. Dayal, *India's Role*, 256.
53. NNRC, "Final Report of the Neutral Nations Repatriation Commission," 33.
54. Dayal, *India's Role*, 244. Hermes, *Truce Tent*, 515, 496.
55. See Chapter 5 of this volume, citations 51–56. Gross exchange numbers include Little Switch and NNRC escapes, taken from Hermes, *Truce Tent*, 514–15, plus 27,000 North Koreans held by President Rhee.
56. Heo, "North Korea's Continued Detention of South Korean POWs," 141–65.
57. Lee and Sang-jin, "The Plight of South Korean POWs." Kwanwoo, "N Korea Prisoner Demand Stuns Seoul."
58. West, "Interior Stories of the Chinese POWs," 180–82. Halliday and Cumings, *Korea*, 208; Millett, *Their War for Korea*, 137. Hermes, *Truce Tent*, 515.
59. Tucker, *Encyclopedia of the Korean War*, 43. Fehrenbach, *This Kind of War*, 414.
60. Alexander, *Korea*, 452. See also Sandler, *Korean War*, 212. Halberstam, *The Coldest Winter*, 624–25. Exceptions who cover forced defections include Foot, *A Substitute for Victory*, Bernstein, "Struggle Over the Korean Armistice," and Stueck, *The Korean War*.
61. Halberstam, *The Coldest Winter*, 624–25.
62. C. H. Peake, 695A.0024 (Dec. 1, 1952), RG 59, in Foot, *Substitute for Victory*, 109.
63. Joy, *Negotiating While Fighting*, 10. Nitze, "NSC 68," 27.
64. *FRUS 1952–1954*, 15:103.
65. Jolidon, *Last Seen Alive*.
66. US Department of State, "Agreement on Ending the War and Restoring Peace in Vietnam."

## Part Two-Chapter 8:   Home to Cheers and Jeers

1. MacArthur, "MacArthur Attacks 'Moral Deterioration,'" 76.
2. Wilson to Dulles (Feb. 19, 1953).
3. Young, "Proposal for Working-Level Plan on Problem of Brainwashed."
4. "D-41: Suggested Guidance for Public Aspects of U.S. Position on Korean Prisoner-of-War Talks."
5. "Some G.I. Captives May Seem Pro-Red."

6. Associated Press, "Ex-Captives, Called Dupes of Reds, Flown to California Amid Secrecy." Beezer, "Trip Report."
7. Brinkley, "Valley Forge GIs," 108. "Dupes" referenced in Beezer, "Trip Report."
8. Brinkley, "Valley Forge GIs," 108.
9. Fink, "To CINCFE Tokyo."
10. Brinkley, "Valley Forge GIs," 121.
11. Ibid., 108. Hayden, "Pass Buck on 'Brain Washing.'"
12. Davis, "Snafu at Valley Forge," 44. David Sentner, "Congressmen Demand Probe in Smear of PWs."
13. "Little Switch," 32. Brinkley, "Valley Forge GIs," 121.
14. Hayden, "Pass Buck on 'Brain Washing.'"
15. Jackson, "To Persons."
16. Craig, "To Godel." Stevens, "To Secretary of Defense."
17. Scofield, "Trip Report." Rogers, "Report of Special Ad Hoc Committee for Korean Captured U.S. Personnel."
18. "National Operations Plan."
19. Clark, "The U.S. Army Welcomes Home United Nations Personnel."
20. UP, "Tight Censorship of freed POWs."
21. "Assess the Problems of Alleged Divergent Actions," *Committee Documentation,* tab 15b.
22. Pate, *Reactionary!* 124. Spiller, *American POWs in Korea,* 16. Segal, "Initial Psychiatric Findings of Recently Repatriated Prisoners of War," 358.
23. Polk, *Ex-Prisoners of the Korean War,* 72. Edwards, *The Korean War,* 166.
24. Notable example: Segal, "Factors Related to the Collaboration and Resistance Behavior."
25. "Lucy Once Registered to Vote Red."
26. Letters, WHCF, box 2503, Prisoners (1) (1953). AP, "PWs Say Pro-Red GIs Return to Propagandize," 3.
27. WHCF, box 2503, Prisoners (1) (1953).
28. *NYT* (March 19, 1954): 1–13.
29. AP, "PWs Blast GIs." "Bitter GIs Out to 'Get' Informers Among PWs." "Buying That Red Stuff." "The Rats."
30. Snyder, *A Soldier's Disgrace,* 119. Biderman, "Effects of Communist Indoctrination Attempts," 306.
31. Malwitz, "Ex-POW Shares Horror of Ordeal in Korean War," 6. Young, *Oral Histories.*
32. "City P.W. 'Played Dumb,' Beat Red Propagandists," 3. Palmer, "The War for the P.O.W.'s Mind," 39, 42
33. Reinhardt, "Frame-Up, Communist Style," 36
34. Beech, "Censorship is Strict at Inchon." UP, "Tight Censorship of Freed POWs." Clark, "The U.S. Army Welcomes Home United Nations Personnel."
35. "Returning Prisoners Tell of Threats."
36. Rogin, "Kiss Me Deadly," 29.
37. "Possible Courses of Action Desirable or Necessary to Satisfy Public Concern," tab 15b:4 *Committee Documentation.*
38. Johnson and Winebrenner, *Captive Warriors,* 235.
39. Robert Alden, "Freed U.N. Captives Tell of Cruelties on 'Death Marches.'" AP, "Clark Charges Reds Still Hold Yank PWs."
40. Whelan, *Drawing the Line,* 331. "Information Agency Sends Out Story by Radio as First Big Project."
41. AP, "P.W. Flyers Reveal Torture by Reds," 2.
42. "What About Reds Among Freed U.S. Prisoners?" 21.
43. Radio Peiping, "American POWs Give Reason Why they Refuse to Go Home."
44. Wills, *Turncoat,* 63.
45. Woerheide and Keeney, "Korean POW Project, Alleged Violations of Treason and Related Statutes."
46. Pasley, *21 Stayed,* 232, 236. Randolph, "POWs Fear Death If They Leave."
47. Prugh, "Justice for All RECAP-K's," 18.
48. "Gov's Radio Appeal," 4.

49. "Parents of 23 GIs," 4.
50. Connolly, "Decisions Come Hard for GI Who Changed His Mind."
51. Prugh, "Justice for All RECAP-K's," 18.
52. "Legion Favors Sending Mothers to GIs," 5.
53. "For the Press."
54. CINCUNC to DEPTAR, CX-65249.
55. "Why Some GIs Stay with Reds," 40.
56. WHTO, Incoming (Sept. 26, 1953), box 104, Mothers to Korea (Oct. 1953).
57. WHTO, Incoming (Oct. 1953), boxes 166–67, Mothers to Korea, Record of Telegrams.
58. WHTO, Incoming (Sept. 26, Oct, 2, 1953), box 104, Mothers to Korea.
59. DEPTAR to CINCFE, DA-473043.
60. CINCUNC to DEPTAR, CX-65249.
61. OCB Minutes (Dec. 9, 1953).
62. Wills, *Turncoat*, 56.
63. AP, "Army Lists P.W. Camp's 'Squealers.'"
64. Wills, *Turncoat*, 78, 67.
65. Pasley, *21 Stayed*, 236.
66. "One Who Won't Return," 27.
67. Pasley, "21 American GIs," 40.
68. Pasley, *21 Stayed*, 1, 53, 238, 243.
69. Ibid., 81.
70. Lech, *Broken Soldiers*, 243.
71. Pasley, *21 Stayed*, 37, 45, 67, 165.
72. Molloy, "Memphis Boy in Foes Hands Turned from American Ideals."
73. "Press and Radio Conference #25," 8.

## Chapter 9:   The Brainwashing Dilemma

1. Marilyn B. Young, "Hard Sell," 113–39. "Korea: The 'Forgotten' War," 21.
2. Lippmann, *The Method of Freedom*, 25, 91–97.
3. More on Lippmann: Gary, *The Nervous Liberals*.
4. Lippmann, *Public Opinion*, 87.
5. Nitze, "NSC-68," 81, 54. Bernhard, "Clearer Than Truth," 563.
6. Osgood, "Form Before Substance," 413, 410, 414.
7. "Draft PCIIA Report."
8. "Exploitation of Soviet, Satellite, and Chinese Communist Psychological Vulnerabilities Before and During the Eighth U.N. General Assembly."
9. Craig, "Subjects for Possible UN Exploitation."
10. Lilly, "Notes for a General Policy Approach to the Lodge Project."
11. Norberg, "Minutes POW Working Group."
12. "National Operations Plan to Exploit Communist Bacteriological Warfare Hoax."
13. Mayo, "Press Release No. 1786."
14. "Information Agency Sends Out Story." Theodore C. Streibert, "U.S. Indictment in the U.N. General Assembly of Communist Treatment of POWs." Miller, "Brainwashing," 50.
15. AP, "Lodge's UN Talk On Red Atrocities." Norberg, "Minutes POW Working Group."
16. "Evidence Supporting the Exclusion of Communist China from the UN."
17. "Puzzlement in the Pentagon," 162. Baldwin, "The Prisoner Issue."
18. Norberg to Enyart. McIlvaine to Norberg.
19. Godel, "Dept. of Army Plan for Exploiting Communist Mistreatment of U.S. Prisoners of War." "Communist Mistreatment of United States Prisoners of War."
20. "Red Murder of 6,000 GI's Finally Angers Us!" 10. "Communist Mistreatment of United States Prisoners of War."
21. Godel, "Dept. of Army Plan." "National Operations Plan," tab B.
22. Bergin to Commanding Generals. Board of Editors, "Misconduct in the Prison Camp," 730.

23. Norberg, "Minutes POW Working Group." MacGhee and Kalischer, "Some of Us Didn't Crack." Norberg, "Meeting of the POW Working Group."
24. Dean, "My Three Years as a Dead Man," 104.
25. Norberg, "Implementation of the National Plan to Exploit Communist BW Hoax."
26. Ulman, "The GI's Who Fell for the Reds," 17–9.
27. Norberg, "Diorama." "Draft Proposal for a Libel Suit." Norberg, "Minutes POW Working Group."
28. Norberg, "Meeting of the POW Working Group." Norberg, "Army Report on Communist-Inspired Atrocities in Korea." "Why They Mourn," 26–27.
29. "Stage Production of The Breaking Point."
30. Norberg, "Exploitation of Communist Atrocities." Norberg, "Minutes POW Working Group."
31. Norberg, "Minutes POW Working Group." Muller, "Potter Report Shocks Senate." "Potter to Push Quiz Into the Fate of PWs."
32. Especially fanciful was Meerloo, "Pavlovian Strategy as a Weapon of Menticide," 595.
33. Hunter, " 'Brain-Washing' Tactics," 2.
34. "Hearings Regarding H.R. 16742," 7581. Marks, *Search for the 'Manchurian Candidate,* 125, 223.
35. Marks, *Search for the Manchurian Candidate,* 126.
36. Taylor, *Brainwashing: The Science of Thought Control,* 6.
37. Hunter, *Brainwashing in Red China,* 4.
38. Marks, *Search for the Manchurian Candidate,* 125. Schein, *Coercive Persuasion,* 16; Kuo, *Comprehensive Glossary of Chinese Communist Terminology.*
39. Hunter, *Brainwashing, From Pavlov to Powers,* 3, 4.
40. Hunter, *Brainwashing in Red China,* 4, 6, 9.
41. Brooks, "Research at Bethesda." Miller, "Brainwashing: Present and Future," 50.
42. Meerloo, "Pavlovian Strategy as a Weapon of Menticide," 809, 813. Hunter, *Brainwashing, From Pavlov to Powers,* 4.
43. Restrained example: Leviero, "For the Brainwashed: Pity or Punishment?"
44. Hunter, *Brainwashing in Red China,* 9.
45. Wilson, *Man in the Gray Flannel Suit.*
46. Gleason, *Totalitarianism,* 93, 103.
47. Small, "The Brainwashed Pilot," 31.
48. Slotkin, *Regeneration Through Violence,* (1973).
49. "Korea Atrocity Film Issued For TV After 3-Week Ban." AP, "Clark Charges Reds Still Hold Yank PWs." Clark, *From the Danube to the Yalu,* 298.
50. Mayo, "Press Release No. 1786."
51. Norberg, "Meeting of the POW Working Group." "Abandoned Americans."
52. July 20, 1954 *Tribune* mentioned in "American Personnel Rumored to Be in Communist Custody." Cole, *POW/MIA Issues,* 226–31.
53. Lawrence, Opinion. UP, "Reds Deny GIs Held," 6. Cole, *POW/MIA Issues,* 238–39.
54. Burns, "MIA Efforts Risk 'Total Failure.' " Kristof, "Reports of American P.O.W.'s in North Korea Persist."
55. Early mention of 944: AP, "Red P.W.'s Who Changed Minds Twice Go Back to North Korea," 2. Norberg, "Minutes POW Working Group."
56. Pelton, *Dead or Alive*; Jolidon, *Last Seen Alive.*
57. McIlvaine to Norberg, (Sept. 11, 1953) PSB box 26, 383.6 (5).
58. Enyart to Jackson; refers to Oct. 28, 1953 *Washington Evening Star.*
59. "National Operations Plan," tab B.
60. Woerheide and Keeney, "Korean POW Project, Alleged Violations of Treason and Related Statutes."
61. Abel, "6 Testify Germ War 'Confessor' Seemed to Be Not in Right Mind," 1.
62. Sam Stavisky, " 'Menticide' Defined At Schwable Trial." Young, "Too Severe, General Says." "Schwable Freed, but is Criticized," 16.
63. AP, "Schwable Getting Desk Job." "Is It a Crime to Crack Up?" 39. UP, "President' View on 'Confessions.' "

64. Leviero, "For the Brainwashed: Pity or Punishment?" 12. Hunter, "Frame-Up, Communist Style," 36.
65. "Possible Courses of Action," tab 15b, *Committee Documentation*.
66. "Is It a Crime to Crack Up?" 41. "Epilogue to the Germ Hoax," B4.

## Chapter 10:  Prosecutions Rile the Nation

1. Johnson and Winebrenner, *Captive Warriors*, 286, 119, 189, 217. Davis, *Long Road Home*, 541.
2. Lone exception Robert Garwood was a special case who stayed with the Vietnamese until 1979, well beyond the Nixon administration's anodyne welcome of returned POWs. He was dishonorably discharged without back pay. Doyle, *Voices from Captivity*, 209–11.
3. "Present Policies on Standards of Conduct," *Committee Documentation*, tab 15a. "Armored Force Cartoons Tell U.S. Soldiers How to Act If Captured," 122.
4. "Courses of Action Desirable or Necessary to Satisfy Public Concern," *Committee Documentation*, tab 15b:5.
5. Carlson, *Remembered Prisoners*, 220. "Status of United States Programs for National Security."
6. Bergin, "RECAP-K Policy." McManus to Adjutant General. Brucker,"RECAP-K Policy."
7. Hoover to Attorney General. Young, *Oral Histories*.
8. Spiller, *American POWs in Korea*, 111. Woerheide and Keeney, "Korean POW Project, Alleged Violations," 3.
9. Riesel, "Brainwashing Still Affects Former POWs." Dickenson trial transcripts, quoted in Lech, *Broken Soldiers*, 193. Ulman, "GIs Who Fell for the Reds," 17.
10. "75 Individuals Who Allegedly Returned to the United States as Trained Agents of Communist Espionage."
11. Chang, *Mao: The Unknown Story*, 377.
12. "75 Individuals," enclosure B, 2–3.
13. Lech, *Broken Soldiers*, 185. In his defense, Lech was undoubtedly unaware of the "75 Individuals" memo.
14. AP, "Some POWs Face Trial." Colegrove, "Army is Probing the Conduct of 3600 U.S. POWs in Korea." Board of Editors, "Misconduct in the Prison Camp," 735.
15. Norberg, "Minutes POW Working Group." AP, "Army Lists P.W. Camp's 'Squealers.'" "Armed Forces: A Line Must Be Drawn," 16.
16. Russell, "For the Prisoners Who Broke," 52. "POWs to Face Ouster If They Collaborated."
17. "Ex-P.O.W. Assails 'Kangaroo' Trial." Pearson, "Unidentified Accusers."
18. UP, "Curb on POW Aid by Army Studied." Lewis, "Claims Unit Finds Korean G.I. Data."
19. Prugh, "Justice for All RECAP-K's," 20.
20. Pasley, *21 Stayed*, 236. AP, "15 Ex-Prisoners Ousted by Army."
21. AP, "Dickenson House Topic" (Jan. 26, 1954; Jan. 27, 1954) clip found in: WHCF, box 102, 3-M D, OF-3M.
22. AP, "Hannah Backs Army Action on Dickenson." Elie Abel, "Eisenhower Urges Tolerance for G.I." AP, "Draft Board Member Quits Over Dickenson."
23. Leviero, "For the Brainwashed: Pity or Punishment?" 16. "Quality of Mercy is Strained by Rank," 603.
24. Gallup, "'Germ Warfare' Signers Should Not Be Punished, Public Says."
25. *Army Times* (Dec. 12, 1953): 6. "Stephen S. Jackson," *Committee Documentation*, tab 15b:2.
26. Sherman Adams, "Letters to the President Referred to the Department of Defense."
27. Prugh, "Justice for All RECAP-K's," 20.
28. Board of Editors, "Misconduct in the Prison Camp," 738.
29. Ibid., 758n., 355. Lech, *Broken Soldiers*, 272.
30. Propaganda conviction: UP, "Colonel Guilty in P.O.W. Trial."
31. Lech, *Broken Soldiers*, 246.
32. Prugh, "Justice for all RECAP-Ks," 18. Board of Editors, "Misconduct in the Prison Camp," 728n., 129.
33. Snyder, *A Soldier's Disgrace*, 188, 62.

34. *Committee Documentation,* tab 5.
35. James E. Godwin, "JAG Memorandum." "Minutes" (March 16, 1956).
36. "Final Report of Ad Hoc Board."
37. Green and McRae to Hall, "Referral by Department of the Army of POW Cases for Prosecution."
38. Woerheide and Keeney, "Korean Prisoner of War Cases." Tompkins to Milton, (June 24, 1957): 2, DOJCSF 146-28-2259 box 151.
39. Woerheide and Keeney, "Korean POW Project," 9. Woerheide (Aug. 8, 1957).
40. Tompkins to Attorney General, "Korean Prisoner of War Cases."
41. Tompkins to Milton (Nov. 12, 1957).
42. Woerheide and Keeney, "Korean POW Project," 6–12.
43. Board of Editors, "Misconduct in the Prison Camp," 782 n., 547.
44. Thompson, *True Colors,* 4.

## Chapter 11:   Target Mom

1. Loosbrock, "Target: Mom," 91.
2. Norberg, "Implementation of the National Plan." Ulman, "The GI's Who Fell for the Reds," 64.
3. Pate, *Reactionary!* Defense Advisory Committee on Prisoners of War, "Code of Conduct Program: First Progress Report." The report included the newspaper clipping by Pate, "Hardest Thing I Ever Had to Do."
4. Young, *Oral Histories.*
5. Gilbert, *Men in the Middle,* 4. Look editors, *Decline of the American Male,* 3–5, 12.
6. "Services Divided on POW Policy," 12. "POWs to Face Ouster If They Collaborated."
7. "The Study of Something New in History," 114–53. "Have We Let Our Sons Down?" 23.
8. Riggs, "Bi-Monthly Report on Status of the Code." Kinkead, "To the Editor," 8.
9. Kinkead, *In Every War But One,* 30, 15–16. Army Security Center, *U.S. Prisoners of War,* 23; Segal, "Factors Related to the Collaboration and Resistance Behavior," 41.
10. "Interrogation Reports of Personnel Returned to Military Control in Operation Little Switch."
11. Leckie, *Conflict,* 389. Similar claims: Bryant, *Khaki-Collar Crime,* 346; Thomis, "How Reds Brainwashed Korea GIs," 10. Favorable escape stories: Blair, *Beyond Courage.*
12. UPI, "General Upholds U.S. Fighting Men," 14. Marshall, "Big Little War," 24.
13. "Communist Interrogation and Indoctrination Methods on Prisoners other than United States," *Committee Documentation,* tab 14. Burgess and Hull, "Press Briefing on Prisoner of War Indoctrination Report."
14. "Briefing by Henry A. Segal," *Committee Documentation,* tab 15a. Carlson, *Remembered Prisoners,* 8, 155.
15. Pincher, *Traitors,* 156.
16. Mayer, "Mind Control."
17. "Briefing by HUMRRO," *Committee Documentation,* tab 15a. Howe, *Valley of Fire,* 159. Ulman, "GI's Who Fell for the Reds," 64.
18. Kupperman, "Apathy and Death in Early Jamestown," 29. Ritchie, "Psychiatry in the Korean War," 902.
19. White, *Captives of Korea,* 86.
20. Ibid., 13. "Briefing by William F. Dean," *Committee Documentation,* tab 15a.
21. "Briefing by Gallery," *Committee Documentation,* tab 15a:5. Sander and Biderman, "Recommendations of Returned USAF Prisoners of War," iii.
22. "Present Policies on Standards of Conduct," *Committee Documentation,* tab 15a. "Services Divided on POW Policy," 12. Young, *Oral Histories.*
23. Nowicki and Muller, "McCain Profile." Schanberg, "McCain and the POW Cover-Up." Kirkpatrick, "In '74 Thesis, the Seeds of McCain's War Views."
24. Trumbull, "G.I.'s in Far East Get Captive Code," 19. Mayer, "Mind Control."
25. Mayer, "Mind Control." Thomis, "How Reds Brainwashed Korea GIs." Mayer, "Mind Control."

26. Ibid. Greenway, "Cracked Record on the Campus," 302. Mayer, *Brainwashing, Drunks & Madness.*
27. Wylie, *Generation of Vipers,* 216, 199, 195. Wylie, "Down With Women! Up With Men!"
28. Box 244(2) Wylie Papers.
29. Wylie, "Down With Women! Up With Men!"
30. Williams, *Klaus Fuchs, Atom Spy,* 153.
31. Carlson, *Remembered Prisoners,* 222.
32. Pollini, *Night,* 103.
33. Lynn, *Turncoat,* 36, 39, 33. More examples of incest in Korean POW fiction: Skomra, *Behind the Bamboo Curtain,* 103; Thorin, *A Ride to Panmunjom,* 37; Steffano, "Nightmare."
34. Rogin, "Kiss Me Deadly," 1–36.
35. "Korea: The Sorriest Bunch," 40. "Armed Forces: A Line Must Be Drawn," 16.
36. Cuordileone, *Manhood and American Political Culture,* 64, 28.
37. *Committee Documentation,* "Memo for the Chairman," tab 3. "Presentation to Secretary of Defense," tab 13.
38. "Presentation to the Secretary of Defense" Part II, *Committee Documentation,* tab 13.
39. "Review of the Ives Committee Report," *Committee Documentation,* tab 15a.
40. "Present Policies on Standards of Conduct," *Committee Documentation,* tab 15a.
41. Marshall, "The Code and the Pueblo," 74.
42. Secretary of Defense's Advisory Committee, *POW,* 39.
43. Prugh, "Code of Conduct for the Armed Forces," 706.
44. Burgess, "Prisoners of War," 676.
45. Secretary of Defense's Advisory Committee, *POW,* 18, 32.
46. Defense Advisory Committee, "Code of Conduct Program: First Progress Report." "G.I.'s in Far East Get Captive Code," 19.
47. Defense Advisory Committee, "Code of Conduct Program: Second Progress Report." Wilson, "To James C. Hagerty."
48. Defense Advisory Committee, "Code of Conduct Program: Third Progress Report." Milton to Chief of Staff, "Pow Code of Conduct." "Code of Conduct Program: First Progress Report."
49. Hoganson, *Fighting for American Manhood.*
50. "Footnote to the Photos;" also "This Strange Business of 'Hardening' By Torture."

## Chapter 12: Missing Action

1. A version of this chapter was previously published as "Missing Action: POW Films, Brainwashing and the Korean War, 1954–1968" in *Historical Journal of Film, Radio and Television.*
2. On Pentagon cooperation see Suid and Culbert, *Film and Propaganda in America;* Shaw, *Hollywood's Cold War.*
3. *The Great Escape; Man at Large; Stalag 17; Von Ryan's Express; The McKenzie Break; Missing in Action.*
4. *King Rat* is a splendid exception. Set in the Pacific war, it does not address collaboration with the enemy, but it is about masculine vulnerability.
5. "Defense Dept. Won't Back Film," 8.
6. *Harrison Reports,* "War Atrocities Pic Limited in Appeal," 3. Knight, *Saturday Review,* 24.
7. Bucklin, *National Parent-Teacher,* 40. Other "documentary" references: Philip T. Hartung, "Screen," *Commonweal,* 15; Harrison, Library of Congress Motion Picture Clip File; *Estimates,* Library of Congress (undated, spring 1954).
8. Walsh, *America,* 229.
9. Knight, *Saturday Review,* 24.
10. "POW Film Denied Army Publicity Aid," 24. "Defense Dept. Won't Back Film on Germ War Issue," 8.
11. Binford to Schooley, (March 23, 1955) box 1, acc.: 59-A949, OASD(PA), WNRC-S. Found in Suid and Culbert, *Film and Propaganda in America, 1945 and After,* 274.

12. CINFO directive.

13. *Estimates* (Nov. 18, 1954) Library of Congress motion picture clip-file. Bucklin, *National Parent-Teacher*; quoted in Suid and Culbert, *Film and Propaganda*, 274–75.

14. Baruch to Louis Shurr.

15. Smith, *Looking Away: Hollywood and Vietnam*, 215.

16. Knight, *Saturday Review*, 47. Kass, *Catholic World*, (April 1954):145. McCarten, "Cinema," *New Yorker*, (Nov. 17, 1956): 102.

17. Hatch, "Films," *Nation*, (Nov. 24, 1956): 467. "Anatomy of Treason," *Newsweek* (June 4, 1956): 99.

18. Board of Editors, "Misconduct in the Prison Camp," 773n., 478.

19. Bassett, *Films in Review*, 463. "Morals of War," *Newsweek* (Oct. 28, 1957): 104.

20. Hatch, "Films," *Nation*, (Nov. 9, 1957): 332.

21. "Service Actions on Repatriated Korean Prisoners of War," *Committee Documentation*, tab 13 II:5.

22. Crowther, "Screen: The Manchurian Candidate," 3:48. Moira Walsh, *America*, 1158.

23. *The Three Stooges Go Around the World in a Daze.*

24. Thompson, "Sergeant Ryker's Back," 2:56.

25. Sanitizing of combat is ubiquitous, for example the censorship of casualty photographs during World War II. See Hallin, *Uncensored War*.

26. Gruner, *Prisoners of Culture*. Franklin, *M.I.A. or Mythmaking in America*.

27. "Jessica Lynch Condemns Pentagon." AP, "Hospital Staff: Forceful U.S. Rescue Operation for Lynch Wasn't Necessary." Kampfner, "The Truth About Jessica." Bragg, *I Am a Soldier, Too*.

## Chapter 13:   The Hidden Reason for Forgetting Korea

1. Some content has already appeared in Young, "POWs: The Hidden Reason for Forgetting Korea," 317–32.

2. Eisenhower, "President's Message to the Nation on the Signing of the Korean Armistice."

3. Halberstam, *Coldest Winter*, 2. "Korea: The 'Forgotten' War," 21. *Army Times* quoted in Kolb, 'Korea's "Invisible Veterans,"' 27.

4. Sandler, *The Korean War: No Victors, No Vanquished*.

5. Piehler, *Remembering War the American Way*, 157.

6. Nitze, "NSC 68," 43.

7. Found in Bernhard, *U.S. Television News and Cold War Propaganda*, 83. Eisenhower, "President's Message to the Nation."

8. Casey, *Selling the Korean War*, 279–93.

9. DOPS (Jan. 24, 1952), found in Casey, *Selling the Korean War*, 285.

10. Browne, "The Strategic Significance of Involuntary PW Repatriation in Korea."

11. Stelle to Nitze, "Alternative Courses of Action on POW Problem."

12. Barrett to Mathews, "Korean Prisoners of War."

13. *FRUS 1952–1954*, 15:715.

14. "Memorandum on Recent Polls on Korea."

15. Wilson to Dulles.

16. Taquey to Irwin, "Prisoners Who Chose Freedom."

17. *NYT* (July 23, 1952).

18. Barrett, "Van Fleet Says Foe Spurns Armistice." Schumach, "Admiral Joy Finds Relief in a Game."

19. Parrot, "Enemy Sees Crisis in Truce Parleys." Hoffman, "Prospect of Truce Dim, U.N. Aide Holds."

20. Barrett to Mathews, "Korean Prisoners of War." *FRUS 1952–1954*, 15:103.

21. Bernstein, "Struggle Over the Korean Armistice," 296–97.

22. "Weekly Summary of Opinion on Far East."

## Conclusion: Two Wars

1. Young, *Oral Histories*.
2. Wade, "A Peek Into the Remarkable Mind."
3. *FRUS 1952–1954*, 15:200. "Koje Generals," 52.
4. *FRUS 1952–1954*, 15:56. Joy, *How Communists Negotiate*, 160.
5. Sang-Hun, "Unearthing War's Horrors."
6. Clark, *From the Danube to the Yalu*, 51, 36.
7. Mayo, "Press Release No. 1786."
8. "National Operations Plan," tab B. McIlvaine to Norberg.
9. Mrozinski, "Board Action of 3 July 1956 Regarding POW Status Report." Corso to Staats; White, *Captives of Korea*, 113.
10. Cole, *POW/MIA Issues*, 237–39.
11. Johnson, *Sorrows of Empire*, 78. Pierpaoli, *Truman and Korea*, 9.
12. Wittner, "How Much Is Enough? America's Runaway Military Spending."
13. Johnson, *Sorrows of Empire*, 4–5, 189.
14. Found in Sherry, *In the Shadow of War*, 235. Eisenhower, "Farewell Address."

# BIBLIOGRAPHY

## Archival Series and Papers

22nd U.S. Army Prisoner of War/Civilian Internee Information Center, Archives II.
Adjutant Generals Office (AGO) RG 407, NARA Suitland.
Boatner, Haydon L. Papers. Hoover Institution, Stanford University, California.
Command Reports 1949-54, AGO CR, 407.3; NARA Suitland, Maryland.
Confidential File (CF), Eisenhower Library.
Department of Justice Classified Subject Files (DOJCSF) RG 60, Archives II.
Jackson, C.D. Papers, Eisenhower Library.
Judge Advocate General, RG 153, Archives II.
Lawton, William S. Papers, Carlisle Barracks, Pennsylvania.
McCardle, Carl W. Papers, Eisenhower Library.
National Security Council Staff Papers 1948-61, Eisenhower Library.
Operations Coordinating Board Central Files (OCB), within NSC Staff Papers, Eisenhower Library.
Pearson, Ralph E. Papers, U.S. Army Military History Research Collection, Carlisle Barracks.
President's Committee on International Information Activities (PCIIA) aka Jackson Committee, Eisenhower Library.
President's Secretary Files (PSF), Truman Library.
PSB Central Files, part of NSC Staff Papers 1948-61, Eisenhower Library.
Records of the Executive Office, RG 330 Office of the Secretary of Defense, National Records Center, Suitland, Maryland.
Records of the Office of the Assistant Chief of Staff, G-3, Operations 1943-58, RG 319, Archives II.
Records of the Office of the Provost Marshal General, 1920–1975, RG 389, Archives II.
RG 338, *nota bene*: this record group has been broken up by the National Archives. Documents listing it may have been reassigned to new groups.
Schooley, C. Herschel Papers, Eisenhower Library.
Staff Member and Office Files (SMOF), Truman Library.
White House Central Files (WHCF), Eisenhower Library.
White House Office Files (WHO), Eisenhower Library.
White House Office Files, Office of the Special Assistant for National Security Affairs, 1952–61, Subject Subseries (WHO OSANSA SS), Eisenhower Library.
White House Telegraph Office (WHTO), Eisenhower Library.
Whitman, Ann File, Papers as President of the United States, 1952–1961 (WF), Eisenhower Library.
Winslett, Edmund J. Papers, U.S. Army Military History Research Collection, Carlisle Barracks.
Wylie, Philip F. Papers, C0059, Firestone Library, Princeton.

216 *Bibliography*

## Libraries and Archival Depositories

Archives II, aka National Archives at College Park, Maryland.
Carlisle Barracks, The U.S. Army Military History Research Collection, Carlisle, Pennsylvania.
Cold War Information Project, Virtual Archive, Korean War, http://wilsoncenter.org.
Eisenhower Library, Abilene, Kansas.
Library of Congress, Washington, DC.
Motion Picture and Television Reading Room, Library of Congress.
National Archives at College Park, Maryland, aka Archives II.
Truman Library, Independence, Missouri.
Washington National Records Center, Suitland, Maryland.

## Web

Beria, L. P. "To G. M. Malenkov and to the Presidium of the CC CPSU. Question Regarding Soviet Role in Falsifying Evidence of American Biological Weapons" (April 24, 1953); Cold War International History Project, Virtual Archive, Korean War http://wilsoncenter.org.

Brown, Lynnita. "Archie Edwards, Korean War Educator Memoirs" (Museum Assoc. of Douglas County [Illinois] Korean War Project, 1996), www.koreanwar-educator.org.

Cline, David. "Wilbert Estabrook Interview" (American Radio Works 2003), www.americanradioworks.publicradio.org.

Haynes, William J. White House General Counsel to Secretary of Defense, "Counter Resistance Techniques" (Nov. 27, 2002), http://en.wikisource.org/wiki/Haynes_Memo_of_Nov_27,_2002.

Hess, Jerry N. "Oral History Interview with John J. Muccio" (February 18, 1971). Truman Library, www.trumanlibrary.org/oralhist/muccio2.htm.

Kim, Young Sik. "Eyewitness: A North Korean Remembers," www.johndclare.net/cold_war10_YoungSKim.htm.

Stalin, Joseph. "Stalin to Mao, Politburo Decision with Approved Message" (Nov. 19, 1951) APRF, Fond 3, Opis 65, Delo 828 [9], Listy 42-43 and AVPRF, Fond 059a, Opis 5a, Delo 5, Papka 11, List 64. Found at: Cold War Information Project, Virtual Archive, Korean War, http://wilsoncenter.org.

Turse, Nick. "Empire of Bases 2.0," www.Tomdispatch.com (Jan. 9, 2011).

Wittner, Lawrence S. "How Much Is Enough? America's Runaway Military Spending" (Aug. 16, 2010) History News Network, www.hnn.us/articles/130258.html.

Yoo, John. "U.S. Dept. of Justice, Deputy Assistant Attorney General John Yoo To Alberto R. Gonzales, White House Counsel" (Aug. 1, 2002), http://news.findlaw.com/wp/docs/doj/bybee80102ltr.html.

Zedong, Mao. "Mao to Stalin" (Nov. 14, 1951), APRF, Fond 45, Opis 1, Delo 342, Listy 16-19. Cold War Information Project, Virtual Archive, Korean War, http://wilsoncenter.org.

## Film

*The Bamboo Prison*, Lewis Seiler, Columbia, US, 1954.
*The Great Escape,* John Sturges, United Artists, US, 1963.
*King Rat*, Bryan Forbes, Columbia, US, 1965.
*Man at Large,* Eugene Forde, Twentieth Century Fox, US, 1941.
*The Manchurian Candidate,* John Frankenheimer, M.C. Productions, US, 1962.
*The McKenzie Break*, Lamont Johnson, United Artists, US, 1970.
*Missing in Action,* Joseph Zito, Cannon, US, 1984.
"Nightmare," *The Outer Limits,* John Erman, ABC, US, 1963.
*The Rack*, Arnold Laven, MGM, US, 1956.
*Prisoner of War*, Andrew Marton, MGM, US, 1954.
*Sergeant Ryker*, Buzz Kulik, Universal, US, 1967.
*Stalag 17,* Billy Wilder, Paramount, US, 1953.

*They Chose China*, Shui-Bo Wang, National Film Board of Canada, 2005.
*The Three Stooges Go Around the World in a Daze,* Norman Maurer, Columbia, US, 1963.
*Time Limit,* Karl Malden, United Artists, US, 1957.
*Von Ryan's Express,* Mark Robson, Twentieth Century Fox, US, 1965.


## Archival Documents

"75 Individuals Who Allegedly Returned to the United States as Trained Agents of Communist Espionage" (Feb. 25, 1959) AGO CCAF, box 344, 383.6.
Adams, Sherman. "Letters to the President Referred to the Department of Defense," WHCF, box 2504, prisoners (2).
Allied Translator and Interpreter Section, Research Report, "Japanese Methods of Prisoner of War Interrogation," SCAP, box 11, 1946, RG 338.
"American Personnel Rumored to Be in Communist Custody" (Jan. 4, 1954) AG, box 252, 383.6, RG 407.
Army Pamphlet 30-101. *Communist Interrogation, Indoctrination, and Exploitation of Prisoners of War* (May 1956), box 19, 22nd US Army Prisoner of War/Civilian Internee Information Center, RG 338, Archives II.
Arpin to Eisenhower (April 19, 1953), WHCF, box 2503, Prisoners (1).
Arzac, Daniel N. Jr. "Intelligence Briefing by Dr. Carleton Scofield" (March 12, 1953), PSB, box 26, 383.6 (1).
Barrett, Edward W. To Mathews, "Korean Prisoners of War" (Feb. 4, 1952), PA Asst SecState Memos, box 2, RG 59.
Baruch, Donald E. To Louis Shurr Agency (March 18, 1954), entry 133, 062.2, OPI, Motion Picture Section, box 135, RG 330.
Beezer, Robert H. "Trip Report: Valley Forge General Hospital" (May 1953), PSB, box 26, 383.6 (2).
Bergin, William E. To Commanding Generals, "Re: Communist Treatment of United States Prisoners of War" (Sept. 9, 1953) AGO, box 4025, 383.6.
——. "RECAP-K Policy" (March 15, 1954): pt. II, AGO, box 4025, 383.6.
Boatner, Haydon L. "Mistakes Made with POW Under 2D Log Command," 22nd US Army POW/CI Information Center, box 19(4), RG 338.
——. *Saga* (Aug. 1963), Boatner Papers, box 1, Koje file, Hoover Institution.
——. To Hoover Institution, "POWs in Asia" (Dec. 5, 1975), Boatner Papers, Hoover Institution.
Bradley, Omar N. "To Secretary of Defense, Policy on Repatriation of Chinese and North Korean Prisoners" (Aug. 8, 1951), SMOF-PSB, box 32, 383.6.
Briggs, Ellis O. "Telegram 604 to Secretary of State" (Dec. 31, 1953), OCB, box 117, 383.6 (5).
Browne, Mallory. "The Strategic Significance of Involuntary PW Repatriation in Korea" (Feb. 1952), SMOF-PSB, box 32, 383.6.
BRSRK, "Minutes," JAG, box 1, v. 1.
Brucker, Wilber M. "RECAP-K Policy" (Sept. 23, 1958), AGO, box 4026, 383.6.
Burgess, Carter L. and John E. Hull, "Press Briefing on Prisoner of War Indoctrination Report" (Aug. 17, 1955): 23, C. Herschel Schooley Papers, box 4, IV (3).
Carroll, Wallace. "Gordan Gray, Repatriation of Prisoners of War" (Dec. 28, 1951), SMOF-PSB, box 32, 383.6.
"Chiang Kai-shek's Letter to Anti-Communist PW's" (July 30, 1953), William S. Lawton Papers, Articles and News Releases from Korea, Korean Prisoner Repatriation Newspapers, 1953–1954.
CINCUNC to DEPTAR, CX-65249 (Sept. 28, 1953), AGO CDF 1953-54, box 4025, 383.6.
CINFO directive (Dec. 15, 1954) AGO, 062.2, entry 363, box 14.
Clark, Mark W. "The U.S. Army Welcomes Home United Nations Personnel" (July 1953), CR AGO, Munsan-Ni Command, box 867, Operation Big Switch.
*Committee Documentation of the Secretary of Defense's Advisory Committee on Prisoners of War* (July 1955), AFPDF 1942–1954, box 441, 383.6 336, RG 341.

"Communist Mistreatment of United States Prisoners of War" (Oct. 23, 1953), AGO 383.6, 9, box 4025, RG 407.

"Communist War in POW Camps: the Background of Incidents Among Communist Prisoners in Korea" (Jan. 28, 1953), FEC, 091.411, RG 389.

"Contingencies for the War in Korea." (June 1953), box 4 Korea (2), C. D. Jackson Records.

Corso, Col. Philip. To Staats (July 2, 1956), OCB, box 118, 383.6(2).

Craig, Horace S. To William H. Godel, "Brain-Washing," PSB, box 29, 702.5 (2).

———. "Subjects for Possible UN Exploitation" (April 28, 1953), OCBS, box 4, Lodge's Human Rights Project.

"D-41: Suggested Guidance for Public Aspects of U.S. Position on Korean Prisoner-of-War Talks" (April 3, 1953), PSB, box 26, 383.6 (2).

Davis. "Special POC Meeting of 16 May" (May 20, 1952), SMOF-PSB, box 32, 383.6.

Defense Advisory Committee on Prisoners of War. "Code of Conduct Program: First Progress Report" (Dec. 1955), WHO OSANSA SS, box 2, Code of Conduct (3).

———. "Second Progress Report" (March 1956).

———. "Third Progress Report" (Dec. 1956).

DEPTAR to CINCFE, DA-473043 (Dec. 11, 1953), box 4025, AGO CDF 383.6.

"Draft PCIIA Report" (May 6, 1953), PCIIA, 1950-1953, box 12 (11).

"Draft Proposal for a Libel Suit" (Oct. 27, 1953), PSB, box 26, 2 (4).

Eisenhower, Dwight D. "President's Message to the Nation on the Signing of the Korean Armistice" (July 26, 1953), Series I Conference and Trip Files, box 1, Korean Truce Negotiations, McCardle Papers.

———. "Farewell Address" (Jan. 17, 1961). www.ourdocuments.gov

Enyart, Byron K. To C.D. Jackson (Oct. 29, 1953), PSB, box 26, 2 (6).

"Evidence Supporting the Exclusion of Communist China from the UN," OCB, box 7, 091 China File 2 (9), 1954.

"Exploitation of Soviet, Satellite, and Chinese Communist Psychological Vulnerabilities Before and During the Eighth U.N. General Assembly" (May 28, 1953), OCBS, box 4, Lodge's Human Rights Project.

Fechteler, William M. Joint Chiefs of Staff to the Secretary of Defense (Oct. 15, 1951), SMOF-PSB, box 32, 383.6.

———. "State-Defense Conference on Korean Armistice Negotiation" (Sept. 17, 1952), PSF, box 243.

"Final Report of Ad Hoc Board" (May 21, 1958), BRSRK, box 1, v. 1.

Fink, J. L. "To CINCFE Tokyo," DA 935630 CX 61741 (1953) OSD, box 34, 383.6.

"For the Press" (Sept. 30, 1953), WHCF, box 822, Non-Repatriated Prisoners of the Korean War, 154-H.

Gallean, Georges. Undated AFP story stapled to "Telegram 604 to Secretary of State" (Dec. 31, 1953) OCB, box 117, 383.6 (5).

Godel, William H. "Dept. of Army Plan for Exploiting Communist Mistreatment of U.S. Prisoners of War" (Sept. 4, 1953), PSB, box 26, 383.6 (4).

———. "Psychological Warfare Operations During the Korean Conflict" (Sept. 17, 1953), WHOF, box 26, 383.6 (6).

Godwin, James E. "JAG Memorandum" (March 16, 1956), BRSRK, JAG, box 1, v. 1.

Green, Dorothy F. and Ernest McRae. To Thomas K. Hall, "Referral by Department of the Army of POW Cases for Prosecution" (Nov. 5, 1954), DOJ CSF 146-28-2259, box 149.

"Hearings Regarding H.R. 16742: Restraints on Travel to Hostile Areas," Committee on Internal Security (Sept. 19 and 25, 1972).

Hess, Jerry N. "Oral History Interview with John J. Muccio," Feb. 18, 1971, Truman Library, www.trumanlibrary.org/oralhist/muccio2.htm.

Highsmith, Patricia. To Philip Wylie, box 244(2), Wylie Papers.

International Committee of the Red Cross. *Third Geneva Convention: Relative to the Treatment of Prisoners of War* (1949), www.icrc.org.

Jackson, C.D. To Persons (May 11, 1953), WHCF, PCIIA, box 50.

Hoopes, Townsend. "The Role of the Defense Department in the Cold War" (Feb. 26, 1953), WHCF PCIIA, box 11(2).

Hoover, J. Edgar. To the Attorney General (March 15, 1954), DOJ CSF 146-28-2259, box 149.

"Interrogation Reports of Personnel Returned to Military Control in Operation Little Switch, 1953," box 1, Records of International and U.S. Military Commands in the Pacific, AGO, G-1.

Joint Chiefs to Johnson, "NSC 74—A Plan for National Psychological Warfare" (Aug. 1, 1950), PCIIA, box 11.

Lilly, Edward P. "Notes for a General Policy Approach to the Lodge Project" (July 22, 1953), OCBS, box 4, Lodge's Human Rights Project (2).

Mayo, Charles W. "Press Release No. 1786" (Oct. 26, 1953), PSB, box 26, 2 (5).

McClure, Robert A. To Army Chief of Staff, "Policy on Repatriation of Chinese and North Korean Prisoners" (July 5, 1951), G-3, 383.6, RG 319, Archives II.

McIlvaine, Robinson. To Norberg (Sept. 11, 1953), PSB, box 26, 383.6 S.

McManus, G. H. To Adjutant General (May 24, 1955), AGO, box 4026, 383.6.

"Measures Required to Achieve U.S. Objectives with Respect to the USSR" (March 30), *FRUS* 1949, 1:276.

"Memorandum for the Executive Officer" (March 16, 1955), OCB, box 118, 383.6 File 2 (1).

"Memorandum on Recent Polls on Korea," box 4, Korea (3), June 2, 1953, C.D. Jackson Records, 1953–1954.

Mickelwait, C. B. "Referral of Prisoner of War Cases to Department of Justice" (Dec. 2, 1955), AG CCAF, box 88.

Milton, Hugh M. To Chief of Staff, United States Army, "Pow Code of Conduct" (Feb. 24, 1958), AGO General Correspondence, box 439, 383.6.

Mrozinski, R. V. "Board Action of 3 July 1956 Regarding POW Status Report," OCB, box 118, 383.6(2).

Muccio, John J. *See* Jerry N. Hess.

NNRC. "Final Report of the Neutral Nations Repatriation Commission" (Feb. 20, 1954), Unclassified Series, box 18 (8), RG 338, 22nd US Army POW/CI Information Center.

"National Operations Plan to Exploit Communist Bacteriological Warfare Hoax, Mistreatment of Prisoners of War, and Other Atrocities Perpetrated by Communist Forces During the Korea War" (Oct. 14, 1953), PSB, box 26, 2 (4).

Norberg, Charles R. "Army Report on Communist-Inspired Atrocities in Korea" (Oct. 22, 1953), PSB, box 26, 383.6 2(4).

———. "Implementation of the National Plan to Exploit Communist BW Hoax" (Oct. 28, 1953), PSB box 26, 383.6.

———. "Diorama" (Jan. 28, 1954), OCB, box 118, 383.6 (7).

———. To Enyart (Sept. 15, 1953), PSB, box 26, 383.6 (6).

———. "Exploitation of Communist Atrocities" (Oct. 6, 1953), PSB, box 26, 383.6.

———. "Implementation of the National Plan to Exploit Communist BW Hoax" (Oct. 28, 1953), PSB box 26, 383.6.

———. To Kenneth Hansen (Sept. 8, 1953), PSB, box 26, 383.6 (4).

———. "Meeting of the POW Working Group" (various dates), PSB, box 26, 383.6, 2(3).

———. "Minutes of the POW Working Group," OCB, box 117, 383.6 (1).

———. "OCB Briefing Note on Plan for Exploiting Communist Mistreatment of UN Prisoners of War" (Sept. 23, 1953), PSB, box 26, 383.6 (7).

OCB Minutes, NSC, box 11, OCB 337.

Osborne, John. "Cable" (approximately June 1, 1953), box 4, Korea (3), C.D. Jackson Records.

———. *Dispatch* 44 (May 30, 1953): 27, box 4, Korea (3), C.D. Jackson Records.

———. "Personal and Confidential," stapled to Jackson to Smith (May 26, 1953), box 4, Korea (3), C.D. Jackson Records.

Peterson, A. Atley. "The Role of the Defense Department in the Cold War, Section II" (Feb. 26, 1953), PCIIA, box 11 Folder (2).

"Petitions," box 205, 383.6, G-3 Army Operations, RG 319.

POW Korea Collaboration Literature, box 13, 22d US Army Prisoner of War/Civilian Internee Information Center, RG 338, Archives II.

Project TROY Report to the Secretary of State. General Records of the Secretary of State, Vol. 1, ix, Lot file 52-283, 1951, RG 59. Found in Allan A. Needell, "'Truth is Our Weapon:' Project

TROY, Political Warfare, and Government-Academic Relations in the National Security State," *Diplomatic History* 17:3 (Summer 1993): 399–420.

"Press and Radio Conference #25" (Jan. 27, 1954), Press Conference Series, WF, 8, box 1.

"PSB Staff Study on Repatriation of Prisoners of War in Korea" (Oct. 18, 1951), SMOF-PSB, box 32, 383.6.

Radio Peiping. "Concerning Repatriation of Chinese and North Korean POWs" (Aug. 18, 1952), G-2 Reports, Japanese Liaison, box 2, binder 1, Winslett Papers.

——, "American POWs Give Reason Why they Refuse to Go Home" (Sept. 24. 1953), G-2 Reports, Japanese Liaison, Concerning Repatriation of Chinese and North Korean POWs, box 2 (2), Winslett Papers.

Report of Boards of Officers-POW Division, Register of Prisoner of War and Civilian Internee Incident Investigation Case Files, FEC G-1, box 1, Records of General Headquarters, Far East Command, Supreme Commander Allied Powers, and United Nations Command, Headquarters U.S. Army Forces Far East, 1952–1957, RG 554.

Ridgway, Gen. Matthew B. To JCS, (April 29, 1952), 6:04 and 11:15 p.m., *FRUS, 1952–1954*, 15:183–84.

Riggs, T.S. "Bi-Monthly Report on Status of the Code of Conduct Program" (Dec. 12, 1955), G-3, box 270, 383.6, RG 319.

Rogers, Henry H. "Report of Special Ad Hoc Committee for Korean Captured U.S. Personnel," (May 8, 1953), PSB, box 26, 383.6 (3).

Sander, Herman J. and Albert D. Biderman. "Recommendations of Returned USAF Prisoners of War on Resisting Enemy Interrogation," Air Force Personnel & Training Research Center: 1957, box 19, RG 338.

Scofield, Carleton F. "Trip Report: Valley Forge General Hospital" (May 1953), PSB, box 26, 383.6 (2).

"Stage Production of The Breaking Point" (May 27, 1954), OCB, box 118; 383.6 (8).

"Status Report on Korea," *Armed Forces Talk 434* (Feb. 2, 1953), Newspapers and News Releases, William S. Lawton Papers.

"Status of United States Programs for National Security" (Dec. 31,1954), Office of the Special Assistant for National Security Affairs Records, NSC Series 1952–1961, box 3, NSC 5509 (8).

Stelle, Charles C. To Nitze, "Alternative Courses of Action on POW Problem" (Jan. 28, 1952), PPS Korea, box 20, RG 59.

——. To Nitze, (Jan. 24, 1952), box 20, PPS, RG 59. Found in Stueck, *Korean War,* 259.

Stevens, Robert T. "To Secretary of Defense: Report of Special Ad Hoc Committee for Korean Captured U.S. Personnel" (June 10, 1953), PSB, box 26, 383.6 (3).

Streibert, Theodore C. "U.S. Indictment in the U.N. General Assembly of Communist Treatment of POW's" (Oct. 26, 1953), PSB, box 26, 2(4).

Taquey, Charles H. To Wallace Irwin, Jr., "The Prisoners Who Chose Freedom" (Aug. 20, 1954), OCB, box 118, 383.6.

Tompkins, William F. To Attorney General, "Korean Prisoner of War Cases" (June 11, 1957), DOJCSF 146-28-2259, box 151.

——. To Hugh M. Milton (June 24, 1957), DOJCSF 146-28-2259, box 151.

——. To Hugh M. Milton (Nov. 12, 1957) DOJCSF 146-28-2259, box 151.

"Transcripts and Related Records Pertaining to Radio Peking Broadcasts Made by U.S. Prisoners of War," G-2, Japanese Liaison Section, 1951–1953, box 1.

"U.S. Army Welcomes Home United Nations Personnel." AGO CR, 1953, Korea, box 867, Operation Big Switch, RG 407.

US Department of State. "Agreement on Ending the War and Restoring Peace in Vietnam," *Department of State Bulletin* (Feb. 12, 1973).

"U.S. Policies, from the Psychological Strategy Standpoint, Governing the Exchange of Prisoners of War and Repatriation of North Korean and Chinese Nationals" (Oct. 2, 1951), SMOF-PSB, box 32, 383.6.

"Weekly Summary of Opinion on Far East" (July 23–29, 1953), WHCF OF, 154-G-4, box 821.

Wilson, Charles E. To Dulles (Feb. 19, 1953), WHCF CF, box 29, PSB 7025.

——. To James C. Hagerty (Aug. 3, 1955), Central Files, OF 3-JJ-1, box 111, 3PP Defense Advisory Committee.

Woerheide, Victor C. and John C. Keeney. "Korean POW Project, Alleged Violations of Treason and Related Statutes" (June 3, 1957), 12, box 151, DOJCSF 146-28-2259.

——. "Korean Prisoner of War Cases" (Aug. 8, 1957), box 151, DOJCSF 146-28-2259.

Wylie, Philip. "Down With Women! Up With Men!" (undated manuscript written for *True* magazine), box 122, Wylie Papers.

——. "The Sissification of America" (undated), 9, box 140 (2), Wylie Papers.

Young, Charles S. *Oral Histories of Korean War POWs* (2009), asc.: 30425101424417, Magale Library, Southern Arkansas University.

Young, Millard C. "Proposal for Working-Level Plan on Problem of Brainwashed U.S. and Other U.N. Prisoners of War" (April 10, 1953), PSB, box 29, 702.5 (2).

### Articles in Journals and Periodicals

"15 Ex-Prisoners Ousted by Army." *NYT* (Oct. 24, 1954).

"12,000 to Join Chiang Forces." *NYT* (April 2, 1954): 8.

"A Complete Account," *Time* (Aug. 28, 1950): 45.

"A Line Must Be Drawn." *Time* (Aug. 29, 1955): 16.

"Abandoned Americans." *Chicago Tribune* (April 22, 1954).

Abel, Elie. "6 Testify Germ War 'Confessor' Seemed to Be Not in Right Mind," *NYT* (Feb. 20, 1954).

——. "Eisenhower Urges Tolerance for G.I," *NYT* (Jan. 28, 1954).

Alden, Robert. "Freed U.N. Captives Tell of Cruelties on 'Death Marches,' " *NYT* (April 22, 1953).

——. "Korea Foe Delays P.O.W.'s Sessions," *NYT* (Oct. 11 1953).

"Anatomy of Treason," *Newsweek* (June 4, 1956): 99.

Anderson, Clarence L. et al. "Medical Experiences in Communist POW Camps in Korea," *Journal of the American Medical Association* 156:2 (Sept. 11, 1954).

"Armed Forces: A Line Must Be Drawn," *Time* (Aug. 29, 1955): 16.

"Armored Force Cartoons Tell U.S. Soldiers How to Act If Captured," *Life* (Oct. 5, 1942): 122.

Associated Press. "Army Lists P.W. Camp's 'Squealers,' " *NYHT* (Jan. 30, 1954).

——. "Clark Charges Reds Still Hold Yank PWs," *Detroit News* (Feb. 3, 1954).

——. "Collins Warns Foe of Bigger Bombing," *NYT* (July 16, 1952).

——. "Curtain on War News," *Philadelphia Inquirer* (Jan. 9, 1951).

——. "Dickenson House Topic," *Baltimore Sun* (Jan. 26, 1954).

——. "Draft Board Member Quits Over Dickenson," *Washington Post* (May 7, 1954).

——. "Ex-Captives, Called Dupes of Reds, Flown to California Amid Secrecy," *NYT* (May 2, 1953).

——. "Fellow Captives of Reds Armed," *San Francisco Chronicle* (Jan. 1, 1954).

——. "Hannah Backs Army Action on Dickenson," *Baltimore Sun* (Jan. 25, 1954).

——. "Hospital Staff: Forceful Rescue of American POW Unnecessary," *USA Today* (May 28, 2003).

——. "India Ignores Red Protest, Gives Allies Prisoners," *Washington Post* (Jan. 20, 1954).

——. "Lodge's UN Talk On Red Atrocities," *Boston Herald* (Dec. 1, 1953).

——. "Neutrals, 3-2, Bar Reds' P.O.W. Plan," *NYT* (Nov. 23 1953).

——. "Noel Knew One of 23," *San Francisco Chronicle* (Sept. 25, 1953): 5.

——. "PW Flyers Reveal Torture by Reds," *NYHT* (Aug. 21, 1953): 2.

——. "PWs Blast GIs Who Aided Reds," *NYHT* (Aug. 12, 1953): 3.

——. "PWs Say Pro-Red GIs Return to Propagandize," *NYHT* (Aug. 11, 1953): 3.

——. "Red MIG-15 Jet Lands Near Seoul," *Louisville Courier* (Sept. 21, 1953).

——. "Red PWs Who Changed Minds Twice Go Back to North Korea," *Louisville Courier Journal* (Sept. 13, 1953): 2.

——. "Schwable Getting Desk Job," *NYHT* (May 12, 1954).

——. "Some POWs Face Trial," *NYT* (Aug. 16, 1953).

"Back from Death Camps, POWs Rediscover Freedom," *Newsweek* (Aug. 17, 1953): 29.

Baldwin, Hanson W. "The Prisoner Issue–III," *NYT* (Jan. 28, 1954).

Barrett, George. "Van Fleet Says Foe Spurns Armistice," *NYT* (May 6, 1952).

Bassett, John M. *Films in Review* (Nov. 1957): 463.

Bauer, Raymond A. and Edgar H. Schein, eds. "Brainwashing, Special Issue," *The Journal of Social Issues* 13:3 (1957).

Beebe, Gilbert W. "Follow-Up Studies of World War II and Korean War Prisoners, II: Morbidity, Disability, and Maladjustments," *American Journal of Epidemiology* 101:5 (1975): 400–22.

Beech, Keyes. "Censorship is Strict at Inchon," *Chicago Daily News* (Aug. 11, 1953).

Benben, John S. "Education of Prisoners of War on Koje Island, Korea," *Educational Record* 36 (April 1955): 157–73.

Bernhard, Nancy E. "Clearer Than Truth: Public Affairs Television and the State Department's Domestic Information Campaigns, 1947–1952," *Diplomatic History* 21:4 (Fall 1997): 545–68.

Biderman, Albert D. "Effects of Communist Indoctrination Attempts," *Social Problems* 6 (Spring 1959): 304–13.

——. "The Image of Brainwashing," *Public Opinion Quarterly* 26 (Winter 1962): 547–63.

"Big Lie," *Time* (May 19, 1952): 24.

"Bitter GIs Out to 'Get' Informers Among PWs" *NYHT* (Aug. 14, 1953): 3.

Board of Editors, "Misconduct in the Prison Camp: A Survey of the Law and an Analysis of the Korean Cases," *Columbia Law Review* 56 (May 1956).

Boatner, Haydon L. "Prisoners of War for Sale," *American Legion Magazine* (Aug. 1962): 39.

Brinkley, William. "Valley Forge GIs Tell of Their Brainwashing Ordeal," *Life* (May 25, 1953): 108–24.

Brooks, Charles G. "Research at Bethesda May Shed New Light on 'Brainwashing' by Reds," *Washington Star* (March 9, 1956).

Bucklin, Mrs. Louis L. *National Parent-Teacher* 48 (Dec. 1954): 39.

——. *National Parent-Teacher*, 48 (May 1954): 40.

Burgess, Carter L. "Prisoners of War," *Columbia Law Review* 56 (May 1956): 676.

Burns, Robert. "MIA Efforts Risk 'Total Failure,'" *AP Impact* (July 8, 2013).

"Buying That Red Stuff," *NYHT* (Aug. 6, 1953): 6.

"Canada Has Koje Sequel," *NYT* (Oct. 8, 1952): 7.

Choe Sang-Hun. *See* Sang-Hun.

"City PW 'Played Dumb,' Beat Red Propagandists," *NYHT* (Aug. 31, 1953): 3.

Colegrove, Albert M. "AF Freed Officer Who Persuaded GIs U.S. Used Germ War," *Washington Daily News* (May 11, 1954): 3.

——. "Army is Probing the Conduct of 3600 U.S. POWs," *Washington Daily News* (April 14, 1954).

——. "They Weren't All Pros," *Washington Daily News* (Oct. 2, 1954): 3.

Connolly, John. "Decisions Come Hard for GI Who Changed His Mind," clip in Sept. 16, 1953 folder, Pearson Papers. Newspaper: *Star*, probably Washington.

"Court Frees Provoo of Treason Charges," *NYT* (Oct. 18, 1955).

Crenson, Sharon L. and Martha Mendoza, AP, "6 of 21 Who Defected After Korean War Now Live Quietly in U.S," *Milwaukee Journal Sentinel* (April 7, 2002).

Crowther, Bosley. "Screen: The Manchurian Candidate," *NYT* (Oct. 25, 1962): 48:3.

Davis, Jamie. "Prisoner of Korean War Shares Story of Capture," *El Dorado Arkansas News-Times* (Nov. 10, 2007).

Davis, R. J. "Snafu at Valley Forge," *Newsweek* (May 18, 1953): 44.

Dean, William F. "My Three Years as a Dead Man," *Saturday Evening Post* (Feb. 27, 1954): 104.

"Death Skims Road in U.S. Jets' Dives," *NYT* (Dec. 10, 1950).

"Defense Dept. Won't Back Film on Germ War Issue," *NYHT* (Mar. 20, 1954): 8.

Editors. "Coercion: A Defense to Misconduct While a Prisoner of War," *Indiana Law Journal* 29 (1954): 607.

"Epilogue to the Germ Hoax," *Washington Post* (Sept. 13, 1953): B4.

Evans, A.M. *Army Times* (Dec. 12, 1953): 6.

"Ex-P.O.W. Assails 'Kangaroo' Trial," *NYT* (Feb. 8, 1956): 20.

Fay, Elton C. "Army Silent On Brainwash Idea's Origin," *Washington Post* (May 6, 1953).

Feather, Carl E. "Life on Prison Island: Local Veteran Took a Risk," *Ashtabula, OH Star Beacon* (June 21, 2010).

Fey, Harold E. "Greatest Victory in Korea, A Review Article," *Christian Century* (May 22, 1957): 655.

"Footnote to the Photos," *New York Post* (Sept. 9, 1955).

Ford, Douglas C. To *Army Times* (Dec. 12, 1953): 6.

Freeman, John. "Talking with: Ha Jin," *Milwaukee Journal Sentinel* (Nov. 21, 2004).

Gallean, Georges. Undated AFP story stapled to "Telegram 604 to Secretary of State" (Dec. 31, 1953), OCB box 117, 383.6 (5).

Gallup, George. " 'Germ Warfare' Signers Should Not Be Punished, Public Says," *Public Opinion News Service* (Feb. 21, 1954).

Gawande, Atul. "Hellhole," *New Yorker* (March 30, 2009), www.newyorker.com.

"Germ Warfare: Forged Evidence," *Time* (Nov. 9, 1953): 22.

"Germ Warfare: The Lie That Won," *Fortune* (Nov. 1953): 92.

"G.I.'s in Far East Get Captive Code," *NYT* (Aug. 12, 1956): 19.

"GIs Freed by Reds Tell of Good Care," *Philadelphia Inquirer* (Nov. 24, 1950).

"Gov's Radio Appeal: Come Home," *Washington Post* (Oct. 4, 1953): 4.

Greenway, John. "Cracked Record on the Campus," *Nation* (Nov. 10, 1962): 302.

Gutteridge, J. A. "The Repatriation of Prisoners of War," *The International and Comparative Law Quarterly* 2 (Jan. 1953): 207–16.

Hanley Charles J. and Martha Mendoza, AP. "U.S. Policy Was to Shoot Korean Refugees," *Washington Post* (May 29, 2006).

Harlow, Harry F., I.E. Farber and Louis Jolyon West. "Brainwashing, Conditioning, and DDD," *Sociometry* 20 (Dec. 1957): 271–85.

*Harrison Reports*, Library of Congress, Motion Picture and Television Reading Room clip file.

Hartung, Philip T. "Screen," *Commonweal* (April 9, 1954): 15.

Hatch, Robert. "Films," *Nation* (Nov. 24, 1956): 467.

———. "Films," *Nation* (Nov. 9, 1957): 332.

Hayden, Martin S. "Pass Buck on 'Brain Washing,'" *Detroit News* (May 8, 1953).

Heo, Man-ho. "North Korea's Continued Detention of South Korean POWs," *The Korean Journal of Defense Analysis* 14:2 (Fall 2002): 141–65.

Hoffman, Michael L. "Prospect of Truce Dim, U.N. Aide Holds," *NYT* (June 4, 1952).

Hinkle, Lawrence and Harold Wolff. "Communist Interrogation and Indoctrination of 'Enemies of the State'—An Analysis of Methods Used by the Communist State Police," *AMA Archives of Neurology and Psychiatry* 76:2 (Aug. 1956): 117–74.

Hughes, John. "Reds Letters Aim at Hearts of Fliers' Kin," *New York Sunday News*, (Feb. 15, 1953).

Hunter, Edward. " 'Brain-Washing' Tactics Force Chinese Into Ranks of Communist Party," *Miami Sunday News* (Sept. 24, 1950): 2.

———. "Frame-Up, Communist Style," *Army Combat Forces Journal* (Oct. 1953): 36.

"Information Agency Sends Out Story by Radio as First Big Project Under New Plan," *NYT* (Oct. 30, 1953).

"Is It a Crime to Crack Up?" *USNWR* (Feb. 26, 1954): 39.

"Jessica Lynch Condemns Pentagon," *BBC News* (Nov. 7, 2003).

Kampfner, John. "The Truth About Jessica," *Guardian* (May 15, 2003).

Karsten, Peter. "The American Democratic Citizen Soldier: Triumph or Disaster?" *Military Affairs* (Spring 1966): 34–40.

Kass, Robert. *Catholic World* (May 1956): 145.

Kinkead, Eugene. "Have We Let Our Sons Down?" *McCall's* (Jan. 1959): 23.

———. "To the Editor," *The Reporter* (April 16, 1959): 8.

———. "The Study of Something New in History," *New Yorker* (Oct. 26 1957): 114–53.

Kirkpatrick, David D. "In '74 Thesis, the Seeds of McCain's War Views," *NYT* (June 15, 2008).

Knight, Arthur. *Saturday Review* (April 17, 1954): 24.

———. *Saturday Review* (May 19, 1956): 47.

"Koje Generals: Clark is Cleaning Up Mess," *USNWR* (May 23, 1952): 52.

Kolb, Richard K. "Korea's 'Invisible Veterans' Return to an Ambivalent America," *VFW* (Nov. 1997): 24–26.

"Korea Atrocity Film Issued For TV After 3-Week Ban," *NYHT* (Jan. 29, 1954).

"Korea: The 'Forgotten' War: Casualties Rise—No End to Conflict in Sight," *USNWR* (Oct. 5, 1952): 21.

"Korea: The Sorriest Bunch," *Newsweek* (Feb. 8, 1954): 40.

Kristof, Nicholas D. "Reports of American P.O.W.'s in North Korea Persist," *NYT* (Sept. 8 1996).

Kristol, Irving. "The Shadow of a War," *The Reporter* (Feb. 5, 1959): 41.

Kupperman, Karen Ordahl. "Apathy and Death in Early Jamestown," *Journal of American History* 66:1 (June 1979): 24–40.

Kwanwoo, Jun. "N Korea Prisoner Demand Stuns Seoul," *The Standard* (Jan. 9, 2006).

Lawrence, David. "Opinion," *NYHT* (Jan. 20 1954).

Lee, Brian and Kim Sang-jin. "The Plight of South Korean POWs," *JoongAng Daily* (Sept. 9, 2009).

"Legion Favors Sending Mothers to GIs," *San Francisco Chronicle* (Sept. 28, 1953): 5.

Leviero, Anthony. "For the Brainwashed: Pity or Punishment?" *NYT* (Aug. 14, 1955): 7:12.

——. "Services Divided on POW Policy," *NYT* (March 8, 1955): 12.

Lewis, Anthony. "Claims Unit Finds Korean G.I. Data," *NYT* (June 17, 1956).

Lieberman, Henry R. "Freed American Tells of Drugging With 'Truth Medicine' in China," *NYT* (July 12, 1952).

Lifton, Robert J. "Home by Ship: Reaction Patterns of American Prisoners of War Repatriated from North Korea," *American Journal of Psychiatry* 110 (April 1954): 732–39.

"Little Switch," *Time* (May 4, 1953): 32.

Loosbrock, John F. "Target: Mom," *Reader's Digest* (May 1953): 91.

"Lucy Once Registered to Vote Red," *Louisville Times* (Sept. 12, 1953).

MacArthur, Douglas. "MacArthur Attacks 'Moral Deterioration,'" *USNWR* (June 22, 1951): 76.

MacGhee, David F. and Peter Kalischer. "Some of Us Didn't Crack," *Colliers* (Jan. 22, 1954).

——. "Tortured in Pak's Palace," *Colliers* (Feb. 5, 1954): 75.

MacGregor, Greg. "3 Neutrals Rebel at Red 'Explaining,'" *NYT* (Nov. 8, 1953).

Malwitz, Rick. "Ex-POW Shares Horror of Ordeal in Korean War," *New Brunswick Home News Tribune* (July 28, 2003): 6.

Mansourov, Alexandre Y. "Stalin, Mao, Kim, and China's Decision to Enter the Korean War," *Cold War International History Project Bulletin* 6 (Winter 1995): 105.

Marshall, S.L.A. "Big Little War," *Army* (June 1960): 24.

——. "The Code and the Pueblo," *Air Force and Space Digest* (July 1969): 74.

Masaharu, Sato and Barak Kushner. "'Negro Propaganda Operations:' Japan's Short-Wave Radio Broadcasts for World War II Black Americans," *Historical Journal of Film, Radio and Television* 19:1 (Jan. 1999): 5–26.

Mayer, William E. "Mind Control." Undated sound recording from the mid-1950s to early 1960s. Available online.

McCarten, John. "Cinema," *New Yorker* (Nov. 17, 1956): 102.

Meerloo, Joost A. M. "The Crime of Menticide," *American Journal of Psychiatry* 107 (1951): 594–98.

——. "Pavlovian Strategy as a Weapon of Menticide," *American Journal of Psychiatry* 110 (May 1954): 809–13.

Miller, James G. "Brainwashing: Present and Future," *The Journal of Social Issues* 13 (1957): 48–55.

Millett, Allan R. "War Behind the Wire: Koje-Do Prison Camp," *Military History Quarterly* (Winter 2009), www.historynet.com.

"Misconduct in the Prison Camp," *Columbia Law Review* 56 (May 1956).

Mitchison, Lois. Untitled, AP (Dec. 15, 1955), found in DOJ Classified Subject Files 146-28-2259, box 150, RG 60.

Molloy, Paul. "Memphis Boy in Foes Hands Turned from American Ideals," *Commercial Appeal* (Sept. 13, 1953).

Moore, Jason Kendall. "Between Expediency and Principle: U.S. Repatriation Policy Toward Russian Nationals, 1944-1949," *Diplomatic History* 24:3 (Summer 2000): 381–404.

"Morals of War," *Newsweek* (Oct. 28, 1957): 104.

Muller, Will. "Potter Report Shocks Senate With Details of War Atrocities," *Detroit News* (Jan. 10, 1954).

Needell, Allan A. "'Truth is Our Weapon:' Project TROY, Political Warfare, and Government-Academic Relations in the National Security State," *Diplomatic History* 17:3 (Summer 1993): 399–420.

Norman, Lloyd. " 'Lightning Joe' Talks," *Army* (June 1960).

Nowicki, Dan and Bill Muller. "McCain Profile," *The Arizona Republic* (March 1, 2007).

"One Who Won't Return," *Time* (Oct. 26, 1953): 27.

"Ordeal by Captivity," *Newsweek* (May 11, 1953): 38.

Osgood, Kenneth A. "Form Before Substance: Eisenhower's Commitment to Psychological Warfare and Negotiations with the Enemy," *Diplomatic History* 24:3 (Summer 2000): 405–33.

Palmer, C. B. "The War for the P.O.W.'s Mind," *NYT Magazine* (Sept. 13, 1953).

"Parents Of 23 GIs Who Chose To Stay Have Our Sympathy, But Men Are Deserters and Traitors," *Knoxville Journal* (Sept. 26, 1953): 4.

Parrott, Lindesay. "Allies Accuse Foe of Outright Lying," *NYT* (May 19, 1952): 2.

——. "Enemy Sees Crisis in Truce Parleys," *NYT* (June 6, 1952).

Pasley, Virginia. "21 American GI's Who Chose Communism," *USNWR* (July 15, 1955).

Pate, Lloyd. "Hardest Thing I Ever Had to Do," *Washington Daily News* (Oct. 10, 1955).

Pearson, Drew. "Unidentified Accusers," *Washington Post* (June 17, 1956).

"Peiping Claims UN Reprisals Against POWs for Germ Confessions," *NYT* (May 19, 1952): 2.

Peters, William. "When the Army Debunks the Army," *Encounter* (July 1960): 78.

"Potter to Push Quiz Into the Fate of PWs," *Detroit News* (Jan. 17, 1954).

"POW Film Denied Army Publicity Aid," *NYT* (Mar. 18, 1954): 24.

"POWs to Face Ouster If They Collaborated," *Evening Star* (Oct. 28, 1953).

Priest, Dana and William M. Arkin. "Top Secret America," *Washington Post* (July 19, 20, 21 2010).

Prugh, George S. "The Code of Conduct for the Armed Forces," *Columbia Law Review* 56 (May 1956): 678–707.

——. "Justice for All RECAP-K's," *Army Combat Forces Journal* (November 1955): 15–26.

——. "Prisoners at War: The POW Battleground," *Dickinson Law Review* 60:2 (1956): 123–38.

"Puzzlement in the Pentagon," *America* 90 (Nov. 13, 1953): 163.

"PW Flyers Reveal Torture by Reds," *NYHT* (Aug. 7, 1953).

"PW In 'Progressive' Group Says He's For Capitalism," *Knoxville Journal* (Sept. 13, 1953).

"Quality of Mercy is Strained by Rank," *Christian Century* 71 (May 19, 1954): 603.

Randolph, John. "POWs Fear Death If They Leave," AP clip in Dec. 28, 1953 folder, Pearson Papers.

"The Rats," *Newsweek* (Aug. 24, 1953): 30.

"Red Charge Bars PTA Election," *NYT* (May 18, 1954): 20.

"Red Murder of 6,000 GI's Finally Angers Us!" *Saturday Evening Post* (Nov. 28, 1953): 10.

" 'Red Rumor' Chills POW's Welcome," *NYT* (Sept. 14, 1953).

"Reds Half Way to Pusan Beachhead," *Philadelphia Inquirer* (Jan. 11, 1951).

"Reds to Quit if Korea Going Gets Tough," *NYT* (July 23, 1952).

Reinhardt, Gough C. "Frame-Up, Communist Style," *Army Combat Forces Journal* (Oct. 1953): 36.

"Returning Prisoners Tell of Threats," *Knoxville Journal* (Sept. 14, 1953): 2.

Richardson, Walton K. "Prisoners of War as Instruments of Foreign Policy," *Naval War College Review* 23:1 (Sept. 1970), 47–64.

Riesel, Victor. "Brainwashing Still Affects Former POWs," *Charlotte Observer* (April 15, 1954).

Ritchie, Elspeth Cameron. "Psychiatry in the Korean War: Perils, PIES, and Prisoners of War," *Military Medicine* 167 (Nov. 2002): 898–903.

Rogin, Michael. "Kiss Me Deadly: Communism, Motherhood, and Cold War Movies," *Representations* 6 (Spring 1984): 1–36.

Roskey, William. "Korea's Costliest Battle: The POW Impasse," *Parameters* 23 (Summer 1993) 96–106.

"Russian Captives Riot at Fort Dix," *NYT* (June 30, 1945).

Russell, Richard B. "For the Prisoners Who Broke—Kindness or Punishment?" *USNWR* (Oct 16, 1953): 52.

Sang-Hun, Choe. "Unearthing War's Horrors Years Later in South Korea," *NYT* (Dec. 3, 2007).

Schanberg, Sidney. "McCain and the POW Cover-Up," *The Nation* (Sept. 18, 2008).

Schein, Edgar H. "Chinese Indoctrination Program for Prisoners of War," *Psychiatry* 19:2 (May 1956): 149–72.

——. "Man Against Man: Brainwashing," *Corrective Psychiatry and Journal of Social Change* 8:2 (1962), found in Mitford, *Kind and Usual Punishment,* 120.

Schumach, Murray. "Admiral Joy Finds Relief in a Game," *NYT* (May 18, 1952).

"Schwable Freed, but is Criticized," *NYT* (April 28, 1954).

Segal, Henry A. "Initial Psychiatric Findings of Recently Repatriated Prisoners of War," *American Journal of Psychiatry* 111 (Nov. 1954): 358–63.

Segal, Julius. "Factors Related to the Collaboration and Resistance Behavior of U.S. Army PW's in Korea," *HumRRO Technical Report* 33, George Washington University, Dec. 1956.

Sentner, David. "Congressmen Demand Probe in Smear of PWs," *New York Journal American* (May 5, 1953).

"Seoul Abandoned to Red Armies," *NYT* (Jan. 4, 1951).

"Sergeant Ryker's Back," *NYT* (Mar. 21, 1968): 2:56.

Small, Sidney Herschel. "The Brainwashed Pilot," *Saturday Evening Post* (March 19, 1955).

"Some G.I. Captives May Seem Pro-Red," *NYT* (April 13, 1953).

Stavisky, Sam. " 'Menticide' Defined At Schwable Trial," *Washington Post* (March 10, 1954).

Strassman, Harvey D. "A Prisoner of War Syndrome: Apathy as a Reaction to Severe Stress," *American Journal of Psychiatry* 112 (1956): 998–1003.

"This Strange Business of 'Hardening' By Torture," *Baltimore Sun* (Sept. 9, 1955).

Thomis, Wayne. "How Reds Brainwashed Korea GIs," *Chicago Tribune* (April 23, 1960): 10.

Thompson, Howard. "Sergeant Ryker's Back," *NYT* (March 21, 1968): 2:56.

"Too Late to Kill Germs," *Economist* (Oct. 17, 1953).

"Tough Prisoners," *Time* (Sept. 21, 1953): 28.

Trumbull, Robert. "GI's in Far East Get Captive Code," *NYT* (Aug. 12, 1956): 19.

Ulman, William A. "The GI's Who Fell for the Reds," *Saturday Evening Post* (March 6, 1954): 64.

"U.N. Captives Plot Charged by Indian," *NYT* (Oct. 2, 1953).

UP. "Colonel Guilty in P.O.W. Trial," *NYT* (Dec. 22, 1955).

——. "Curb on POW Aid by Army Studied," *NYT* (Dec. 19, 1955).

——. "Fliers Ready to Die Rather Than 'Confess' Germ Warfare," (Macon) *Telegraph* (Sept. 5, 1953).

——. "Freed Men 'Burned Up,' Army Says," *San Francisco Chronicle* (May 3, 1953).

——. "President' View on 'Confessions,'" NYHT (March 11, 1954).

——. "Reds Deny GIs Held," *Washington Post* (Sept. 13, 1955): 6.

——. "Tight Censorship of Freed POWs," *NYHT* (Aug. 1, 1953).

UPI, "General Upholds U.S. Fighting Men," *NYT* (March 16, 1962): 14.

"U.S. the New Hitler: USSR," *Time* (June 30, 1952): 25.

"Veterans Groups Divided On 'Sgt. Flanary Case,'" *Knoxville Journal* (Sept. 14, 1953).

" 'Voice' Taunts Foe Over 'Volunteers,'" *NYT* (May 4, 1952).

Wade, Nicholas. "A Peek Into the Remarkable Mind Behind the Genetic Code," *NYT*, (July 11, 2006).

Walsh, Moira. *America* 91 (May 22, 1954): 229.

——. *America* 107 (Nov. 24, 1962): 1158.

"War Atrocities Pic Limited in Appeal," *Hollywood Reporter* (Mar. 24, 1954): 3.

"War and Disease," *Newsweek* (Mar. 17, 1952): 43.

Weathersby, Kathryn. "To Attack, or Not to Attack? Stalin, Kim Il Sung, and the Prelude to War," *Cold War International History Project Bulletin* 5 (1995): 1–9.

"What About Reds Among Freed U.S. Prisoners?" *Newsweek* (Aug. 17, 1953): 21.

"Where Yanks Suffered Disaster," *Philadelphia Inquirer* (Nov. 3, 1950).

Whitehead, Don. "Withdrawal Inevitable," *Newark Sunday News* (Jan. 14, 1951).

"Who Won the War?" *USNWR* (July 13, 1951): 14.

"Why Some GIs Stay with Reds," *USNWR* (Nov. 13, 1953): 40.

"Why They Mourn," *Life* (Nov. 2, 1953): 26–27.

Young, Charles S. "Missing Action: POW Films, Brainwashing and the Korean War, 1954–1968," *Historical Journal of Film, Radio and Television* 18:1 (March 1998): 49–74.

——. "POWs: The Hidden Reason for Forgetting Korea," *Journal of Strategic Studies* 33:2 (April 2010): 317–32.

Young, Robert. "Too Severe, General Says," *Chicago Tribune* (March 9, 1954).

Zellers, Lawrence. "I Was a Prisoner in Korea," *Christian Century* (June 17, 1953): 713.

Zweiback, Adam J. "The 21 'Turncoat GIs:' Nonrepatriations and the Political Culture of the Korean War," *The Historian* 60:2 (Winter 1998): 345–61.

## Books

Adams, Clarence. *An American Dream: The Life of an African American Soldier and POW Who Spent Twelve Years in Communist China.* Amherst: University of Massachusetts Press, 2007.

Alexander, Bevin. *Korea: The First War We Lost.* New York: Hippocrene, 2000.

Allen, Michael J. *Until the Last Man Comes Home: POWs, MIAs, and the Unending Vietnam War.* Chapel Hill: University of North Carolina Press, 2012.

Allen, William M. *My Old Box of Memories: Thoughts of the Korean War.* Self-published, 1999.

Army Security Center. *U.S. Prisoners of War in the Korean War: Their Treatment and Handling by the North Korean Army and the Chinese Communist Forces,* 1954; reprinted by Arden A. Rowley. Paducah, KY: Turner Publishing, 2002.

Bailey, Sydney D. *The Korean Armistice.* New York: St. Martins, 1992.

Bassett, Richard M. and Lewis H. Carlson. *And the Wind Blew Cold: The Story of an American POW in North Korea.* Kent, Ohio: Kent State University Press, 2002.

Berens, Robert J. *Limbo on the Yalu and Beyond.* St. Petersburg: Southern Heritage, 2000.

Bernhard, Nancy E. *U.S. Television News and Cold War Propaganda, 1947–1960.* New York: Cambridge University Press, 1999.

Bernstein, Barton. "Struggle Over the Korean Armistice: Prisoners of Repatriation?" In *Child of Conflict.* Bruce Cumings ed.

Biderman, Albert D. *March to Calumny: The Story of American POW's in the Korean War.* New York: Macmillan, 1963.

——. and Samuel M. Meyers, eds., *Mass Behavior in Battle and Captivity: The Communist Soldier in the Korean War.* Chicago: University of Chicago Press, 1968.

Blair, Clay Jr. *Beyond Courage.* New York: David McKay, 1955.

Bragg, Rick. *I Am a Soldier, Too: The Jessica Lynch Story.* New York: Vintage, 2004.

Bryant, Clifton D. *Khaki-Collar Crime: Deviant Behavior in the Military Context.* New York: Free Press, 1979.

Burchett, Wilfred and Alan Winnington. *Koje Unscreened.* Peking, 1953.

Carlson, Lewis H. *Remembered Prisoners of a Forgotten War: An Oral History of the Korean War POWs.* New York: St. Martins, 2002.

Carson, Jerry. *The Guilty of the Korean War.* Georgetown, TX: Word Wright, 2002.

Casey, Steven. *Selling the Korean War: Propaganda, Politics, and Public Opinion in the United States, 1950–1953.* New York: Oxford University Press, 2008.

Chang, Jung and Jon Halliday. *Mao: The Unknown Story.* New York: Knopf, 2005.

Clark, Conley. *Journey Through Shadow, 839 Days of Hell.* Charlotte, NC: Heritage, 1988.

Clark, Mark W. *From the Danube to the Yalu.* New York: Harper, 1954.

Cole, Paul M. *POW/MIA Issues, Volume 1, The Korean War.* Santa Monica: Rand, 1994.

Crane, Conrad C. *American Airpower Strategy in Korea, 1950–1953.* Lawrence: University Press of Kansas, 2000.

Cumings, Bruce, ed. *Child of Conflict: The Korean-American Relationship, 1943–1953.* Seattle: University of Washington Press, 1983.

——. *Korea's Place in the Sun: A Modern History.* New York: Norton, 1997.

——. *The Origins of the Korean War Vol. II: The Roaring of the Cataract, 1947–1950.* Princeton, NJ: Princeton University Press: 1990.

Cuordileone, K. A. *Manhood and American Political Culture in the Cold War.* New York: Routledge, 2005.

Daws, Gavan. *Prisoners of the Japanese: POWs of World War II in the Pacific.* New York: William Morrow, 1994.

Davis, Vernon E. *The Long Road Home: U.S. Prisoner of War Policy and Planning in Southeast Asia.* Washington, DC: Office of Secretary of Defense, 2000.

Dayal, Shiv. *India's Role in the Korean Question: A Study in the Settlement of International Disputes Under the United Nations*. Delhi: S. Chand, 1959.

Deane, Philip. *I Was a Captive in Korea*. New York: Norton, 1953.

DeRosa, Christopher S. *Political Indoctrination in the U.S. Army: From World War II to the Vietnam War*. Lincoln: University of Nebraska Press, 2006.

Dower, John W. *War Without Mercy: Race and Power in the Pacific War*. New York: Pantheon, 1986.

Doyle, Robert C. *Voices from Captivity: Interpreting the American POW Narrative* Lawrence: University Press of Kansas, 1994.

Endicott, Stephen and Edward Hagerman. *The United States and Biological Warfare: Secrets from the Early Cold War and Korea*. Bloomington: Indiana University Press, 1998.

Edwards, Paul M. *The Korean War*. Westport, CN: Greenwood Press, 2006.

Fehrenbach, T. R. *This Kind of War: A Study in Unpreparedness*. Washington, DC: Brassey's, 1963.

Foot, Rosemary. *A Substitute for Victory: The Politics of Peacemaking at the Korean Armistice Talks*. Ithaca, NY: Cornell University Press, 1990.

*Foreign Relations of the United States. See* US Department of State.

Forrestall, James. *The Forrestall Diaries*, Walter Millis and E. S. Duffield, eds. New York: Viking, 1951.

Franklin, H. Bruce. *M.I.A. or Mythmaking in America*. New Brunswick, NJ: Rutgers University Press, 1993.

*FRUS. See* US State Department, *Foreign Relations of the United States.*

Funchess, William H. *Korea POW: A Thousand Days of Torment*. Self published, 1997.

Furmanski, Martin and Mark Wheelis. "Allegations of Biological Weapons Use." In *Deadly Cultures: Biological Weapons Since 1945*, Mark Wheelis and Lajos Rozsa, eds. Cambridge, MA: Harvard University Press, 2006.

Futrell, Robert F. *The United States Air Force in Korea, 1950–53*. New York: Duell, Sloan and Pearce, 1961.

Gacek, Christopher H. *The Logic of Force: The Dilemma of Limited War in American Foreign Policy*. New York: Columbia University Press, 1994.

Gary, Brett. *The Nervous Liberals: Propaganda Anxieties from World War I to the Cold War*. New York: Columbia University Press, 1999.

Gilbert, James. *Men in the Middle: Searching for Masculinity in the 1950s*. Chicago: University of Chicago Press, 2005.

Gittings, John. *The Role of the Chinese Army*. Oxford: Oxford University Press, 1967.

Gleason, Abbott. *Totalitarianism: The Inner History of the Cold War*. New York: Oxford University Press, 1995.

Goncharov, Sergei N., John W. Lewis and Litai Xue. *Uncertain Partners: Stalin, Mao, and the Korean War*. Palo Alto: Stanford University Press, 1993.

Grant, Lee Booth. "Operation Big Switch: Medical Intelligence Processing." 1953 pamphlet, reprinted in Stan Sommers, ed. *The Korea Story*. Marshfield, WI: American Ex-Prisoners of War Medical Research Committee, 1981.

Gruner, Elliott. *Prisoners of Culture: Representing the Vietnam POW*. New Brunswick, NJ: Rutgers, 1993.

Ha Jin. *See* Jin.

Halberstam, David. *The Coldest Winter: America and the Korean War*. New York: Hyperion, 2007.

Halliday, Jon and Bruce Cumings. *Korea: The Unknown War*. New York: Pantheon, 1988.

Hallin, Daniel C. *The "Uncensored War:" The Media and Vietnam*. Berkeley: University of California, 1986.

Hanley, Charles J. and Sang-Hun Choe. *The Bridge at No Gun Ri: A Hidden Nightmare from the Korean War*. New York: Henry Holt, 2001.

Hansen, Kenneth K. *Heroes Behind Barbed Wire*. Princeton, NJ: Van Nostrand, 1957.

Hearst, Patricia. *Every Secret Thing*, Garden City. New York: Doubleday, 1982.

Hermes, Walter G. *Truce Tent and Fighting Front: United States Army in the Korean War*. Washington, DC: US Government Printing Office, 1966.

History Book Club, ed. *Remembering the Forgotten War, Korea: 1950–1953*. New York, 2000.

Hogan, Michael. *The Irish Soldiers of Mexico*. Intercambio Press, 2011.

Hoganson, Kristin L. *Fighting for American Manhood: How Gender Politics Provoked the Spanish-American and Philippine-American Wars*. New Haven: Yale University Press, 1998.

Howe, Charles. *Valley of Fire*. New York: Dell, 1964.

Hunter, Edward. *Brainwashing, From Pavlov to Powers*. New York: Bookmailer, 1960.

——. *Brainwashing in Red China: The Calculated Destruction of Men's Minds*. New York: Vanguard, 1951.

Jacobson, Matthew Frye and Gaspar Gonzalez. *What Have They Built You to Do?: The Manchurian Candidate and Cold War America*. Minneapolis: University of Minnesota Press, 2006.

Jin, Ha. *War Trash*. New York: Vintage, 2004.

Johnson, Chalmers. *The Sorrows of Empire: Militarism, Secrecy, and the End of the Republic*. New York: Metropolitan, 2004.

Johnson, Sam and Jan Winebrenner. *Captive Warriors: A Vietnam POW's Story*. College Station: Texas A & M University Press, 1992.

Jolidon, Laurence. *Last Seen Alive: The Search for Missing POWs from the Korean War*. Ink-slinger Press, 1995.

Jones, Francis S. *No Rice for Rebels: A Story of the Korean War*. London: Bodley Head, 1956.

Joy, C. Turner. *How Communists Negotiate*. New York: Macmillan, 1955.

——. *Negotiating While Fighting: The Diary of Admiral C. Turner Joy at the Korean Armistice Conference*, Allan E. Goodman ed. Stanford: Hoover Institution Press, 1978.

Jung Chang. *See* Chang.

Kaufman, Burton I. *The Korean Conflict*. Westport, CT: Greenwood, 1999.

King, O. H. P. *Tail of the Paper Tiger*. Caldwell, ID: Caxton, 1961.

Kinkead, Eugene. *In Every War But One*. New York: Norton, 1959.

Knox, Donald. *The Korean War: Uncertain Victory, An Oral History*. New York: Harcourt, 1988.

Kuo, Warren. *Comprehensive Glossary of Chinese Communist Terminology*. Taipei: National Chengchi University, 1978.

Latham, William C. *Cold Days in Hell: American POWs in Korea*. College Station: Texas A&M University Press, 2012.

Laurie, Clayton D. *The Propaganda Warriors: America's Crusade Against Nazi Germany*. Lawrence: University Press of Kansas, 1996.

Lech, Raymond B. *Broken Soldiers*. Urbana: University of Illinois Press, 2000.

Leckie, Robert. *Conflict: The History of the Korean War, 1950–1953*. New York: Putnam, 1962.

Lee, Steven Hugh. *The Korean War*. London: Pearson, 2001.

Leffler, Melvyn. *A Preponderance of Power: National Security, the Truman Administration, and the Cold War*. Palo Alto: Stanford University Press, 1992.

Li, Xiaobing, Allan R. Millett, and Bin Yu, eds. *Mao's Generals Remember Korea*. Lawrence: University Press of Kansas, 2001.

Lifton, Robert J. *Thought Reform and the Psychology of Totalism: A Study of Brainwashing in China*. London: Gollancz, 1961.

Lippmann, Walter. *The Method of Freedom*. New York: MacMillan, 1934.

——. *Public Opinion*. New York: Harcourt, 1922.

Look editors. *The Decline of the American Male*. New York: Random House, 1958.

Lucas, Scott. *Freedom's War: The American Crusade Against the Soviet Union*. New York: NYU Press, 1999.

Lutz, Catherine. "Epistemology of the Bunker: The Brainwashed and Other New Subjects of Permanent War." In *Inventing the Psychological: Toward a Cultural History of Emotional Life in America*, Joel Pfister and Nancy Schnog, eds. New Haven: Yale University Press, 1997.

Lynn, Jack. *The Turncoat*. New York: Delacorte, 1976.

MacDonald, Callum A. *Korea: The War Before Vietnam*. New York: Free Press, 1986.

Maffioli, Len and Bruce H. Norton. *Grown Gray in War: The Len Maffioli Story*. New York: Random House, 1997.

Marks, John. *The Search for the 'Manchurian Candidate:' The CIA and Mind Control*. New York: Times Books, 1979.

Mayer, William E. *Brainwashing, Drunks & Madness: Memoirs of a Medical Icon*. Westerville, OH: Winterwolf Publishing, 2004.

McCoy, Alfred W. *Torture and Impunity: The U.S. Doctrine of Coercive Interrogation*. Madison: University of Wisconsin Press, 2012.

Meerloo, Joost A.M. *The Rape of the Mind*. New York: World Publishing House, 1956.

Millett, Allan R. *Their War for Korea: American, Asian, and European Combatants and Civilians, 1945–1953*. Washington, DC: Brasseys, 2002.

Mitford, Jessica. *Kind and Usual Punishment: The Prison Business*. New York: Knopf, 1973.

Mitrovich, Gregory. *Undermining the Kremlin: America's Strategy to Subvert the Soviet Bloc, 1947–1956*. Ithaca, NY: Cornell University Press, 2000.

Nitze, Paul H. "NSC 68: United States Objectives and Programs for National Security." In *American Cold War Strategy: Interpreting NSC 68*, Ernest R. May, ed. Boston: Bedford, 1993.

Oh, Se Hee. *Stalag 65: A Memoir of a Korean POW*. Portland, OR: Artwork Publications, 2000.

Osgood, Kenneth and Andrew K. Frank, eds. *Selling War in a Media Age: The Presidency and Public Opinion in the American Century*. Gainesville: University Press of Florida, 2011.

Pasley, Virginia. *21 Stayed: The Story of the American GI's Who Chose Communist China*. New York: Farrar, Straus, 1955.

Pate, Lloyd W. with B. J. Cutler, *Reactionary!* New York: Harper, 1956.

———. *Reactionary, Revised 2000*. New York: Vantage, 2000.

Pelton, Robert W. *Dead or Alive: An Explosive Expose of the Shameful Betrayal of American POWs*. Iuniverse, 2000.

Peters, Richard and Xiaobing Li. *Voices from the Korean War: Personal Stories of American, Korean, and Chinese Soldiers*. Lexington: University Press of Kentucky, 2004.

Piehler, G. Kurt. *Remembering War the American Way*. Washington, DC: Smithsonian Institution, 2004.

Pierpaoli, Paul G. Jr. *Truman and Korea: The Political Culture of the Early Cold War*. Columbia: University of Missouri Press, 1999.

Pincher, Chapman. *Traitors: The Anatomy of Treason*. New York: St. Martins, 1987.

Polk, David. *Ex-Prisoners of the Korean War*. Paducah, KY: Turner, 1993.

Pollini, Francis. *Night*. Paris: Olympia Press, 1960.

Prasad, S. N. *History of the Custodian Force (India) in Korea 1953–54*. Delhi: Armed Forces of the Indian Union, 1976.

Qiang Zhai. *See* Zhai.

Rawnsley, Gary D. ed. *Cold-War Propaganda in the 1950s*. New York: St. Martins, 1999.

Robin, Ron. *The Making of the Cold War Enemy: Culture and Politics in the Military-Intellectual Complex*. Princeton, NJ: Princeton University Press, 2001.

Rowley, Arden A. *Korea POW: A Thousand Days with Life on Hold*. Tanner Publishing, 1997.

Sandler, Stanley. *The Korean War: No Victors, No Vanquished*. Lexington: University Press of Kentucky, 1999.

Schaller, Michael. *The American Occupation of Japan: The Origins of the Cold War in Asia*. New York: Oxford University Press, 1985.

Schein, Edgar H. *Coercive Persuasion: A Socio-Psychological Analysis of the "Brainwashing" of American Civilian Prisoners by the Chinese Communists*. New York: Norton, 1961.

Secretary of Defense's Advisory Committee on Prisoners of War. *POW: The Fight Continues After the Battle*. Washington, DC: US Government Printing Office, 1955.

Se Hee Oh. *See* Oh.

Shaw, Tony. *Hollywood's Cold War,* Amherst: University of Massachusetts Press, 2007.

Sherry, Michael S. *In the Shadow of War: The United States Since the 1930s*. New Haven: Yale University Press, 1995.

Simpson, Christopher. *Science of Coercion: Communication Research and Psychological Warfare, 1945–1960*. New York: Oxford University Press, 1994.

Skomra, Fred. *Behind the Bamboo Curtain: A Novel of the Air War Over Korea Skies*. New York: Greenwich Book Publishers, 1957.

Slotkin, Richard. *Regeneration Through Violence: The Mythology of the American Frontier, 1600–1860*. New York: HarperCollins, 1973.

Smith, Julian. *Looking Away: Hollywood and Vietnam*. New York: Scribner, 1975.

Snyder, Don J. *A Soldier's Disgrace*. Dublin, NH: Yankee Books, 1987.

Spiller, Harry, ed. *American POWs in Korea: Sixteen Personal Accounts*. Jefferson, NC: McFarland, 1998.

Springer, Paul J. *America's Captives: Treatment of POWs from the Revolutionary War to the War on Terror*. Lawrence: University Press of Kansas, 2010.

Stueck, William. *The Korean War: An International History*. Princeton, NJ: Princeton University Press, 1995.

——, ed. *The Korean War in World History*. Lexington: University of Kentucky Press, 2004.

——. *Rethinking the Korean War: A New Diplomatic and Strategic History*. Princeton, NJ: Princeton University Press, 2002.

Suid, Lawrence H. and David Culbert, eds. *Film and Propaganda in America: A Documentary History, vol. 4, 1945 and After*. Westport, CT: Greenwood, 1991.

Taylor, Kathleen. *Brainwashing: The Science of Thought Control*. New York: Oxford University Press, 2004.

Thompson, James. *True Colors: 1004 Days as a Prisoner of War*. Port Washington, NY: Ashley, 1989.

Thorin, Duane. *A Ride to Panmunjom*. Chicago: Regenry, 1956.

Toland, John. *In Mortal Combat: Korea, 1950–1953*. New York: William Morrow, 1991.

Tomedi, Rudy. *No Bugles, No Drums: An Oral History of the Korean War*. New York: Wiley, 1993.

Tucker, Spencer, ed. *Encyclopedia of the Korean War: A Political, Social, and Military History*. Santa Barbara: ABC-Cleo, 2000.

US Department of State. *Foreign Relations of the United States, 1950*. Vol. 7: *Korea*. Washington, DC: Government Printing Office.

——. *Foreign Relations of the United States, 1951*. Vol. 7: *Korea and China*.

——. *Foreign Relations of the United States, 1952–1954*. Vol. 15: *Korea*.

Vetter, Hal. *Mutiny on Koje Island*. Rutland, VT: Charles E. Tuttle, 1965.

Weintraub, Stanley. *War in the Wards: Korea's Unknown Battle in a Prisoner-of-War Hospital Camp*. New York: Doubleday, 1964. Reprint, San Rafael: Presidio, 1976.

West and Li Zhihua, "Interior Stories of the Chinese POWs in the Korean War." In *Remembering the "Forgotten War": The Korean War Through Literature and Art*, Philip West and Suh Jimoon eds. Armonk, NY: M. E. Sharpe, 2001.

Whelan, Richard. *Drawing the Line: The Korean War, 1950–1953*. Boston: Little, Brown, and Co., 1990.

White, William Lindsay. *The Captives of Korea: An Unofficial White Paper on the Treatment of War Prisoners; Our Treatment of Theirs: Their Treatment of Ours*. New York: Scribner, 1957.

Williams, Robert Chadwell. *Klaus Fuchs, Atom Spy*. Cambridge, MA: Harvard University Press, 1987.

Wills, Morris R. and J. Robert Moskin. *Turncoat: An American's 12 Years in Communist China*. Englewood Cliffs: Prentice-Hall, 1968.

Wilson, Sloan. *The Man in the Gray Flannel Suit*. New York: Simon and Schuster, 1955.

Wiltz, John Edward. "The Korean War and American Society." In *The Korean War: A 25-Year Perspective*, Francis H. Heller ed. Lawrence: University Press of Kansas, 1977.

Wood, Richard. *Film and Propaganda in America: A Documentary History, 1945 and After*. Westport, CT: Greenwood, 1991.

Wylie, Philip. *Generation of Vipers*. New York: Rinehart, 1955.

Xiaobing Li. *See* Li.

Young, Charles S. "Voluntary Repatriation and Involuntary Tattooing of Korean War POWs," in James I. Matray, ed., *Northeast Asia and the Legacy of Harry S. Truman*. Kirksville, MO: Truman State University Press, 2012, 146–67.

Young, Marilyn. "Hard Sell: The Korean War." In *Selling War in a Media Age*. Kenneth Osgood and Andrew K. Frank, eds. Gainesville: University Press of Florida, 2011, 113–39.

Zellers, Larry. *In Enemy Hands*. Lexington: University of Kentucky, 1991.

Zhai, Qiang. *The Dragon, the Lion, and the Eagle: Chinese, British, American Relations, 1949–1958*. Kent, OH: Kent State University Press, 1994.

# INDEX